# THE TYPOLOGY OF THE EARLY CODEX

# THE TYPOLOGY OF THE EARLY CODEX

ERIC G. TURNER

WIPF & STOCK · Eugene, Oregon

Wipf and Stock Publishers
199 W 8th Ave, Suite 3
Eugene, OR 97401

The Typology of the Early Codex
By Turner, Eric G.

ISBN 13: 978-61097-008-2
Publication date 10/8/2010
Previously published by University of Pennsylvania Press, 1977

# Contents

# List of Books and Abbreviations

This is not a bibliography of the codex, but an aid to identification of works cited in the text. A detailed list of abbreviations used by papyrologists is set out in the works of R. A. Pack (below) and in my *Greek Papyri* (see below), pp. 157-71 (brought up to date in an Italian edition now at press at Lemonnier, Florence, 1975). Abbreviations employed by New Testament scholars will be found in detail in the works of K. Aland and B. M. Metzger below.

K. Aland, *Kurzgefasste liste der gr. Handschriften des Neuen Testaments*. Berlin, 1963.

H. I. Bell and T. C. Skeat, *Fragments of an Unknown Gospel*. London, 1935.

*Cambridge History of the Bible*. Cambridge, 1963–70: Vol. I ed. P. R. Ackroyd and C. F. Evans, 1970; Vol. II ed. G. W. H. Lampe, 1969; Vol. III ed. S. L. Greenslade, 1963.

G. Cavallo, *Ricerche sulla maiuscola biblica*. 2 vols. Florence, 1967.

R. Devreesse, *Introduction á l'étude des manuscrits grecs*. Paris, 1954.

Sir Frederic Kenyon, *Books and Readers in Ancient Greece and Rome* (abbrev. *Books and Readers*$^2$). 2nd ed. Oxford, 1951.

W. H. P. Hatch, *The Principal Uncial Manuscripts of the New Testament*. Chicago, 1939.

P. L. Hedley, Unpublished list of Biblical manuscripts (compiled 1934).

E. A. Lowe, *Codices Latini Antiquiores* (abbrev. *CLA*). 11 volumes plus supplement. Oxford, 1934–73.

J. Mallon, *Paléographie romaine*. Madrid, 1952.

B. M. Metzger, *The Text of the New Testament*. 2nd ed. Oxford, 1968.

R. A. Pack (abbrev. Pack$^2$), *The Greek and Latin Literary Texts from Greco-Roman Egypt*. 2nd ed. Ann Arbor, 1965.

C. H. Roberts, "The Codex," *Proceedings of the British Academy* XL (1954): 169–204. (A revised edition is in preparation.)

W. Schubart, *Das Buch bei den Griechen und Römern* (abbrev. *Das Buch*$^2$). 2nd ed. Berlin and Leipzig, 1921. (The 3rd edition of 1962 is useless to scholars.)

———*Griechische Paläographie*. Munich, 1925 (in *Handbuch d. Altertumswissenschaft*).

———*Papyri Graecae Berolinenses.* Bonn, 1911.
R. Seider, *Paläographie der griechischen Papyri.* 2 Bände. Stuttgart, 1967, 1970.
E. G. Turner, *Greek Papyri: An Introduction.* Oxford and Princeton, 1968.
———*Greek Manuscripts of the Ancient World* (abbrev. *GMAW*). Oxford and Princeton, 1971.
———*The Papyrologist at Work.* Duke University, 1973.

ABBREVIATIONS

*ADIK* = *Abhandlungen des Deutschen archäologischen Instituts.* Cairo, 1958—.
*ARCHIV* = *Archiv für Papyrusforschung und verwandte Gebiete.* Leipzig/Berlin, 1901—.
*BASP* = *Bulletin of the American Society of Papyrologists.* New Haven/Toronto, 1963—.
*BICS* = *Bulletin of the Institute of Classical Studies.* Univ. of London, 1954—.
*BIFAO* = *Bulletin de l'Institut français d'Archéologie orientale.* Cairo, 1901—.
*BKT* = *Berliner Klassikertexte.* Berlin, 1904—.
*Cd'E* = *Chronique d'Egypte.* Brussels, 1925—.
*CLA* = E. A. Lowe, *Codices Latini Antiquiores.* Oxford, 11 volumes plus supplement.
*CQ* = *Classical Quarterly.* 1907—.
*CR* = *Classical Review.* Oxford, 1887—.
*DJD* = *Discoveries in the Judaean Desert* [*of Jordan*]. Oxford, 1960—.
*GRBS* = *Greek, Roman and Byzantine Studies.* Cambridge, Mass., 1958—.
*HTR* = *Harvard Theological Review.* Cambridge, Mass., 1908—.
*JEA* = *Journal of Egyptian Archaeology.* 1914—.
*JHS* = *Journal of Hellenic Studies.* 1880—.
*JNES* = *Journal of Near Eastern Studies.* Chicago, 1942—.
*JTS* = *Journal of Theological Studies.* New Haven, 1900—.
*MIFAO* = *Mémoires publiés par les membres de la Mission Archéologique Française au Caire.* Cairo, 1884—.
*MPER* = *Mitteilungen aus der Sammlung der Papyrus Erzherzog Rainer.* Vienna, 1887-97. Bände i-vi. The same abbreviation covers the new series, I. Folge 1932—.
*PGM* = *Papyri Graecae Magicae,* ed. K. Preisendanz. 3 vols. Leipzig/Berlin, 1928, 1931, 1941.
*PSI* = *Papiri greci e latini.* Florence, 1912—.
*PTA* = *Papyrologische Texte und Abhandlungen.* Bonn, 1968—.
*SB* = *Sammelbuch griechischer Urkunden aus Ägypten.* Strasbourg etc., 1913—.
*SHA* = *Scriptores Historiae Augustae.*
*SIFC* = *Studi italiani di filologia classica.* Florence, 1893—.
*TU* = *Texte und Untersuchungen zur Geschichte der altchristlichen Literatur.* Leipzig/Berlin, 1883—.
*Stud. Pal.* or *SPP* = *Studien zur Palaeographie und Papyruskunde,* ed. C. Wessely.
*VBP* = *Veröffentlichungen aus den badischen Papyrus-Sammlungen.* Demotic, Coptic, and Greek texts at Heidelberg, edited by W. Spiegelberg, F. Bilabel, and G. A. Gerhard.
*YCS* = *Yale Classical Studies.* New Haven, 1928—.
*ZAW* = *Zeitschrift für die alttestamentliche Wissenschaft.* Berlin, 1881—.
*ZNTW* = *Zeitschrift für neutestamentliche Wissenschaft.* Giessen, 1923—.
*ZPE* = *Zeitschrift fur Papyrologie und Epigraphik.* Bonn, 1967—.

# Illustrations

No. 1
An early codex written in one broad column: PSI 158, Astrological treatise (**341**), 3rd century A.D.

No. 2
An early papyrus codex written in two columns: Paris suppl. gr. 1120 (**244**; cf. page 35), 3rd century A.D.

No. 3
An early parchment codex written in two columns: BM Add MS 34473 (1) (**47**)

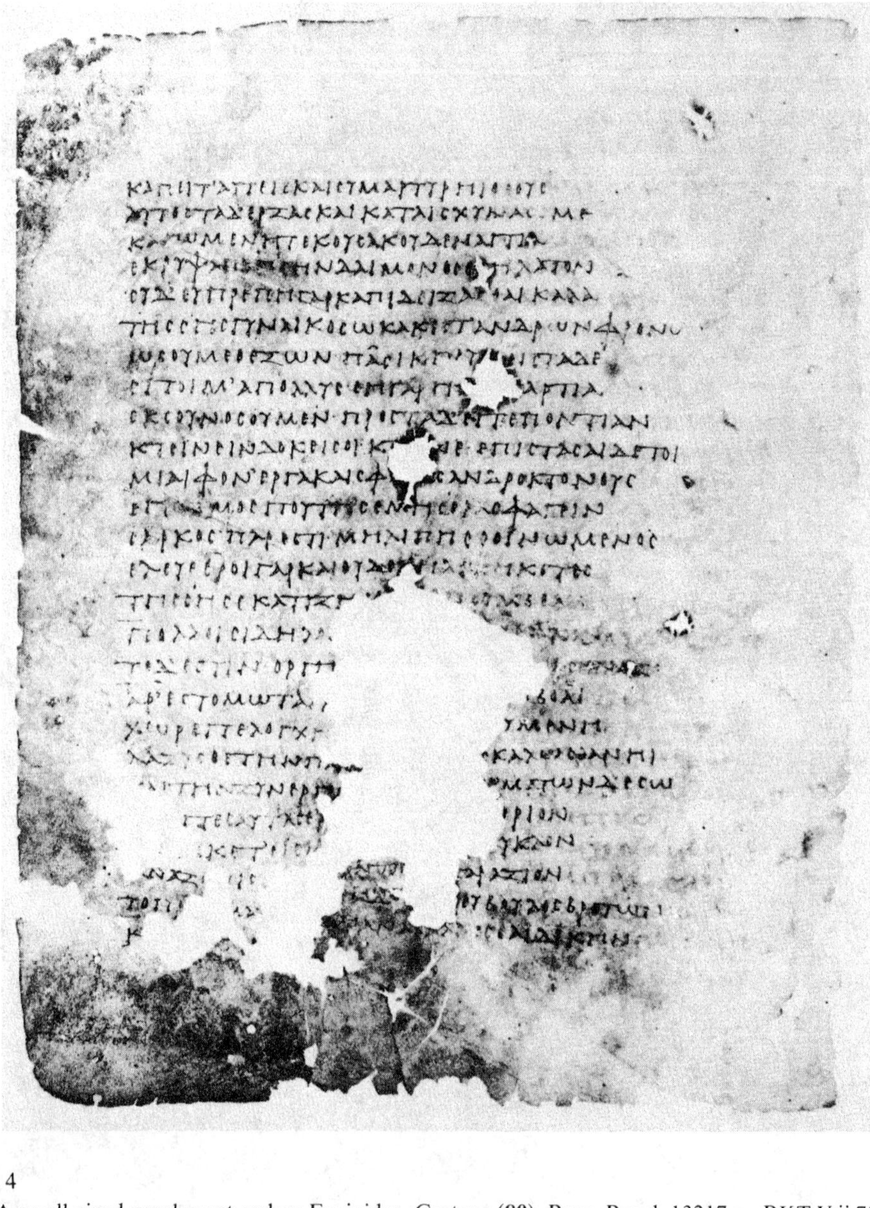

No. 4
(a) A small-sized parchment codex: Euripides, Cretans (**80**), Perg. Berol. 13217 = BKT V ii 73.
See page 41.

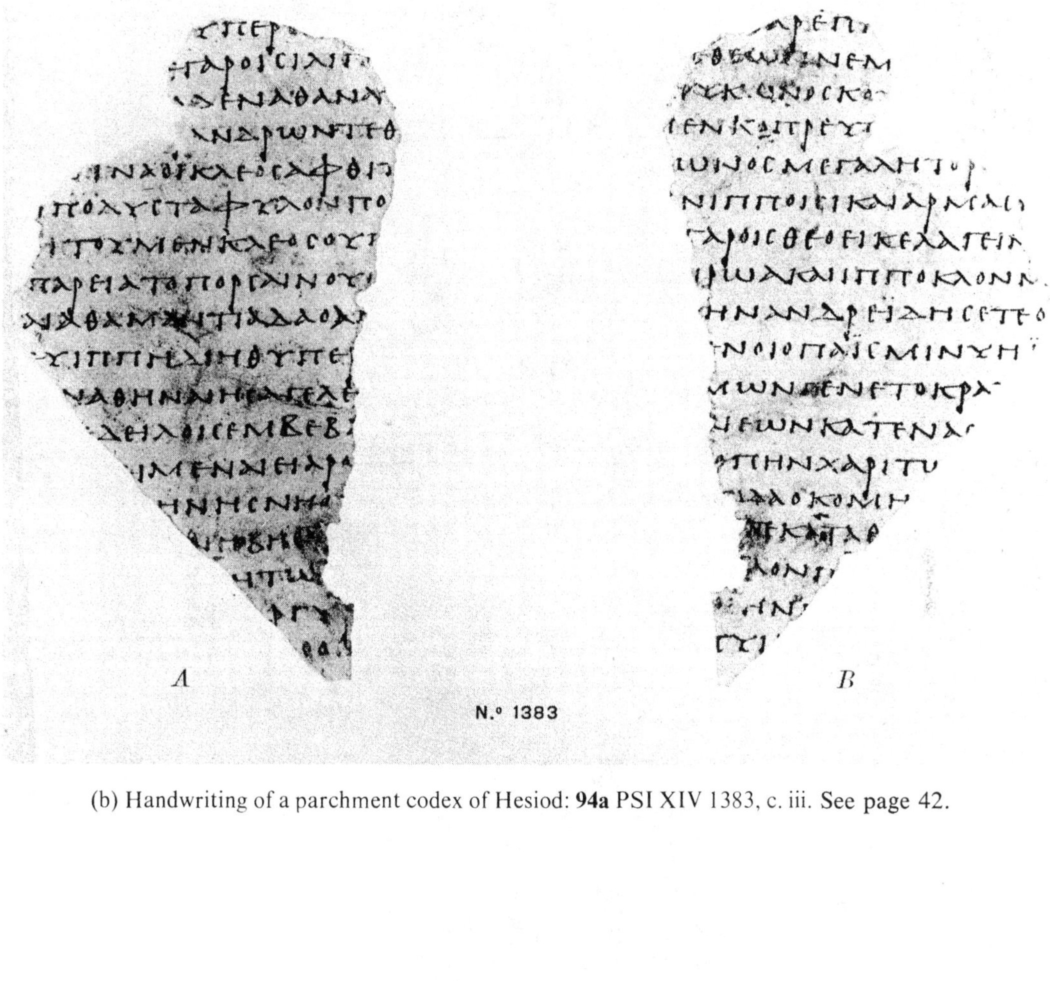


(b) Handwriting of a parchment codex of Hesiod: **94a** PSI XIV 1383, c. iii. See page 42.

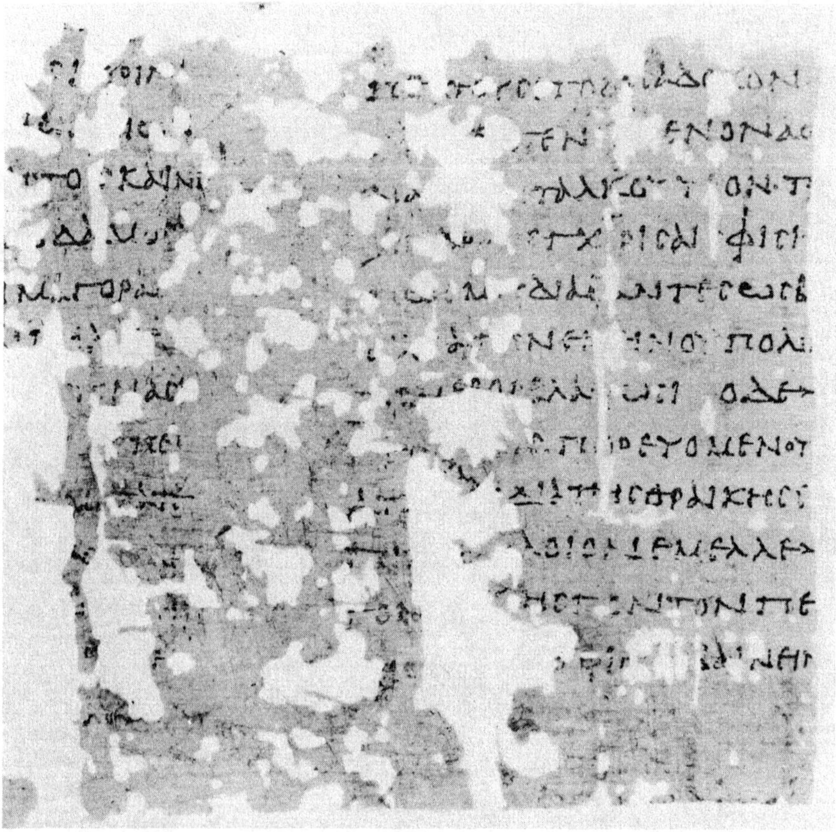

No. 5

(a) Handwriting of a papyrus roll of Thucydides, before A.D. 148: P. Oxy. xiii 1622. See page 42.

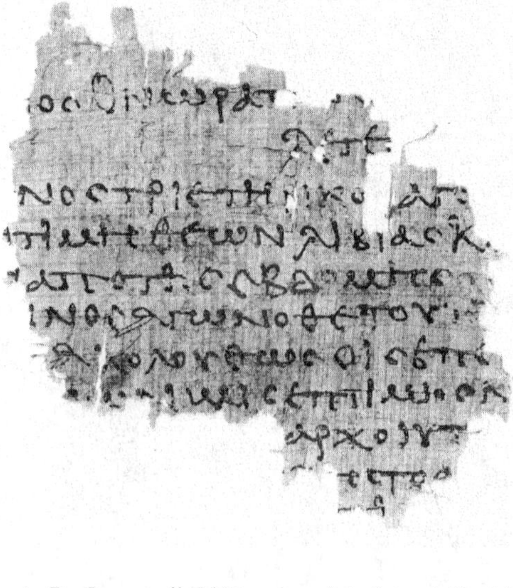

(b) A misdated document: P. Oxy. xvii 2105, once dated to A.D. 148, now dated to A.D. 231–36. See page 4.

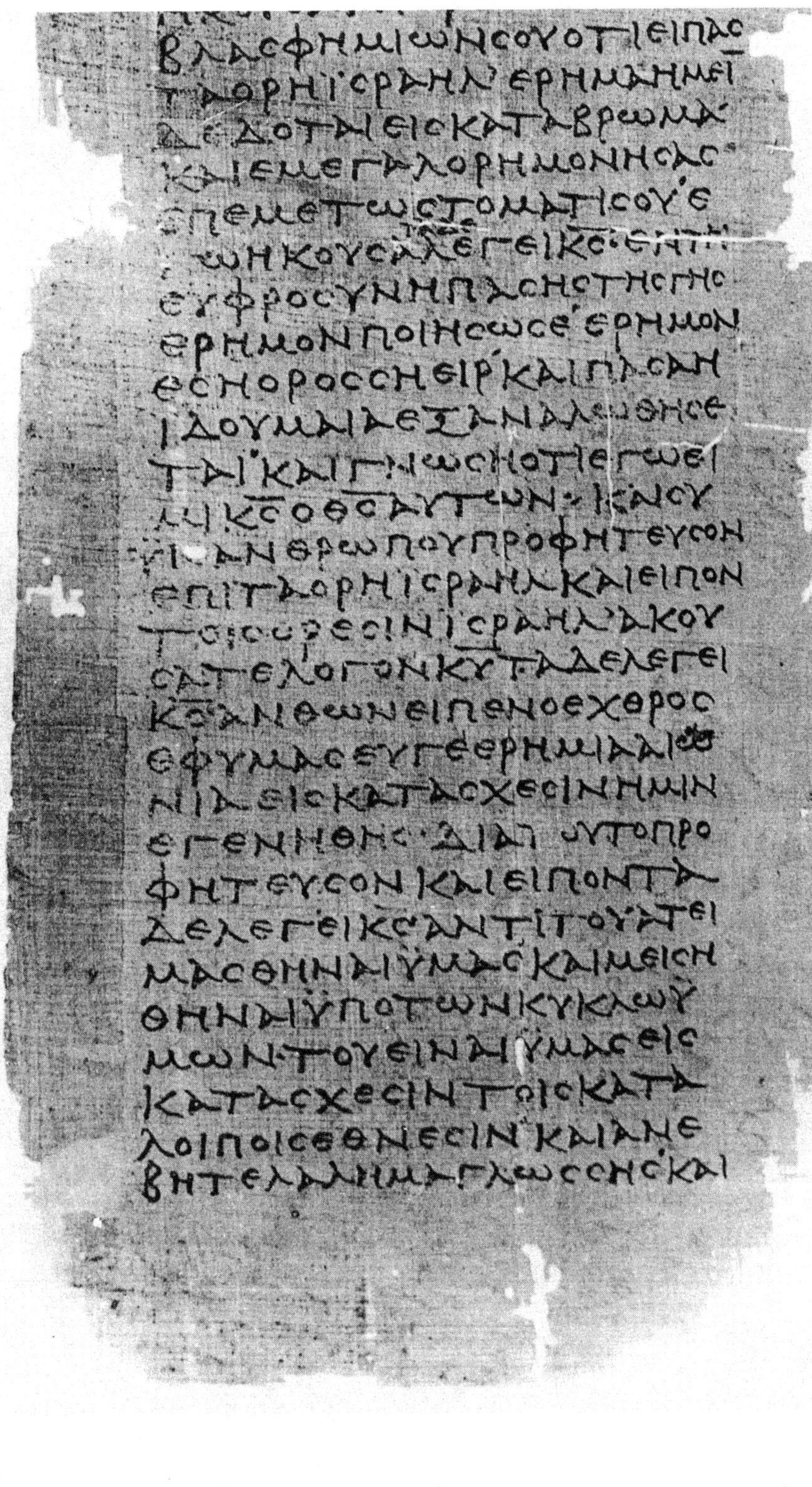

No. 6
An early single-quire codex, lower portion (note the *kollesis*). Cf. **OT 183 + 207A** (P. Princeton Scheide containing Ezekiel 30). Full height is about 35 cm. See page 49.

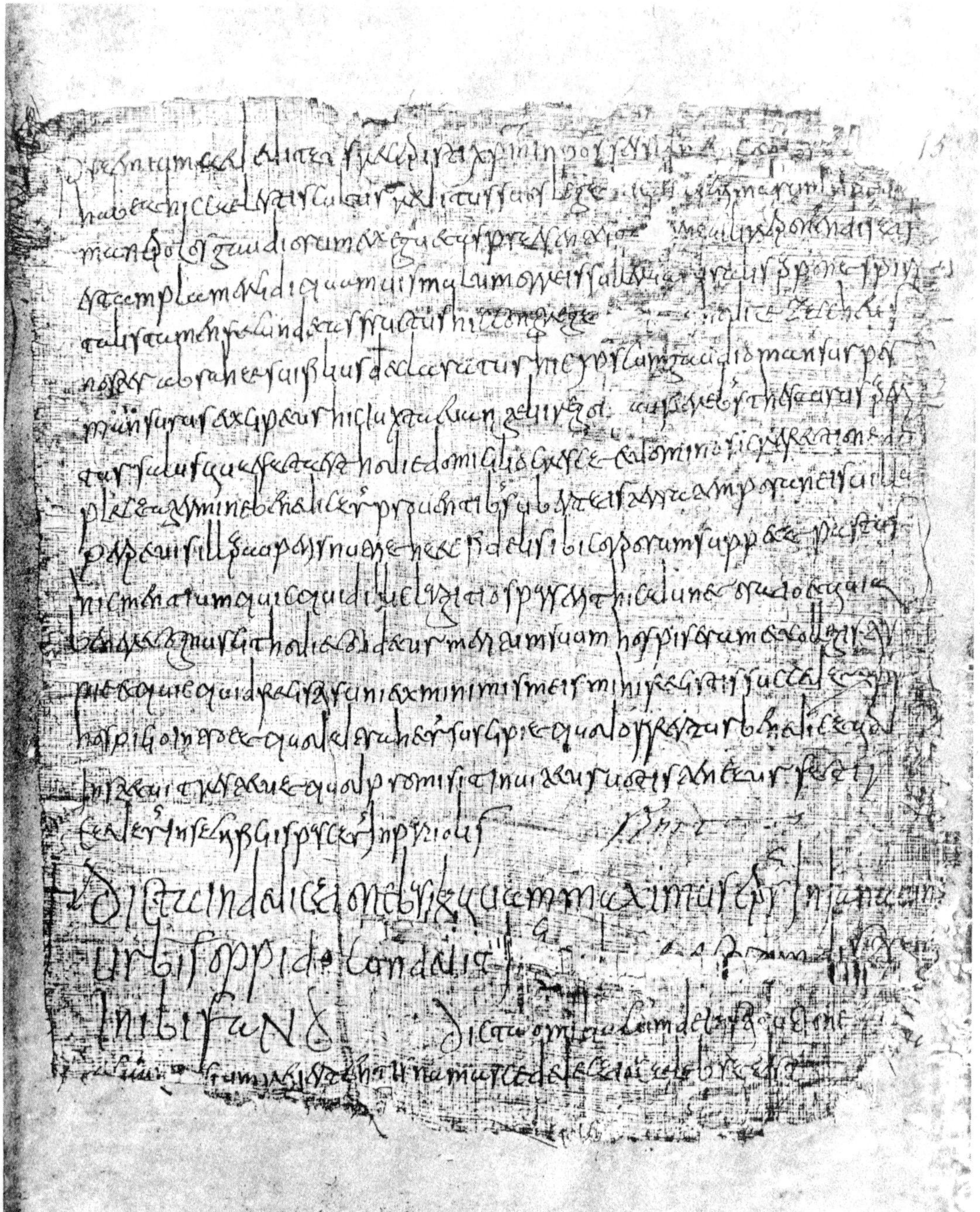

No. 7

A papyrus codex of century vi after Christ: Paris Avitus B. N. Lat. 8913 (**Lat. 2**). Reduced by 48%; original size 29B x 30H. Each gathering contains both parchment and papyrus.

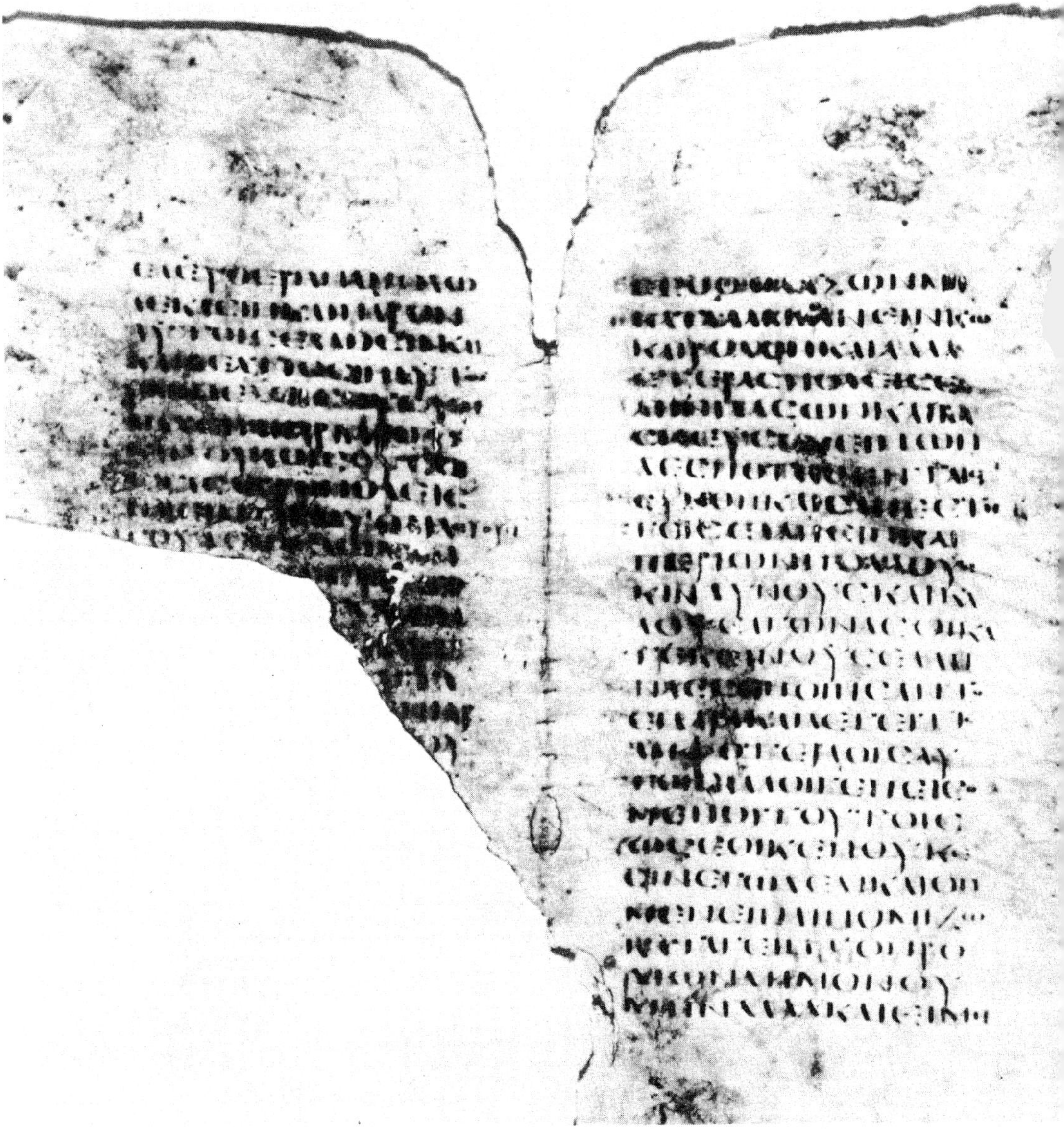

No. 8
An unusual format of parchment codex: Cairo 274B (= **42**), Demosthenes, 5th century A.D.

# Preface

My first task (and a pleasant one it is) is to thank the Provost and the University Library of the University of Pennsylvania for the invitation to take up the University's Rosenbach Fellowship for 1970–71 and to deliver the Rosenbach lectures in bibliography in 1971. The University has doubled the obligation under which it puts me by undertaking to publish these lectures from a manuscript that has been much extended since they were given. The giving of the lectures was a very pleasant occasion, made warmer by the hospitality of Professor Lloyd and Mrs. Betty Daly, and of many other Philadelphia friends. I should also particularly like to acknowledge the help given me by Mrs. Neda Westlake and Dr. David O'Connor.

I am very conscious that these lectures offer provisional results only—an inchoate study in an important field of scholarship. As I worked at them I have become sharply aware that such a task as I have embarked on can properly be based only on a personal examination of all the manuscripts and fragments of manuscript involved. I have indeed myself examined a large number of them, and others I have studied in good photographs. But for too many I have to depend on the statements of editors, which have frequently offered data that I could not reconcile with each other. However, I have decided to publish an imperfect study simply because it is a beginning. It may perhaps encourage other scholars to look at the manuscripts concerned, correct the data, and thereby provide the basis for firmer hypotheses than have been possible for me to reach. During the writing of the book I have had the pleasant experience of finding some of my suggestions refined, some refuted, and some confirmed by investigators to whom I have shown parts of the manuscript. I should like to mention particularly the help received from Professor James M. Robinson, the Director of the Institute for Antiquity and Christianity, Claremont, California, who has experimentally tested some of my theories on the Nag Hammadi codices (of which also he has kindly provided me with detailed measurements). Chapter Four, and indeed my whole investigation, would have taken a different form if I had been able at an earlier stage to draw on his knowledge of the Nag Hammadi finds, and if I had been able to read the remarkable study of L. Gilissen in *Scriptorium* xxvi (1972): 3ff. (cf. p. 87, n.1).

A pioneer work such as this is also bound to be incomplete. I am conscious of areas of study that should have been treated in it. My work has, for instance, nothing to say on the subject of bindings, and that is a weakness. The decision to exclude the great mass of codices written in Latin was taken deliberately, after exploration of the splendid material assembled in E. A. Lowe's *Codices Latini Antiquiores* (see the Appendix to Chapter Two). The development of the codex to contain writing in Latin is a subject in its own right. I have not the qualifications to undertake it, and in any case it will contribute only marginally to the principal problem to which this book addresses itself. But I am aware that inadequate attention has been paid to the great parchment manuscripts in Greek of the fourth to the seventh centuries; and that even in my field of primary concern, the fragments of papyrus and parchment preserved in Egypt, I have failed to include a number that ought to have made their appearance, and which might, if studied, modify the conclusions reached. I have indeed at times felt that my task was like that set to the Danaides, and that it would not be possible to present even provisional results unless I made a firm stop at some point. The point chosen was November 1973. No codex published after that date will find a place in this book. Much, alas, published before that date ought to be in it and is not.

I am aware that there are risks involved in bringing together codices of Greek and Latin literature, copies of the scriptures in these languages and in Coptic, and then treating the material as unitary for the purposes of analysis. This is a point to which future investigators will have to pay attention. The original research sheets on which the list of codices has been drawn up have now been deposited in the Institute of Classical Studies of the University of London (31–34 Gordon Square, London WC1H OPY, England), where they will be available for other researchers. One further warning should be given. I have used "Christian" as a blanket term to describe theological, religious, polemical or scriptural works that are obviously not "Greek literature." I wish I had used a more neutral terminology. Dr. K. Treu has recently pointed out, in *Kairos* ii (1973): 142, that a number of anomalies make it less certain that has been generally supposed that the use of the codex form and certain standardized *nomina sacra* are firm evidence that the text concerned is of Christian ambience.

In three provisional studies I have attempted to set out and justify some of the ideas discussed in this book. They are: (1)"Akten des XIII int. Papyrologenkongr.", *Münch. Beiträge* lxvi (1974): 427ff.; (2) "La Paléographie hébraique médiévale," *Colloques intern. CNRS* dxlvii (Paris, 1974): 137-52, P1. cxvii-viii; (3) Proceedings of the XIV Int. Congress of Papyrologists (Oxford, 1974), pp. 309–12. Wherever these studies and this book are in conflict, the reader should assume that this book contains my later opinion.

I am indebted for help to many scholars. First of all, I should like to thank Professor Lloyd Daly, for continuous commentary as the lectures were given and afterwards; and especially for generously giving up much time to put in order an untidy manuscript. Then I should like particularly to name those who sent me photographs: Professor K. Aland of Berlin; Mr. Adam Bülow-Jacobsen of Copenhagen; Dr. R. A. Coles from the papyrology rooms of the Ashmolean Museum, Oxford; Professor Frank Gilliam of the Institute for Advanced Study, Princeton; Dr. R. W. Hunt, Curator of Western Manuscripts in the Bodleian Library; Professor L. Koenen of the Institut für Altertumskunde in Cologne; Dr. D. O'Connor of the University of Pennsylvania Museum; Professor A. Orlandi of Milan; Mr. T. S. Pattie of the British Museum; Dr. H. Riad, Director of the Cairo Museum; Dr. O. Sullivan, formerly Librarian of Trinity College Dublin; Dr. M. A. Vandoni of Milan; M. Jean Vezin of the Bibliothèque Nationale, Paris; Professor W. H. Willis of Duke University; Dr. A.

Wouters of Louvain. Professor Manfredo Manfredi of the Instituto Papirologico G. Vitelli, Florence, Dr. Wolfgang Müller of the Berlin Museum, and Dr. Helene Loebenstein of the Papyrusabteilung der Nationalbibliothek in Wien have not only sent a considerable number of photographs, but have courteously answered a whole series of questions.

Similarly I should like to thank the following for information or for inspecting manuscripts on my behalf: Professor K. Aland of Berlin and Münster, Professor G. Cavallo of Rome, Professor A. Henrichs of Harvard University, Professor R. Kasser of Geneva, Professor L. Koenen of Cologne, Professor A. Orlandi of Milan, Professor A. Petrucci of Rome, Dr. John Rea of Oxford, Professor J. M. Robinson of Claremont, California, and Professor Kurt Treu of Berlin.

Curators of libraries and collections to whom I have a particular obligation are: Mr. Martin Amt of the Smithsonian Institution in Washington; Professor C. F. Buhler of the Pierpont Morgan Library, New York; Dr. David O'Connor of the University of Pennsylvania Museum; the Keeper of Rare Books in the Firestone Library in Princeton. In Paris I have received much help from Messieurs C. Astruc, M. Thomas, J. Vezin in the Bibliothèque Nationale and M. Jacques Vandier of the Louvre; in Cairo from Dr. H. Riad and Dr. Selim of the Cairo Museum.

With Mr. C. H. Roberts I have maintained a continuing exchange of photographs and ideas throughout the preparation of this manuscript. Parts of it have been seen by Mr. T. C. Skeat and Dr. W. E. H. Cockle, and benefitted thereby. Professor A. F. Shore helped me with Coptic codices, and made suggestions that I have tried to follow up. Suggestions of value have also been made by Professor L. Koenen, Dr. John Rea, by Mrs. Dorothy and Professor Homer Thompson and by the late Professor Douglas Young. Last of all I should wish to thank my close colleagues in University College London. Mr. E. Hitchcock has photographed many texts for me with his accustomed skill. Mr. David Thomas helped me in the early stages of this enterprise by collecting material. Dr. W. E. H. Cockle has shown a deep interest throughout, and has constantly drawn my attention to things I might have missed. The manuscript has been typed and retyped through successive redactions by Miss Frances Mills. The editorial staff of the University of Pennsylvania Press has maintained an alert watchfulness throughout. To all of these benefactors—and to all my predecessors in palaeographical studies, who alone have made this book itself possible—I am under an obligation that can be discharged only by rigorous critical effort.

May 1975 E. G. Turner

*Supplementary note:* At the moment of reading the galley proofs I learn of the imminent publication of two repertories of 'Christian'/biblical texts, one compiled by J. Haelst, the other by Kurt Aland (*Repertorium d. gr. christlichen Papyri*). I wish they had been available six years ago! At least reviewers will now be able to check my lists of these manuscripts against theirs, for I do not expect us to be always in agreement.

I should like also to acknowledge a grant made from the Sir John Rose Bradford Bequest to University College London as a contribution towards the cost of corrections.

January 1976 E. G. T.

CHAPTER

# 1

# Towards a Typology of the Codex

The greatest benefactors of mankind are unsung and unknown—the inventor of the wheel, the deviser of the alphabet. Among their number we should place the inventor of the codex. In this form of book the sheets of papyrus or of cut and treated skin are not pasted or stitched together to form a long roll but are superimposed on each other, folded across the middle, and then secured by stitching so that they open into pages. The outside pages can be protected by binding covers and the whole ensemble then forms a durable, sturdy book, easy to store, easy to open and refer to, easy to carry about, and withal capacious since it uses both sides of the writing material. Once this new form gained acceptance, the days of the bookroll were numbered. It had served well to record the thoughts and imaginings of men for more than three thousand years; but it had some of the same disadvantages as the roll of microfilm. True, you did not need a special apparatus to use it, but it also was relatively fragile, tore easily across its length, was difficult to refer to, must be rewound after use, and could easily wrap itself in knots.

It seemed to me therefore that a Rosenbach Fellow (whose duty is to advance the study of bibliography) might very appropriately investigate the early development of the codex as a book form. Let me be quite clear. I do not mean to reopen the question of the origins of the codex. C. H. Roberts in his British Academy paper on "The Codex" of 1954[1] has set out a series of attractive hypotheses which are likely to hold the field until new evidence is forthcoming. Pointing to the fact that almost all Christian texts found in Egypt (beginning in the second century of the Christian era) are in codex, not roll form, at a time when parallel finds from the same source show that the codex form was scarcely used at all for Greek and Latin literature, he has suggested that the codex was a deliberate innovation of Christian evangelists, who evolved it from the parchment notebook. The investigation I have set myself to carry out in preparing these lectures is one into the bibliographical form of surviving codices from the ancient world. They make their earliest appearance in the second century, and examples in Greek and Latin still on papyrus from the eastern and western Mediterranean world can be found down to the seventh and even the eighth century. I shall concern myself especially with the earlier part of this period (say down to and including the sixth century A.D.) and this area, and with texts in Greek and Latin. Coptic and Manichaean books may occasionally be appealed to. But the story of the codex in the Latin west of the Empire will not be my concern except that I shall refer to those Latin codices that are written on papyrus. Manuscripts written on paper will not be discussed.

The history of the codex was described by C. H. Roberts as "a familiar but still unmapped territory."[2] His own study provided, as indicated, a brilliant suggestion about origins, a thorough discussion of the literary evidence, and an outline of the development. But it still did not map the territory—or rather it provided a general map on a very small scale. Much detailed surveying had been done, of course, as a basis for generalization:[3] but a mariner at sea in the world of the codex, wishing to find a "fix" for a new fragment, still lacks a detailed chart. And the coastline is constantly changing. When C. H. Roberts wrote he could take into account the Chester Beatty (Ch. B.) codices—twelve of them—and the sensational fragment of St. John's Gospel in the John Rylands Library. The great find of Coptic Gnostic material at Nag Hammadi was known about by scholars, but few details were available; the books of Origen and Commentaries of Didymus the Blind from Tourah were also whispered about, but exact acquaintance with them was still in the future. So also was the great corpus assembled by M. Bodmer (twenty-five books in 1970 but not twenty-five separate manuscripts; P. Bodmer I is excepted because it is a roll) which provided earlier and more complete books than many of those in Sir Chester Beatty's collection. And only in 1970 the Papyrological Institute of Cologne has made known a sensational treasure—a "butterfly" codex (the opened pages are the size of a butterfly's wings) containing on parchment in Greek a long lost work by Mani (**Misc. 4**). Generalizations in this area of work are therefore particularly liable to be upset—and any I may make during the course of these investigations must themselves take their chance. Statements based on a negative are particularly vulnerable to new information. Let me quote (not in scorn, for I have a great respect for Schubart's imagination and integrity) a statement made in 1921 about miniature codices by a great authority: "The examples known to me are not earlier than the fourth century, are mostly on parchment, and show no special care in their writing."[4] More recent finds have rendered the first and last of these statements out of date and untrue.

The practical impulse to reopen this question came in 1968 when I essayed to discover what shape of codex had been the parchment book of Menander in Leningrad that contains parts of the *Epitrepontes* and the *Phasma*.[5] Jernsted in 1891 had laid it down that the pages of this codex had originally contained not more than thirty or so verses, and the point was material to the sequence of the two sides which contain separate scenes of *Phasma*. Every subsequent editor of Menander had accepted Jernsted's results. Did they still hold after eighty years of manuscript discoveries? The search to control them revealed to me how empty was the chart of this territory. Yet the problem I was facing was one that confronts the papyrologist almost every day as he wrestles with small fragments of ancient books. Each time he has to begin almost at the beginning in his search for parallels.

A second impulse to investigate came from a consideration of the possible chronological utility of a study of the formats (the physical shape) of codices in this period. Might not such a study reinforce the somewhat hit-and-miss datings assigned by palaeographers to books on the basis of their handwritings? Every palaeographer is aware of his fallibility on this score. The person without palaeographical skill will have observed with interest a number of recent examples of incompatible dates. It will suffice to quote three examples here. In 1958 I had the good luck to see the original of a passage of Demosthenes *De Corona* (P. Oslo ii 10) preserved in Oslo, and recognized it as part of the very same sheet of papyrus manuscript of Demosthenes which had happened to pass through my hands a year or so before, and which is published as P. Harris 45. In the original edition of one piece the date assigned by the editor was third century A.D., in that of the other late first century A.D. Both could not be right! The second example is even more striking since it shows different datings assigned by the same editor: it is the Ch. B. Biblical Codex IX (**OT 183**), containing the Septuagint text of Esther. Sir Frederic Kenyon assigned it to the late third century A.D. Ch. B. Biblical Codex X (**OT 207A**), containing Daniel, was allocated to the early third century by him.[6] Shortly after the preliminary publication, Professor A. S. Hunt showed that only one manuscript is involved. The scribe is not the same in the two portions, but it is unlikely that there is a difference of seventy-five to one hundred years in the time the two portions were written. Once again the two datings cannot both be right. Yet they are repeated without change in R. Seider's *Paläographie d. gr. Papyri* II, nos. 45 and 55, published in 1970.

The third is the case of a mutilated document, P. Oxy, xvii 2105, published first by Professor A. S. Hunt in 1927. It is the edict of a prefect read by Hunt as Petronius Honoratus, prefect in A.D. 148. In 1967 Dr. John Rea reread this name as that of Maevius Honoratianus, prefect in A.D. 231–36, i.e., almost ninety years later![7] The hand can in fact be easily paralleled from documents of the middle of the third century, e.g., P. Oxy. ix 1200 (A.D. 266). This example is especially instructive since it is the error of an outstanding palaeographer; and concerns a documentary hand, a type of writing which it has often been claimed is easier to date with confidence than a book hand. Any practicing palaeographer will be able to think of similar errors in which he has himself been caught out and will be humble in consequence.

The helplessness felt by palaeographers when they have to rely on the morphological analysis of letter forms is well illustrated by the lack of agreement on the dating of the Ambrosian *Iliad,* and more recently of the Duke University fragment of Plato Parmenides **253**-*GRBS* xii (1971): 539ff. I cannot bring myself to date this latter fragment in c. ii A.D. as Professor W. H. Willis does, and throughout this study I have treated it as of iii/iv A.D. Other palaeographers of my acquaintance assign it to c. vi A.D.

An objection will at once come to mind to the procedure suggested: papyrus manuscripts (codices included) are arranged chronologically on the basis of the dates assigned to their handwriting. If a system of codex-formats erected on the basis of handwriting dates is used to correct these dates, the argument proceeds in a circle and can have no validity. The objection is a just one, and it is easy to see how circularity has distorted the truth in the past. Just because the *communis opinio* down to the 1930s was that the codex was late in invention and acceptance, not really at home till the fourth century after Christ, papyrologists tended to give late dates to papyrus manuscripts in codex form.[8]

Then in the 1930s the growing mass of material, the analyses of the Rylands Library St. John (P. Ryl. Gk. 457 = **P 52**) by C. H. Roberts and of the British Museum *Unknown Gospel* (**N. T. Apocrypha 7**) by H. I. Bell and T. C. Skeat, and above all the publication by Sir Frederic Kenyon of the Chester Beatty Codices (especially Codex VI, Numbers and Deuteronomy = **OT 36**) offered a solid base for the view that the codex was well established for Christian writings in the second century A.D. and for Greek literature in the third. Earlier datings were revised, and codices were allowed to be older than their first editors had suggested. This reaction really gained momentum in the 1950s and 1960s and has in my view now gone a great deal too far. I have already quoted the case of Ch. B. Biblical Codices IX and X (**OT 183, 207A**): of the alternative dates proposed for these (either early third century or the end of the third century) the later one seems to me to come nearer to the truth. Similarly, Bodmer Papyrus II (**P 66**), a codex of St. John in relatively small square format dated by its first editor to about A.D. 200 has been placed in the middle of the second century A.D. by Professor H. Hunger.[9] I have elsewhere given palaeographical reasons for thinking this redating wrong, and that the better placing is c. A.D. 200–250; as I have also for dating Bodmer Papyrus IV (and XXV, XXVI) (**225**), the Menander codex, not to the early or middle part of the third century, but to about A.D. 300 or even to the early fourth century. Some firmly dated examples of calligraphic handwriting of this later period have recently turned up, and they seem to me to justify my view of the later dating of the manuscripts just discussed. These examples (enumerated in *Greek Manuscripts of the Ancient World* on no. 70) include a precisely dated document (A.D. 298/9) in a large and careful rounded handwriting; a rounded book-hand of similar size and care, and of great beauty, which cannot be earlier than A.D. 306 since the manuscript is an account of the appearance of Phileas, Bishop of Thmuis, before the prefect of Egypt Culcianus, whose dates are known; and a private letter belonging to a circle of friends existing between A.D. 320 and 340 which is a beautiful example of the "mixed" style of handwriting.

Is the objection of circularity, then, to deter us from attempting our task at all? A moment's reflection on the instance just given will show that this "circularity" is complex: it is not a matter of simple opposition between an independent date for handwriting on one side and a resultant date for a codex on the other. In the dating of a papyrus manuscript by a scholar a large number of elements are taken into account. I have tried to describe them in *Greek Manuscripts.* They are a real farrago, a rag-bag of indications: for the palaeographer, like Hercule Poirot, will seize on any clue that seems likely to help him forward. The rigorous palaeographer will try to derive each single element from a certainly dated source. But the quantity of *certain* data is in fact insufficient for his needs. The certain data have to be linked to each other by extrapolation, by hypothetical extension and combination; however conscientiously the palaeographer tests out and refines his apparatus of criteria, it is unlikely that he will succeed in eliminating a subjective factor. And the important point is that (certainly in the past, and probably still) his views about the origin and growth of the codex have already entered into his apparatus of criteria for determining dates.

In this chaotic situation the palaeographer is not isolated. The archeologist and the historian of art are similarly placed. Archeologists find a way out by resort to typology. They attempt an arrangement of their pots in a series according to the hard physical factors of size and shape (and such features as rims, handles, feet). At certain points what appears to be a series is firmly anchored in time, and from the anchors dates are given to the remainder of the series.

It is in fact a typology of the (early) codex that I propose to undertake. The utility of such a study will not be restricted to the areas from which came the impulse to study, but will flow out into wider fields. And it may well be that in spite of my originally restricted aims, some light may fall on the early stages of the codex, and on the interaction of the materials papyrus and parchment in that development.

An obvious physical feature of the codex is its format, which can be simply expressed in terms of the breadth and height of a single page. I have already hinted that formats are likely to play an important part in this investigation. Examination of them will indeed be a principal part. But an attempt will be made also to take account of other physical features, prominent among which will be the make-up of the gatherings of the codex: how many sheets go to a gathering (and how many gatherings to a book); what is the order in which these sheets are arranged (if papyrus, of pages with vertical ↓ and horizontal → fibers; if parchment, of flesh and hair side).[10]

Earlier scholars have not entirely neglected formats. C. H. Roberts has some remarks on the formats of early codices. He characterizes them in terms of the proportion between breadth and height of the page. In selecting this proportion as the feature for comparison, he is treading in the same path as Wilhelm Schubart, the only other scholar known to me to have essayed this kind of investigation, and from whose thoughtful pages (though I have come utterly to disagree with them) I have learned much. In *Das Buch*[2] Schubart writes:

> To bring the measurements of codices into order, one must give first place to the aspect natural to the codex, namely the proportion of breadth to height. From this there results in the first place a group whose dimensions are equal or approximately so (small divergencies in measurement are often to be explained by damage to the margins and need not to be taken into account). . . . A contrast is provided by a format in which the breadth is about half the height. . . . Finally I believe myself able to distinguish a series of codices in which the dimensions are related in the approximate proportion 2:3 or 4:5. It seems to be no accident that many of them are of considerable size and exceed a height of 25 cm., though there are also smaller ones. Such a survey proves the general point that fixed sizes apppear here as rarely as they do in the case of the roll, perhaps even less frequently: it is the proportion between its dimensions that gives the codex its external characteristics. . . .

The argument is then supported by adducing some supposed examples of the creation of new formats by halving existing pages (we shall need to return to this argument in a later chapter, for it seems to me to prove something different from Schubart's conclusion). He then continues:

> Formats should not be entirely without value for dating codices. . . . As far as my knowledge goes, the first and second classes of formats seem to be of fairly considerable age. Admittedly, we are using a circular argument if we use formats to date handwritings when we have used handwritings to date formats. But from the mere fact that the characteristics of early handwriting strikingly coincide with approximate equality of breadth and height or with extreme differences between these two dimensions, these two formats may belong to a period down to and including the fourth century. In this same period, in spite of a great diversity of formats, a predominance of small formats is also to be observed. By way of contrast I believe I can recognize an increase in large formats from the fifth century on; "folio" sizes such as the Berlin Aristophanes codex measuring 25 x 36 cm. or the later Nonnus codex which is 28 x 40 cm. are hardly likely to be paralleled in c. iv. Still more clearly does it seem to result that in this period formats in the proportion 3:2 become established. Naturally every such observation can only be an observation of the establishment of a fashion.[11]

This passage was used by J. Manteuffel, *JJP* ii (1948), to date a fragment of Euripides *Andromache* in a Berlin papyrus codex (Inv. P. 13418) (**67**). The fragment (of which he gives no picture, but states the measurements as 11 x 17 cm.) seems to have had thirty lines on each page since this is the interval between the preserved top lines on each side; it actually preserves parts of only nine lines, plus the inside and outside margin across the breadth, and the upper margin above the writing. Manteuffel works out that thirty lines would occupy 21 cm. (I cannot, incidentally, understand his arithmetic, or follow the way he reaches his conclusion). In his statement that the fragment measures 11 x 17 cm., I suppose he means to give the height first, the width second. The distortion is still greater if he intends the opposite.[12] "Add," he says, "the upper margin of 3 cm., suppose the height of the lower margin to be identical, and the resulting total height of the page is 21 + 3 + 3 = 27 cm., and the restored page will be 17 cm. broad x 27 cm. high," i.e., a proportion he takes to be roughly 2:3. He then appeals to Schubart's "demonstration" (as he calls it) that such proportions were especially in favor in the fifth century, and dates the codex to the fifth century.

This is a rough and ready procedure, and one can have doubts about it right away. Firstly, Manteuffel adduces as a parallel for the handwriting of his papyrus codex Schubart, *Gr. Pal.* Abb. 101, a text which (since it was written by Dioscorus of Aphrodite, whose lifespan is closely dateable) must belong to the mid-sixth century A.D. (the parallel is adduced only with this caveat, that in the *Andromache* fragment the letters are upright, not inclined as in the Dioscorus).

Secondly, Schubart's generalization had been made on the basis of a very small collection of instances (thirty examples altogether ranging over four centuries). When I came to spread the net wider myself, I quickly discovered a variation in the proportion which seemed to reveal a gap in his generalization. The page size of an important though damaged codex of Callimachus, of which seven leaves survive in P. Oxy. vii 1011 (**34**), is given as 18 x 30 cm., and this codex was dated by its editors (a little hesitantly) to the fourth century: 18 x 30 is of course the proportion 3:5 not 2:3; perhaps, therefore, it is not to be considered parallel to Manteuffel's Euripides (yet it must go into Schubart's and Manteuffel's division as 2:3. Their division is tripartite, allowing only the approximate proportions 1:1, 1:2, or 2:3, 4:5). But the Oxyrhynchus codex has been dated to the fourth century. Shall we then redate Manteuffel's codex? Or should the redating be applied rather to the Oxyrhynchus codex? While thinking this over, I observed a further point: the dimensions given for the Oxyrhynchus codex, 18 x 30 cm., are identical with the dimensions quoted by A. Körte, and given for most of its pages by G. Lefebvre for the famous Cairo codex of Menander (**227**). Is it possible that this coincidence is an accident? Whatever the date we may want to assign to Manteuffel's Euripides, the Oxyrhynchus Callimachus and the Cairo Menander codex, the discovery in the latter of two papyrus codices of large format having the same dimensions is striking. It is clearly a matter requiring investigation. We can no longer dismiss as incidental and unimportant the absolute sizes of papyrus codices. It must be our business to explore the whole of the evidence to see if there are more examples of this size; and whether there are multiple examples of other sizes too. It seems, indeed, quite uncertain whether the basis from which Schubart started, that there is no rhyme nor reason in the absolute heights of papyrus roll, is not also false. No one has yet done the complicated work of reconstruction and comparison that will allow us to have any confidence in Schubart's assumption. And positive reasons may be urged why, as an assumption, it is unlikely: we know from the elder Pliny's account that papyrus sheets were manufactured to certain standard sizes, of which Pliny gives us the trade names and measurements. It is not impossible that the sizes of these sheets changed over the ages—but Egyptian craftsmen, above all others, were governed by tradition and indeed made excellent products so long as they abode by traditional methods. We may also think that individual scriptoria might have offered books in a fixed range of sizes, and wonder whether our investigations might help us to conclusions about provenance.

To this particular point we shall we need to return later on, for there is a good deal more to be said on it. But the coincidence of size discovered seems to make it quite clear that a possible source of information will remain unexplored if we do not take note of absolute sizes of codices,[13] not merely of proportions between page breadth and height. The same proportion may subsist in a codex of small absolute dimensions and one of large absolute dimensions. But we may find good evidence for dating one type early, and one late. Moreover, the system of no more than three proportions between breadth and height of page, though useful as an initial tool, is a gross simplification of the data. It omits those relations in which the breadth is greater than the height; and it omits such proportions (also not uncommon) as B3:H4, or B3:H5.

It will appear in the upshot that I have abandoned recording relations of proportion in favor of giving absolute dimensions of page size (from which, of course, the reader can himself work out the proportions). The relations of proportion have still a considerable importance for classification. But one is made aware that there are certainly many different groups (arranged by absolute dimensions) inside which the relationships of proportion apply; and that it is vital to distinguish between codices of parchment and papyrus, which will be found to give quite different results in regard to proportional relationships. The analysis of papyrus and parchment codices in an undiscriminated group, and application of the results obtained from one kind to the other, is the factor which principally vitiates Schubart's careful account of the evolution of the codex.

Our first task in the new situation will be to compile a much fuller list of examples than Schubart used. We shall wish to utilize, as far as we can have access to them, the codices which have survived nearly complete—or of which some pages are complete. From such books figures can be elicited in which one may have some sort of confidence. But the much larger number of fragmentary examples must also be taken into account. This is what I have endeavored to do in compiling my numbered list of codices in Table 16. For Greek and Latin "literary" texts I have followed the order and arrangement of R. A. Pack, *The Greek and Latin Literary Texts from Greco-Roman Egypt,* 2nd ed. 1965, but I have added texts published since 1965, giving them "A" numbers and interpolating them at appropriate points. New Testament papyri are quoted according to their "P" numeration in the lists of Von Soden, Aland, Metzger. I have used an unpublished list compiled about 1934 by H. L. Hedley for parchment manuscripts of the New Testament, giving my own numeration (**NT Parch.** ) and for both parchment and papyrus manuscripts of the Old Testament (**OT** ). Both of these lists have been crosschecked against similar lists in O. Montevecchi, *La Papirologia* (Milan, 1973). I am aware that none of my lists can be complete.

If the scholar is forced to rely on published editions, he will often be helpless. Some early twentieth-century editors (especially the Berlin editors in *BKT*) give no dimensions, no number of pages, no number of lines per column, and often no dating—or else some omnibus label such as "late." More and more it has become clear to me that ideally the present task requires an inspection of the originals: at the very least, a good photograph. In the table of codices I have marked with an asterisk the examples of which I have seen a photograph or inspected the original.

One of the obstacles to be met faces us in regard to the reconstructed measurements of Manteuffel's Euripides (**67**), which he worked out as 17B:27H cm. This was taken to be a proportion of 2:3 by adding 1 cm. to the breadth, to give a relationship of 18:27. But how can one be sure that the height of 27 cm. is not itself arbitrary? I presume the upper margin survives in this piece (Manteuffel does not say so) and that it measures 3 cm. But the height of the column of writing, namely 21 cm., was a calculation; and the height of the lower margin was assumed to be 3 cm. (I suppose because the upper margin is; actually lower margins are usually considerably higher than upper ones). Suppose the error were of 3 cm. (i.e., 3 cm. too small) for the height, and we add 1 cm. to the calculated breadth, we reach a total of 18:30, which was the size of the Callimachus and Menander codices. Let us note here four different possible sources of error which cumulatively might completely vitiate our conclusions:

(1) The errors in the assumed dimensions on which we base our calculations will, if the assumptions are erroneous, be multiplied by the multiplier we use in trying to reconstruct a whole page from a small scrap. If we have decided we have a third of the possible text and multiply by 3, any error in that assumption will be multiplied by a factor of 3.[14]

(2) It has still to be discovered whether there is any established relationship between the written space and the complete page (that is, upper, lower, and side margins around the written space).

(3) The precise size of a codex page may be uncertain if we have only one page surviving from which to judge: 18 x 30 is the size of the Menander codex given by Körte and Schubart (**227**). This is the size of many of the leaves. But some are stated by Lefebvre to be 18 x 31; Seider says 18.5 x 31.5 of the one he illustrates. We remember Schubart's warning of the liability of edges to damage. Within what tolerance can we allow for such damage? And is the hypothesis of damage enough to account for a variation between 18 x 30 and 18 x 31? The question of what deviation in size is acceptable will recur, in the next chapter, and throughout our enquiry.

On size it is worth noting that the composite Bodmer codex (of which more later pp. 79f.) had one section bound into it, in which the gatherings were 0.5 cm. higher than the preceding and following sections. This relatively small difference in dimension did not worry the maker or the user of this codex. It would seem to follow from this observation that a knife or guillotine was not used to trim the sheets to identical size, but that in c. iv A.D. in such an ancient papyrus book small differences in page or sheet sizes were readily tolerated. We should not therefore look for absolute regularity of page size.

(4) Mention of the binder's knife is a reminder of a further possible difficulty. We know that parchment MSS preserved in the great libraries were often rebound, and usually cut down in the process. This offers an additional unknown.

And after all our work on these fragments of codices, we shall not (unless we have at least a pair of conjugate leaves) be able to elicit from them what was the make-up of the codex of which they are the wretched survivor.

In the list I have drawn up I use the symbol $\alpha$ to denote the dimensions (breadth first, height second) of the complete page (given in square brackets [ ] when there is an element of reconstruction involved, i.e., the dimensions stated by the original editor or measured by me on original or facsimile photograph are less than of a complete page, so that the size of the latter has had to be calculated). I use $\beta$ to denote the area of the written portion (again in square brackets when it is reconstructed, not measured).

When one is dealing with fragments it may well seem unprofitable to attempt to reconstruct complete page sizes; and useless to compare written areas with each other. Often the most that will be possible will be to calculate the number of verses or lines contained on each page. Even this result is only a rough and ready guide. When we have a choice of several pages of a codex to explore, we note that there is commonly a variation in the figure of lines per page: e.g., the Vienna Hesiod (**91**) has 30 or 32 or 33 lines per page, the Cairo Menander (**227**) a number which varies between 32 and 37. In the Pierpont Morgan *Iliad* (**140**) the range is between 21 and 42 (average 34/35). A single figure must therefore be treated as an approximation (from which the expected variation may be as much as 5 lines). These figures, which in any case will be of interest for editors who have to restore unpublished papyri, may possibly themselves even tell a certain story, and the figures elicited from restoring codices of known authors such as Homer are likely to be valuable.

Of course the reconstruction even of the number of lines per page can only be done with the texts of known authors, where we can assume that the lines we restore from other manuscripts were once written on our fragment. New fragments of Greek literature, however interesting in themselves, will tell us nothing in this respect. And the assumption that the missing piece of text was of identical length to our medieval text (without which we cannot operate on this material) may be unjustified. The scribe may have omitted or added lines, have repeated sections, have left spaces between sections, etc. In the case of small fragments it may even be uncertain whether we are dealing with codices at all. A small scrap (the Rylands St. John itself, for instance) may be identified as a codex because the papyrus is written both front and back by the same scribe, and one passage (after a gap) continues the other. But suppose for some reason a page were left empty (such was the case with the Harris Homer, for instance), and then only that particular page survived, how could we recognize it for a codex? This difficulty may be observed in the case of P. Oxy. iii 449, the opening verses of Euripides *Andromache,* which the editors supposed to be a codex, though one side of it contains only two letters which the editors read as *ρη*[ and restored as ῥῆ[σις 'Ανδρομάχης. But Jean Bingen, *Cd'E* (1965), p. 484, has re-examined the original. No other example can be produced of a blank page before the opening lines of a play containing such a title, and in such spacing: the thesis that a codex is involved must be discarded.

One example may be given where the assumption of continuity between the two sides of a fragmentary sheet can be shown to be unjustified. P. Princ. iii 109 is a strip of papyrus 3.8 cm. broad x 21 cm. high dated by its editor to v A.D., containing on ↓ *Iliad* i 216–37, on → *Il.* i 574–97. The editor comments "the codex apparently consisted of four columns to a page and had 50 to 54 lines to a column." He is assuming that his fragment contained a complete text of *Iliad* Book i. But a quick reconstruction will show that the assumption is unjustified. The greatest surviving width, 3.8 cm., carries at most twelve, usually less than ten, letters of a hexameter line which normally reaches a length of thirty-five to forty letters; taking the figure most favorable to the editor, each line therefore would be about 11.4 cm. wide; four parallel columns would require the page to be 46 cm. wide, without counting the spaces between the columns or the inner and outer margins. This width (to anticipate) is far in excess of any other width recorded in our list; indeed, it is so unlikely, that the original assumption must be wrong. The sheet must have held not a continuous text but selected passages from *Iliad* i. The passage on one side is the crisis of the quarrel on earth between Achilles and Agamemnon; the passage on the other is the quarrel in Heaven between Zeus and Hera, precipitated by Thetis' appeal, and composed by Hephaestus. We might indeed have felt the editor's reconstruction to be suspect on the basis of C. H. Roberts' axiom ("The Codex," p. 190 n.1) that poetic texts were always written in single columns. (Cf. p.35). The practical reconstruction empirically confirms the generalization.

A further case where writing on both sides of the material by the same scribe does not justify the assumption that a fragment of a codex is concerned arises with passages from the scriptures used in the liturgy. It is not uncommon to find a single sheet, of either papyrus or parchment, on which, for example, a psalm is written. The writing may or may not continue on the back; even if it does, other evidence is desirable to prove that a codex is involved. It is known from the list in the Codex Alexandrinus that certain psalms were used in the liturgy at particular hours of the day or night. A psalm from this list will need careful inspection.[15]

The fact that a fragment is of small size may also cause difficulty, since the portion of the back preserved may not have happened to be that part on which there was once writing. The reader who wishes to note the difficulties can carry the examination further by considering the following cases in the table: **7** (Appian, from Doura-Europos: nothing visible on the back), **45** (a quaternio of Demosthenes, but page one is blank, and there are omissions between each page thereafter such as to cause the editors to label the text an exercise), **307** (small size), **396** (medical prescription on one side of a vellum leaf), **399**. Latin juridical literature offers particular difficulties, which can be seen in Pack's lists, when single leaves, double leaves, opisthograph sheets are all in theory possible descriptions of unknown and unidentified texts.

This chapter may conclude with an example of an error of the opposite kind, to which I have recently drawn attention.[16] A papyrus fragment found by John Johnson in 1914 at Antinoe contains a beautiful drawing in ink and colored washes of a group of charioteers. Its first editor, S. J. Gasiorowski, correctly called the fragment part of a papyrus codex, but for some reason (possibly because he worked from a photograph) stated that there was no writing on the back. It was therefore supposed that Gasiorowski was mistaken, and the fragment was taken to be an example of an illustrated roll, and dated two centuries too early. One has in fact only to turn the papyrus over to see that on the other side it does have writing, almost certainly by the same scribe. It is therefore an illustrated codex on papyrus, dated by its handwriting to about A.D. 500; and its page-size is calculable as at least 18 cm. wide, and very probably as much as 28 cm. wide. It therefore joins the small company of books in codex form which have illustrations: the "Alexandrian chronicle" (**370**) on papyrus, P. Berol. in v. 13296 (H. Leitzmann, *Quantulacumque* (1937), pp. 339–69; the Ambrosian *Iliad* and Vienna Genesis on parchment. The sizes of these known illustrated books seem to have been respectively about 25 cm.B x 33 cm.H (my estimate); [16+ x 28+], 28.8 cm.B x 32.6 cm.H (Bianchi Bandinelli); and 27 cm.B x 33.3 cm.H (Gerstinger, as a minimum).[17] I have argued that the illustration in the charioteers papyrus ran right across the width of the page, as do the illustrations in the Ambrosian *Iliad* and the Vienna Genesis.

## NOTES

[1] *Proc. Brit. Acad.* xl (1954): 169–204. A revised edition of this paper is planned.

[2] Roberts, "The Codex," p. 169, n.1.

[3]Among which one would specially mention W. Schubart, *Das Buch bei den Griechen und Römern*[2] (Berlin and Leipzig, 1921) (the third edition of 1962 is useless); and Sir Frederic Kenyon's chapter on "The Codex" in *Books and Readers in Ancient Greece and Rome*, 2nd ed. (Oxford, 1951).

[4]*Das Buch*[2], p. 130.

[5]See *GRBS* x (1969): 311–12. The manuscript is **227a** in my list.

[6]And U. Wilcken, *Archiv* xi 113, actually dated it to the second century after Christ.

[7]See P. Oxy. xxxviii p. xiv. Cf. Plate 5b.

[8]It is instructive to document this assertion. Grenfell and Hunt made a number of remarks in passing in their editions of *Oxyrhynchus Papyri*. For instance, on P. Oxy. iii 459 = **54** Demosthenes, "we should attribute it to c. iii. It is therefore an unusually early example of a classical text in codex form"; P. Oxy. iv 697 = **280**, Xenophon, is nevertheless assigned to c. A.D. 200. This dating is perhaps a little too late, but is remarkably honest from these editors in view of their comments on iv 656 = **OT 9**, "The MS. was carefully written in round upright uncials of good size and decidedly early appearance, having in some respects more affinity with types of the second century than of the third. To the latter, however, the hand is in all probability to be assigned." (H. I. Bell and T. C. Skeat, *Fragments of an Unknown Gospel*, p. 6, confidently date it to c. ii.) On vi 873 = **93** Hesiod, they remark "the character of the handwriting . . . points to a date not very late in the 3rd cent., in which the codex form is somewhat uncommon except for theological works." Oxy. vi 849 = **NT Apocrypha 13**, is dated to c. iv rather than c. iii because it is on parchment. "Had the material been papyrus we should have been more disposed to assign it to late c. iii rather than to c. iv." The same reason is given in regard to vii 1007 = **OT 2** (Latin Genesis on parchment), because the material is parchment, and the BM Demosthenes 34473(1) (= **47**) and Berlin Euripides *Cretans* (**80**) are grouped along with it in the third century. A. S. Hunt writes of P. Oxy. x 1226 = Psalms (**OT 65**), 'a papyrus-book of early date'; and similarly on xiii 1596 = (**P 28**); these should probably be dated earlier than by their first editor.

General criticism of Grenfell and Hunt's conservative attitude was voiced (after the discovery of the Chester Beatty papyri) by H. I. Bell and T. C. Skeat, *Fragments of an Unknown Gospel*, p. 6; by H. I. Bell, *HTR* xxxvii (1944): 201; and C. H. Roberts, *HTR* xlvi (1953): 234. J. Mallon has criticized relatively late dating of Latin handwritings for different reasons in *Paléographie romaine*, p. 182 on plate XXI (specifically commenting on Latin documents of first half of c. iv in the Abinnaeus archive): "d'une manière générale il semble que les monuments de basse époque qui, pendant longtemps, ont été seuls connus, ont exercé une sorte d'attraction vers le bas dans la datation de nombreux exemples plus anciens qui ont apparu ensuite."

[9]*Anzeige der Wien. Akad.* (1960), pp. 12–13. Cf. *Greek Manuscripts of the Ancient World (GMAW)*, no. 63.

[10]Very few scholars have surveyed these problems as a whole. The chief exceptions are W. Schubart and C. H. Roberts. Early in the twentieth century, A. Deissmann and his technical assistants won much useful information in their restoration of a papyrus codex of the Minor Prophets. Mention should also be made of the careful description and attempt to reconstruct the form of the original codex in the editorial work of H. Gerstinger and P. Sanz of Vienna and Jacques Schwartz of Strasbourg.

[11]*Das Buch*[2] (1921), 2: 131–32.

[12]In my tables, this manuscript (**67**) is shown as 32 cm. high. The figure is a recalculation by me, attempting to reconcile Manteuffel's data. The original papyrus is not now traceable in either Warsaw or Berlin.

[13]It will also be possible to reject reconstructed sizes of codex for which no parallel can be discovered. The Isocrates in *MPER* iv p. 137 (**219**) is an example. No papyrus codex is as high as the 45 cm. estimated for the complete leaf of this ms.

[14]P. Oxy. xx 2258 (= **28**) offers an instructive warning on the dangers attendant on calculation. See the remarks of E. Lobel, P. Oxy. xx p. 79n.

[15]See H. B. Swete, *An Introduction to the Old Testament in Greek* (Cambridge, 1900), p. 359; P. Sanz on *MPER* iv 14.
[16]*JHS* xciii (1973), with colored plate = **370a**.
[17]See below, Chapter Two, n.1.

CHAPTER

# 2

# The Dimensions of Papyrus and Parchment Codices

In this chapter I am going to examine tabulations of absolute dimensions of codices made of papyrus first, of codices made of parchment second, and then to institute a comparison between them. I hope to show that it is possible to classify both classes of codices into coherent and meaningful groups simply on the basis of the absolute dimensions of their pages.

Table 1 contains a provisional list of papyrus codices (papyrus only, not parchment) grouped according to the size of the complete page (or leaf, which for these purposes is identical). The B(readth) is given first, the H(eight) second. Perhaps I may interpolate that I realize the traditional palaeographer's rule has been to put H(eight) first, B(readth) second.[1] But even papyrologists who have set out to make this their rule have broken it with sufficient frequency to make it desirable each time to characterize in some such way as I am doing those measurements which are of B(readth), and those which are of H(eight). When the page appears to be complete, the sizes are of the actual measurements (or the largest measurements, when there are several pages) without addition to account for hypothetical loss of margins. Sizes on this list that are obtained by reconstruction (that is, because no complete page survives that can be measured) are placed inside square brackets. The sizes are always of *complete* pages (whether surviving or reconstructed), never of the fragments themselves. The Roman figure at the end of each entry is the date by century after Christ. It is the date given by its editor, unless I have explicitly substituted my own assessment, and marked it by the initials E.G.T.

It is right to say here that it was an arbitrary choice on my part to put B(readth) first, H(eight) second, and to make the classification in descending order of B(readth). Since, as will be seen later, if the groups are real groups, they are probably derivative from the height of the roll available to the scribe who wrote them, it might have been thought more natural to give H(eight) first, and arrange the list in descending order of H(eight). I have indeed tried this order, and compiled a list in which H is set out first. In fact it makes the groupings produced by arranging dimensions in the opposite order harder to observe. There appears to be a continuous progression from the maximum height of 41 cm. to the minimum height of 2.9 cm. Inside that progression it is not easy to seize a correlation of heights with breadths, or even to divide it arbitrarily into blocks for which any satisfactory unifying feature, such as date or function, can be suggested. If breadth is put first, however, unifying reasons spring to the mind at once, as I hope to show in the next two chapters. This suggests that there may be a real importance for understanding in giving priority of place to breadth. I shall return to this point later.

## TABLE 1

### Papyrus Codices Grouped by Dimensions

Sizes given are of page (leaf) by B(readth) first, H(eight) second. Sizes inside square brackets are obtained by reconstruction. The small Roman figure at the end of the line is the editor's date by century after Christ. The arrangement is by descending order of breadth.

*Group 1 The Largest Sizes*

| | | | |
|---|---|---|---|
| VERY BROAD | [37B x 28H] | **28** | Callimachus, P. Oxy. xx 2258, vi-vii |
| | [30 x 40] | **447** | Cicero, *In Cat.* + Greek glossary (school book), P. Vindob. G. 30885, iv-v |
| | 30 x [36?] | **465** | Virgil glossary, *PSI* vii 756, iv-v |
| | [27.5 x 41] | **457** | Virgil, P. Ant. i 29, iv |
| | [28 x 40] | **236** | Nonnus, *BKT* v, 1, 94, vi |
| | 27 x 36 | **C22** | Sahidic Sirach, etc., viii |
| BROAD AND VERY TALL | [26/25 x 36] | **480** | Digest, P. Ryl. iii 479, vi |
| | 26 x 33.8 | **Misc. 1** | Tax register, P. Lond. iv 1419, viii |
| | 25 x 37/6 | **10** | Aristophanes, *BKT* v, ii, 99, vi |
| | 24 x 35 | **189** | Homer, *PSI* xiii 1299, vi |
| | 24 x 34 | **Lat. 6** | Josephus, Milan Ambrosiana Cimelio I, vi |
| LESS BROAD, STILL VERY TALL (35 cm. H and more) | [25/20 x 40/35] | **223a** | Lollianus, *Phoenikika,* ii |
| | [ x 39] | **158** | P. Flor. ii 110, iii (E. G. T.) |
| | [ x 36](E. G. T.) | **93** | Hesiod, *Theogony,* P. Oxy. vi 873, iii |
| | [23 x 36.5] | **OT57A** | Psalms, *Stud. Papyrol.* iv, 91, v/vi |
| | [22.4 +? x 34.3+?)] | **481** | Index to *CJ*, P. Oxy. xv 1814, vi |
| | 21.5 x 40.4 | **84** | Galen, *Göteborgs Högsk. Årskr.* 31. 201, vi |
| | [21.5 x 35.5] | **97** | Himerius, *Classica et Med.* 17, 23, v |
| | 21.5 x 35.5 | **507** | St. Cyril, Louvre E. 10295, + U. C. L. + Vienna, vi |
| | [21 x 37] | **247** | Pindar, P. Oxy. xiii 1614, v-vi |
| | [21 x 36/5] | **257** | Plutarch, P. Ant. ii 85 + 213, iii |

| | | | |
|---|---|---|---|
| | 20.6 x 37.7 | **478** | Index of Stephanus to Digest, *PSI* i 55 (Wodke, *Christentum am Roten Meer*, pp. 122ff.), vi |
| | [20 x 35] | **459** | Virgil glossary, P. Ryl. iii 478 + P. Med. 1 + P. Cairo, iv/v |
| *Group 2* | | | |
| LESS TALL | [28 x 33] | **99** | Hippocrates, P. Ant. ii 86, vi/vii |
| | [27 x 33](?) | **127** | Homer, *PSI* viii 977, iv-v |
| | [27 x 34/33] | **132** | Homer, *PSI* i 10, v/vi |
| | 25.5 x [33] | **C35** | Pauline Epp. (Sahidic), *SB Wien* 1914, no. 5, v or vi |
| | [25 x 33](E. G. T.) | **25** | Aristophanes, P. Oxy. xi 1374, v or vi |
| | [25 x 33(?)(E. G. T.)] | **16** | Aristophanes, P. Oxy. xi 1371, v or vi |
| NEARLY SQUARE | 29.6/29 x 30.3/30 | **Lat.2** | Avitus, Paris BN Lat. 8913, vi |
| | [27 x 30/29] | **466** | Virgil glossary, P. Fouad i 5, iv/v |
| | [25 x 31] | **279** | Thucydides commentary, *Denkschr. Wien. Ak.* 1925, Abt. 2, iii |
| | 25 x 30(ed.) | **383** | Rhetorical catechism, *Wien. Stud.* 1937, 68, v-vi |
| | 24.5 x 27/26.5 | **514** | Didymus, *in Psalmos* (P. Tourah V), vi |
| | 23.5 x 29 | **148** | Homer, *PSI* xiii 1298, v-vi |
| | 23.5/24 x 27.5/27 | **512** | Didymus, *in Ecclesiastem* (P. Tourah III), vi |
| | [23 x 30+] | **444** | Cicero, P. Oxy, viii 1097, x 1251 (BM 2057), v? |
| | 23 x 27 | **513** | Didymus, *in Genesim* (P. Tourah IV), vi |
| | 22.5 x 27 | **515** | Didymus, *in Zacchariam* (P. Tourah VI), vi |
| | 22 x 28.5 | **517** | P. Tourah VIII, vi |
| | [22 x 28] | **P33 + P58** | Acta Apostol., Vienna, vi |
| *Group 3* (c.23/21 x 32/31) | [23.5 x 32?] | **170** | Homer, P. Oxy. xv 1818(E. G. T.), v or vi |
| | [23 x 33] (E. G. T.) | **482** | Codex Justinianus, *PSI* xiii 1347, vi |
| | 22 x 33/32 | **Lat.1** | Augustine, Paris BN Lat. 11641, vii-viii (E. A. Lowe) |
| | [22 x 32] | **250** | Pindar, *PSI* ii 147, ii |
| | [22] x 31 | **455** | Terence, *Andria*, P. Oxy. xxiv 2401, iv? |
| | [ x 30] | **77** | Euripides, *Phoenissae*, P. Rain. iii 21, vi |

| | | | |
|---|---|---|---|
| | 21 x [32] | **149** | Homer, *Il.* xiii, *BASP* X (1973):47, v |
| | [20 x 32.5] (E. G. T.) | **67** | Eur. *Orestes,* P. Berlin Manteuffel, v-vi (E. G. T.) |
| | [20 x 33.5] | **324** | Pastoral poetry, *MPER* i 4, ii/iii |
| | [20 x 30+] | **409** | Aristotelian Physics, *PSI* xiv 1400, vi/vii |
| | [ ] x 34 | **302** | Epic, *BKT* V, 1, 67, iv |
| ABERRANTS | [20/19 x 30/29] | **464** | Virgil ii-vi, P. Colt 2, vi? |
| (cf. Group 5) | [20/19 x 30/29] (E. G. T.) | **467** | Virgil, *PSI* i 21, v |
| | [19/18 x 34] | **279a** | Thucydides i 99-105, P. Oxy. ined., iii |
| | [20 x 30+] (Welles) | **52** | Commentary on Dem., *YCS* (1957), 181, ii/iii |
| | [19/18 x 33] | **OT36** | Numbers etc., Ch. B. VI, iii(E. G. T.) |
| | 19 x 33.5 | **C13** | Sirach(Coptic), *BIFAO* viii 64, vi? |
| *Group 4* | [22 x ] | **317a** | Epikedeia, *BKT* v, 1, 82, iv |
| (c. 20 x 25) | [20.4 x 25.4] | **P45** | Gospels and Acts, Ch. B. I, iii |
| | 20 x 26 | **NT Apocryph. 9** | *Praxeis Paulou* (Hamburg), iii/iv |
| | [20 x 25] | **157** | Homer, P. Rain. iii 4, v |
| | [20 x 25] | **222** | Josephus, P. Rain. iii 36, iii |
| | 19.8 x 24.5 | **535** | Hermas, P. Oxy. xiii 1599, iv |
| ABERRANTS | 21 x 28.4+ | **266** | Theocritus, P. Antinoe, v-vi |
| | [20.5] x 29 | **445** | Cicero glossary, P. Ryl. iii 477, v |
| | 20.4 x 27.2 | **Lat. 5** | Hilarius de Trinitate, Vindob. Lat. 2160, vi |
| | 20 x 27.5 | **458** | Virgil glossary, P. Colt 1, vi |
| | [20/19 x 27/26] | **176** | Homer, P. Oxy. iv 777, iv |
| | 19 x 26.5 | **499** | Latin-Greek-Coptic Conversation Manual, Klio 13, 27, vi |
| *Group 5* | 19.5 x 31 | **537** | Ignatius, *BKT* vi 1, v |
| (18 x 30) | 19 x 31 | **P74** | Acts, Epp., P. Bodmer xvii, vi or vii |
| | 19 x 29.5 (J. Rea) | **91** | Hesiod, P. Rain. 19815, v (E. G. T.) |
| | [19/18 x 32/31] | **224** | Lysias, P. Lond. + P. Ryl. iii 489, iii/iv |
| | 18.8 x 28.3 | **104a** | Homer, P. Oxy. xxxvi 2747, v or vi |
| | 18.7 x 28 | **OT91** | Psalms 36, *PSI* xiv 1371, iv |
| | [18.5 x 31.5](E. G. T.) | **161** | Homer, P. Oxy. xv 1817, v or vi |
| | 18.5 x 30 | **P63** | Biblical Hermeneia, v or vi |
| | 18 x 31.5 | **C32** | Coptic *Manichaean Homilies,* iv or v |

| | | | |
|---|---|---|---|
| | 18 x 31.5 | **C31** | Coptic *Manichaean Kephalaia,* iv or v |
| | 18 x 30 | **34** | Callimachus, P. Oxy. vii 1011 iv/v |
| | 18 x 30 | **227** | Menander, Cairo 43227, iv/v |
| | [18 x 30] | **74** | Euripides, *Medea,* P. Ant. i 23, v-vi |
| | [18 x 30] | **230** | Menander, *Georgos,* P. Genève, v(E. G. T.) |
| | [18 x 29.5] | **72** | Euripides, P. Oxy. xi 1370, v |
| | 18 x 29 | **133a** | Homer, *Iliad,* P. Ant. iii 160, iii/iv |
| | [18 x 28] | **OT5** | Ch. B. IV, Genesis, 961, iv |
| | [18 x 28] | **146** | Homer, *BIFAO* 61, 169, iv |
| | 18 x 27.5 | **551** | Origen, *Contra Celse, Commentaire* . . . (Tourah Codex II), vi/vii |
| | [18] x 26.5 | **P15** | 1 Corinthians, P. Oxy. vii 1008, iv(E. G. T.) |
| | [17.8 x 26.7] | **OT181** | Ch. B. XI, Sirach, iv |
| | 17.5 x [30] (E. G. T.) | **OT191** | Heidelberger Septuaginta Pap. 1, vi-vii |
| | 17.5 x 27.5 | | Homer, Berlin P. 13230 (Schubart, *Das Buch*[2] 187) |
| | [17.5 x 26.5] | **Lit.2** | Deir el Balaizah Euchologium, vi |
| | 17.5 x 27 | **C33** | Coptic, Ch. B. *Manichaean Psalm Book,* iv or v |
| | [17 x 32/31] | **233** | Menander, P. Oxy. vii 1013, v-vi |
| | [18.5] x 31 | **78** | Scholia to Euripides *Phoenissae,* P. Wurzb. 1, vi |
| | 17 x 30 | **M4** | P. Leiden "X," Chem. Receipts, iv |
| | [17 x 30] | **23** | Aristophanes, P. Oxy. xiii 1617, v |
| | [17 x 29] ? | **P81** | i Peter, P. Barc. Inv. 20, v(E. G. T.) |
| | 17.3/17.5/15.2 x 29.1 | **C47** | Nag Hammadi Coptic Codex VII (Krause), iv? |
| | 16.6 x [31] | **26** | Aristotle, *Philologus* 44, 21, vi–vii |
| SUBCLASS OF GROUP 5 18 x 25 | [18.5/17] x 25.6 | **211** | Isocrates, P. Oxy. viii 1095, iv |
| | 18 x 25 | **OT1** | Berlin Genesis, 911, iv |
| | 18 x 25 | **C12** | Coptic Exodus, *BIFAO* viii 43, v or vi |
| | [18/17 x 24] | **548** | Origen, P. Giss. Univ. Bibl. ii 17, iii/iv or iv |
| | [17.5 x 25] | **446** | Cicero, *PSI* i 20, v-vi |
| | [17] x 24.5 | **129** | Homer, P. Oxy. iv 763, iii |

| | | | |
|---|---|---|---|
| ABERRANTS OF GROUP 5 | 18.5 x 20.5 | **421** | Shorthand manual, P. Ant. 1, iv |
| | [18 x 21.3] (E. G. T.) | **P52** | St. John, P. Ryl. iii 457, ii |
| | [18/17 x 23] | **OT88** | Psalms 33, *Stud. Pal.* ix no. 8, vi-vii |
| | 17.5 x 22 | **OT71** | Psalms codex "U" = BM Pap. 37, vii |
| | [17 x 23] | **453** | Sallust, P. Oxy. vi 884, v |
| | [17] x 21 (E. G. T.) | **OT11** | Ch. B. Pap. V, 962, Genesis, iii/iv |
| ABERRANTS OF GROUP 8 RATHER THAN 5? | [17 x 34] (Lenaerts) or [16 x 32] (Oellacher) | **8** | Aratus, P. Lit. Lond. 34, iv ? |
| | [17 x 32] | **275** | Thucydides, P. Berol. 13236, ii/iii |
| *Group 6* (c. 16B x 28H) | 16 x [29] (E. G. T.) | **15** | Aristophanes, *Lysistrata, Mél. Nic.* 217, v (ed.), iv (E. G. T.) |
| | [16 x 28.7] (E. G. T.) | **59** | Dio Chrysostom, *JEA* 16, 187, iv ? |
| | 16 x 28 | **Lit.8** | Christian liturgy, Schmidt, *Studien Heinrici,* v (E. G. T.) |
| | 16.5 x 27.5 | **C7** | Coptic Letters of St. Paul, P. Milan Vogl. V, v? |
| BROADER AND TALLER | 16.5 x 29.3 | **C1** | Coptic BM Ms Or. 7594, iv |
| | 16.5 x 30/29 | **M 5** | P. Holm., iv |
| LESS BROAD (some examples to be classified as Group 8?) | [15.6 x 28] | **391** | Medical, P. Ryl. iii 529, iii |
| | [15.5 x 27] | **153** | Homer, Seider, *Pal.* ii 32, iii |
| | [15.5 x 26.5] (to Group 7 ?) | **OT189** | Amos, P. Oxy. vi 846, vi |
| | 15 x 32 | **406** | Panegyric, *MPER* i 14, iv-v |
| | [15+ x 29.8] | **OT65** | Psalms, P. Oxy. x 1226, early iii (E. G. T.) |
| | [15 x 29] (E. G. T.) | **22** | Aristophanes, P. Oxy. xi 1373, v? |
| | 15 x [29] | **151** | Homer, *PSI* x 1169, iii |
| | [15 x 28] | **171** | Homer, *PSI* ii 140, iii |
| ABERRANT | 16.5 x 25 | **131a** | Homer, *Iliad* viii, P. Ant. iii 158, iii |
| | 16.5 x 19.7 | **Lit.9** | Liturgical Book, *VBP* iv 58, viii? |
| | [16] x 25.6 | **P39** | John, P. Oxy. xv 1780, iii |
| | [16 x 25] | **240** | Pamprepius, *SB Wien* (1928), v/vi |
| | [16] x 23 | **P19** | Matthew, P. Oxy. ix 1170, iv/v(E. G. T.) |
| | [16 x 22] | **523** | Anthology from Gregory of Nyssa, *BKT* vi 38, v |
| | 16 x 19 | **Lit.4** | Liturgical Book, P. Egerton 5, iv-v |
| | 15.8 x 22.3 | **C19** | Pierpont Morgan Coptic 636, ix |

| | | | |
|---|---|---|---|
| *Group 7* (c. 15B x 25H) | 16/15 x 27/26.5 | **M3** | Magic, *PGM* II pap.xiii = P. Lug. Bat. "W," iv (E. G. T.) |
| | 15.6/15.7/14.1 x 25.7 | **C43** | Nag Hammadi III (Krause), iv |
| | [15.5 x 23.5] | **410** | Philosophical, P. Lit. Lond. 163, iii |
| | [15.5 x 22] | **504** | St. Basil, *BKT* vi 21, v |
| | 15.3 x [26] | **OT195** | Ch. B. VII, Isaiah 965, iii |
| | 15.1 x 25.7 | **C49** | Nag Hammadi IX (Krause), iv |
| | [15 x 25] | **128** | Homer, *BIFAO* 61, 151, iv |
| | [15] x 25 | **C15** | Coptic Luke, *BIFAO* viii 76, iv or v |
| | [15 x 24.5?] | **69** | Euripides, *Bacchae,* P. Ant. ii 73, v-vi |
| | [ x 24.5] | **32** | Callimachus, P. Oxy. 2168 + P. Berlin 13417A, iii? |
| | 15 x 23.5 | **420** | Shorthand Manual, BM Inv. 2561, iii-iv |
| | 14.7/14.9/12.0 x 24.2 | **C48** | Nag Hammadi VIII (Krause), iv |
| | [14 x 24.2] | **P47** | Ch. B. III, Revelation, iii? |
| ABERRANTS 1 | 15.5 x 22.5 | **Lat.7** | Isidorus, St. Gall.Stiftsbibl. 226, vii |
| | [15] x 21+ | **111** | Homer, *PSI* vii 746, iii (E. G. T.) |
| | [15 x 20] | **P32** | Titus, P. Ryl. i 5, iii (E.G.T.) |
| | 14.8 x 22.5 | **334** | Astronomical table, Proc. Am. Philos. Soc. 1962, 385, iv |
| | 14.5 x [21+] | **416a** | Schoolbook, *Anc. Society* i (1970): 20, iv |
| | 14 x 21.7 | **C29** | Coptic Liturgy, "Ms d'Anastasy," vi or vii |
| | 14 x 21 | **341** | Astrological treatise, *PSI* ii 158, iii |
| | 14 x [20] | **OT7** | Yale Genesis, P. Yale 1, ii/iii (E. G. T.) |
| | 14 x 18.5 | **C16** | Coptic Phillips codex a, vii/viii |
| | 13.7 x 19.7 | **210** | Isocrates, P. Oxy. xv 1812, v or vi |
| | [13.5 x 20] | **530** | Hermas Pastor, P. Oxy. ix 1172, iv |
| | [13.5 x 20] | **C30** | Coptic Isaiah, P. Bodmer xxiii, iv |
| | 13.1 x 19.5 | **503; OT175** | Aristides, *Apologia,* etc., P. Lit. Lond. 223, iv |
| | [13/12 x 20.5] | **P28** | St. John, P. Oxy. xiii 1596, iii (E. G. T.) |
| ABERRANTS 2 (cf.Group 6 "less broad") | 15.5/14.5 x 33 | **516** | Didymus, in Hiob (= P. Tourah VII), vi |
| | 14.8 x [32/30] | **354** | Glossary, P. Oxy. xv 1803, vi (may be taller) |

| | | | |
|---|---|---|---|
| | 14.5 x 32 | **550** | Origen, Dialogue (= P. Tourah I), vi |
| | 14 x [32] | **OT187** | Freer Minor Prophets ("W"), iv (E. G. T.) |
| | [14 x 30] (to Group 8 ?) | **46** | Demosthenes, de Fals. Leg., P. Lit. Lond. 126, iii |
| *Group 8* (B half H, B14/12 x H 30/25) | 15.4/14.5-13.8/13.5 x 28.4 | **C42** | Nag Hammadi II (Krause), iv |
| | [15.2 x 30.5] | **OT202** | Jeremiah, Ch. B. VIII, iv (E. G. T.) |
| | 15.2/13.5 x [27/26.5] | **P46** | Pauline Epp., Ch. B. II, iii |
| | 14.7/14.9/12.9 x 27.9 | **C46** | Nag Hammadi IV (Krause), iv |
| | 14.5 x [29] | **199a** | *Odyssey,* P. Ant. iii 174, vi ed., iv E. G. T. |
| | 14.4 x 30 | **C41** | Nag Hammadi I (Krause), iv |
| | 14.3/14.2/13.7 x 28.2 | **C51** | Nag Hammadi XI (Krause), iv |
| | 14 x 30+ | **234a** | Menander, *Misoumenos,* P. Oxy. xxxiii 2656, iv |
| | [14/13 x 27.5/26.5] | **60** | Dionysius, *Bassarika,* P. Lit. Lond. 40, iv ? |
| | 14 x [27] | **OT222; 543** | Enoch, Melito, Ch. B. XII, iv |
| | 14/12.5 x 27 | **140** | Pierpont Morgan *Iliad,* iv |
| | 13.8 x 27.2 | **C53** | Nag Hammadi XIII (Krause), iv |
| | 13.5 x [23+] | **90** | Hesiod, *SB Berlin* (1887), 809, iv/v |
| | [13.5/13] x 24.5 | **224a** | Lysias Hypotheses, P. Oxy. xxxi 2537, ii/iii |
| | 13 x 27.5 (V. Martin) | **225** | Bodmer Menander, iv |
| | 13 x 26 | **P75** | Luke, John, P. Bodmer xiv/xv, iii (E. G. T.) |
| | [13 x 26] | **100a** | Homer, *Cd'E* 1971, 313, iii (E. G. T.) |
| | 12.5 x 25 | **C2** | Coptic St. John ("Q"), iv |
| | [12.5 x 25] | **P5** | P. Oxy. ii 208 + xv 1781, St. John in Greek, iii |
| | [12+ x 25] | **P37** | St. Matthew, P. Mich. iii 137, iv |
| | 12.1/11.4 x 26.6/25.6 | **C50** | Nag Hammadi X (Krause), iv |
| | 12 x [24.7] | **P1** | St. Matthew, P. Oxy. i 2, iii |
| | 12 x 25 | **C8** | Coptic 1st Ep. Clement, *TU* 1908, iv ? |
| | 12 x 24.5 | **419** | Shorthand Manual, BM Inv. 2562, iii-iv |
| | 12 x 23 | **79** | Euripides, *Rhesus,* P. Achmim 4, iv/v (cut down ?) |
| LESS THAN 12 cm. BROAD | 11/9.5 x 25 | **C11** | Sahidic Apocalypse, *TU* (1899), 4, v ? |
| | 11.5 x 25 | **529** | Hermas Pastor, Mich. inv. 917, iii |

| | | | |
|---|---|---|---|
| | 11+ x 24.3 | **OT9** | Genesis, P. Oxy. iv 656, ii/iii (E. G. T.) |
| | 11 x 21.5 | **Misc.2** | Land-tax register, *Forsch. u. Fortschritte* XXXV (1961): 23, vii |
| | 11 x 20 | **OT19a** | Genesis, P. Erlangen 1, iv-v (may be larger) |
| | 10 x 23.5 | **Lit. 6** | Legend of St. George, P. Colt ii 6, vii |
| ABERRANT 1 (much higher than broad) | 13.7 x [32.5] | **150** | Homer, P. Merton i 3, iii |
| | 13/9.5 x 30.5/27 | **M1** | Magic, *PGM* I pap. iv, Paris, iv |
| | 13 x 29.5 | **106** | Harris Homer, P. Lond. 126, iii |
| | [13/12 x 33] | **P69** | St. Luke, P. Oxy. xxiv 2383, iii |
| | 12.8 x 34.4 | **OT207a** | Daniel, Esther, etc., P. Chester Beatty IX-X, ii (Wilcken), iii (E. G. T.) |
| | 12.5 x [33.1] | **280** | Xenophon, P. Oxy. iv 697, ii |
| | [12.5 x 31] | **263** | Sophocles, P. Oxy. i 22, iv or v |
| | 12.3/11.3 x 28 | **M2** | Magic, *PGM* I pap. v = P. Lond. 46, iv |
| | [11 x 30/29] | **21** | Aristophanes, *PSI* vi 720, iii |
| ABERRANT 2 (H not quite twice B) | [13.5 x 23 (E. G. T.)] | **281** | Xenophon, P. Varsov. + P. Ryl. iii 549, iii |
| | 13.3/12.3/11.3 x 24 | **C45** | Nag Hammadi V (Krause),* iv |
| | 10.7/12.3-13.2/12.4 x 23.6 | **C44** | Nag Hammadi IV (Krause), iv |
| | 13 x 24 | **OT75a** | Psalms, P. Bodmer xxiv, iii/iv |
| | 13.2 x 23 | **OT223** | 'Ascension of Isaiah,' P. Amh. I 1, v |
| *Group 9* ("Square", Schubart: e.g. 15 x 17, 14 x 16 or 13/12 x 15/13) | 16.5 x 17.8 | **244** | Philo, Paris BN Suppl. gr. 1120, *MIFAO* ix, 2, iii |
| | 15 x 17.5 | **243** | Philo (P. Oxy. + P. Haun. + PSI xi 1207), iii |
| | 14.2 x 16.2 | **P66** | St. John, P. Bodmer II, iii |
| | 14.2 / 14.6 x 15.5 / 16.0 | **OT87a** etc. | Composite Bodmer V, VIIff., XII, XX, iv (see p. 79 and Table 12) |
| | [14 x 16.6 (E. G. T.)] | **214** | Isocrates, *PSI* i 16, v ? |
| | [14 x 16 (E. G. T.)] | **208** | Isocrates, P. Ross Georg. i 16, iv |
| | 14 x 15 | **C9** | Coptic *Epistula Apostolorum*, TU 1919, iv |
| | 13.5/10 x 15 | **C34** | Coptic Gnostic, Berlin P. 8052, TU 60, v |
| | 13/12.5 x 15.5/14.5 | **C10** | Achmimic Elias Apocalypse, TU 1899, iv or v |

*Nag Hammadi codex XII (Krause) (**C52**), surviving measurements 15.2 x 23.8, is manifestly incomplete; J. M. Robinson restores as c. [19 x 26].

| | | | |
|---|---|---|---|
| ABERRANT 1 (NOT SQUARE i.e., range in B is similar, but difference between B and H is 3 cm. or more) | [14] x 18 | **OT 180** | Sirach, P. Oxy. xiii 1595, vi |
| | [14/13.5 x 17] | **OT22** | Genesis, P. Lit. Lond. 202, iii/iv |
| | 13.5 x 17 | **P4** | St. Luke, P. Paris Suppl. gr. 1120, iii |
| | 13 x 18 | **355B** | Grammatical and lexical study book, P. Chester Beatty inv. Ac 1499, *Ancient Society* iii: 259, iv |
| | [13/12 x 18/17]?? | **P 64 + P 67** | St. Matthew (Oxford and Barcelona), ii |
| | [12.8] x 16.7 | **134** | Homer, P. Oxy. iii 548, iii |
| | [12.4 x 16.6] | **OT15** | Genesis, P. Oxy. ix 1167, iv |
| | [12 x 17] | **OT 165** | Proverbs, P. Ant. i 8, iii |
| | [12 x 17/16] | **OT51** | ii Paralipomena, P. Barc. inv. 3, iii (E. G. T.) |
| | 11.5 x 16 | **OT43** | Judges, *PSI* ii 127, iii (E. G. T.) |
| ABERRANT 2 (broader than high) | 15.2 x 14.6 | **C3** | Coptic Melito, Mississippi Crosby, iii or iv |
| | 14.3 x 12.2 | **C6** | Achmimic Proverbs, P. Berlin Or. 987, iv ? |
| *Group 10* (less than 11 cm. B, and "square") | 11.4 x 12.6 | **446a; Lat.4** | Cicero, Cat. i, ii, *Psalmus Responsorius,* P.Barc., iv |
| | 10.2 x 15.7 | **45** | Demosthenes, P. Ryl, i 58, v, exercise? |
| *Group 11* ("Miniature," defined as less than 10 cm. broad) | 8 x 9 | **415** | Schoolbook, P. Bouriant 1, iv |
| | 7.7 x 11.5 | **OT58** | Psalms, P. Oxy. xv 1779, iv |
| | 7 x 10 | **OT56** | Psalms 1ff., P. Erzh. Rainer, Führer p. 5, v |
| | 6.6 x 7.5 | **350** | Palmomancy, P. Ryl. i 28, iv |
| | [6.3] x 7.3 | **OT60** | Psalms, P. Lit. Lond. 204, iii ? |
| | 5.6 x 6.6 | **P62** | Greek-Coptic Lectionary, Symbolae Osloenses 1945, 121, ? iv |
| | 5.3 x 2.9 | **P78** | Epistle of Jude, P. Oxy. xxxiv 2684, iii/iv |
| | 4.5 x 6 | **Lit.10** | Christian Acrostic Hymn, *BKT* vi p. 125, iv |
| | 4.3 x 5 | **OT85** | Schoolbook, incl. Psalm 32, 9-15, *MPER* iv 24, iv-v |
| | 2.6 x 4 | | Lord's prayer (amulet?), P. Ant. ii 54, iii ? |

Before calling attention to some characteristics of these groupings, one should perhaps first ask whether they are *real* groupings at all. Does the range of deviation from the postulated norm undermine their credibility? There has already been some general discussion of this difficulty in Chapter One, p. 8. Three points may be made here:

(1) It is quite unclear what allowance must be made for the wear and tear of time. The edges of pages of papyrus may have been broken off, or been pared down at the

time of the first binding or of later rebindings[2] (as it is certain that some surviving parchment codices have been pared down). The only way to proceed is to assume that when they preserve a straight edge the present dimensions of a page (leaf) are the original ones, and to see how far this assumption may require modification. One can in fact be really satisfied about a size only if one has several pages of a codex. Even then, if it is a thick codex in a single quire, the inside sheets will be less broad than the outside. The variation, for instance, in the Pierpont Morgan *Iliad* (**140**) is from 14.0 cm.B for the outer leaves to 12.5 cm. for the inner; in Berlin Coptic 8502, a composite codex (**C 34**), the variation is between 13.5 and 10 cm.H. Ibscher has claimed that in P. Ch. B. II (**P 46**) the variation is as much as 5 cm., though I cannot find an example of more than 3 cm.

(2) It seems quite possible that the ancients were not troubled (any more than the readers of early printed books) by unevennesses in page sizes. Some pages of the Cairo Menander codex (**227**) which appear to have their original margins measure 18 x 30 cm., others 18.5 x 31.5 cm. (the former is slightly the commoner). L. Doutreleau has further observed that in the Tourah codices "variations between one leaf and another may be of the order of 1 cm."[3] A variation of 1.5 cm. in a dimension of 30, 0.5 cm. in a dimension of 15, is therefore attested even in a codex which is not in single-quire form.

(3) As we shall be reminded later, papyrus is a hand-made product, the finished sizes of which are not governed by any more definite physical limitation than the skill of the craftsman and the size of the papyrus stem that he can handle. There is no physical restriction comparable to that imposed by the papermaker's tray on the papermaker. It is, in consequence, acceptable in itself that the manufactured sizes of papyrus sheets should not be constant.

Taking these factors into account it seems possible to accept the groupings in the table of dimensions as significant groupings about a norm. A deviation from the norm of 1 (or in the larger groupings, of 2) cm. in each of breadth and height may be regarded as insufficient to cause the grouping to break down. When the relationship between breadth and height is also found to be constant (as it is in Group 8, where B = ½ H), the grouping may confidently be taken to embody the intentions of the original makers of the books in question. In such cases (and this applies also to Group 9 and Group 5) the factor of proportion between breadth and height retains its importance; but it is instructive (and as I shall hope to show, useful for chronology) to observe the absolute limits within which the proportion is observed.

The range of deviation just mentioned does not well apply to the first three groups. They are meant to display the largest sizes of papyrus codex; and though these codices are not by any means all of late date, they reveal a fondness for large formats attested equally in codices of parchment. But beginning from Group 4, when the range of deviation exceeds 2 cm. in either breadth or height, I have classed the codex as "aberrant." It will be the task of scholars to find an explanation of the "aberrancy," and to assess whether or not the anomaly is significant.

It will be noted that in Group 1 the dates are predominantly vi.[4] But there are a number of interesting exceptions, some of them enormously broad and high codices which belong to the formative period of the papyrus codex. Such are P. Flor. ii 110 (**158**), *Iliad* (a reconstruction from a tiny surviving fragment); P. Oxy. vi 873 (**93**), Hesiod *Theogony;* P. Cairo inv. 47268 (**171a**), Homer; *PSI* ii 147 (**250**), Pindar *Paeans* (on the strength of the correspondence of a fragmentary text with that of P. Oxy. v 841); the Cologne codex of Lollianus (**223a**); the Antinoopolis Plutarch (**257**); the

Vienna codex of pastoral poetry, *MPER* i no. 4 (**324**). The Old Testament codices are also to be placed in this category: P. Ch. B. VI (**OT 36**) and P. Ant. i 9 (**OT 164**), Proverbs. In Chapter Seven Table 14, will be found a list of codices with many lines to a page, most of them of relatively early date. These very big early codices just mentioned will have, at a later stage, to be compared with the aberrants class 1 of Group 8.

Compared with Group 1, Group 2 also shows a degree of chronological spread. However, only one dating is of iii, there are some of iv, while vi is predominant. In Group 3, if the Pindar (**250**) is rightly assigned to ii and rightly restored, the spread is from ii to vi.

By contrast, Group 4 (20 x 25) is predominantly of iii to iv, except for its aberrants. Group 5, a large group (32 entries), has 2 apparent examples of iii/iv, seven of iv, five of iv/v, ten of v (including examples listed as "v or vi") and eight which are later. In its pure form its proportions are B : H : : 3:5, and the type examples are the Cairo Menander or the Oxyrhynchus Callimachus (18 x 30). The aberrants of this Group have been reclassified since I first listed them at Marburg in 1971; there are enough examples of the size 18 x 25, date iii–vi, to form a sub-group. That done, the remaining aberrants form a second sub-group of about 17/18 x 23/21, a format that could be thought of as approximating to "square," with a wide spectrum of dates, beginning in ii. It will be found that a format of this size is well paralleled in parchment (p. 31). It is also to be borne in mind that the examples in Group 6 could also be reclassified, so as to treat codices of say 16.5 x 29 as special cases of Group 5, and to class the less broad examples separately. As set out, however, (assuming a mean 16 x 28) the dates are predominantly iii–iv (several examples of iii, some of v). The dates assigned to codices in Group 7 and its first set of aberrants are predominantly iii-iv, but note P. Ant. ii 73 (**69**) (assigned v–vi) and the St. Gallen Isidorus (**Lat. 7**) (vii). It is interesting to observe that in the first list of aberrants there are almost sufficient examples to make a sub-group size 14/15 x 21/22, in which two astronomical books and a school book figure. In Chapter Seven we shall call attention to the closeness of this format to that of the Yale Genesis. The second set of aberrants appended to Group 7 are later (iii/iv to vi/vii).

Group 8 contains 25 examples (31 if one is allowed to count breadths between 12 and 10 cm.) of one characteristic type of papyrus codex, that in which the height is double the breadth. Maximum breadth is about 15 cm., minimum 10. One of the 25 is ii/iii, and 22 are of iii or iv (accepting my redating, first suggested by its format, and then checked on a photograph, of P. Ant. iii 174, from vi to iv). All except 10 of these examples are known to be single-quire codices (see p. 58 below), and even those ten may be of single-quire form. Characteristic examples of this group are the Bodmer Luke/John (**P 75**, iii) among Christian texts, or the Bodmer Menander (iv) among books of Greek literature. They are usually quickly written, have narrow margins, and are often executed in small handwriting that allows many (50-60) long lines to the page.[5] Attention may be particularly called to the four Gospel codices, two of John, two of Matthew, of practically identical format (12.5 x 25). In the case of the two former, one in Coptic, one in Greek, the same number of sheets was used to make the manuscript. The first class of aberrants from this group exaggerates further the disproportion between breadth and height, offering a very narrow, tall page in which B:H :: 4:10. Some of these aberrants are certainly to be dated to ii. They will come up for discussion in Chapter Seven.

Group 9, though not constituted of so many members, is also a characteristic type of papyrus codex, nearly square according to the description given by Schubart (a proportion B:H :: 7:8). Many examples of this group are not later than iii. As types of the group, one might select the Bodmer St. John (**P 66**, iii, 14 x 16) or the two Philo manuscripts (16.5 x 17.8 and 15 x 17.5 respectively). The scribe has usually allowed himself a more generous spacing for his handwriting (and at times also for margins) than is the case with Group 8. The 10 aberrants in Class 1 show a difference between B and H of 3 cm. or more, so that the definition "square" will have to be stretched excessively if it is to cover them. Nevertheless, the range of breadths of these aberrants is similar to that of the "square" manuscripts. I have therefore included them under Group 9, while drawing attention to their aberrancy. Their dates are also predominantly iii and iv; indeed one of them (**P 64 + 67**, an early codex of St. Matthew's Gospel) may be as early as ii. It is therefore open to us to regard this subclass in which B:H roughly corresponds to 2:3 as competing with Group 8 for the distinction of being the earliest format of the papyrus codex.[6] The two Coptic manuscripts composing aberrant Class 2 have the distinction of being broader than they are high.[7] Group 10 is only a special case in a slightly smaller format of Group 9. Under Group 11 I have collected all papyrus codices which are less than 10cm. broad, using that breadth as a conventional upper limit for codices termed "miniature." When compared with the similar category of parchment codices, two points will stand out: [1] there are no papyrus codices which match the common parchment format of c. 9/10 x 9/12; [2] the number of miniature codices on papyrus (10) is small compared with the number of parchment codices in the same class (45). It was no doubt of parchment manuscripts that Schubart was thinking when he wrote that "in the early period of the codex there is a predominance of small formats."[8] The statement is just not true of papyrus manuscripts.

This brief review of the classification of papyrus codices by format has been made in order to support the contention that groupings by absolute—not only by relative—sizes can be made, and that within chronologically definable periods scribes favored one or other of such groupings sufficiently for these groupings themselves to offer a chronological aid to the researcher. Of course the groups call for further analysis than this; for instance, the relationship between size of written area (the $\beta$ measurements) and complete page (the $\alpha$ measurements) deserves investigation; so does an account of the number of lines per page, and whether the lines are long, written in a single column, or relatively short, written in two or more columns. On some of these points more will be said shortly. The basic information according to which such an analysis can proceed is collected in the Consolidated List of Codices Consulted (Table 16). It will not be possible in the compass of this book to provide an exhaustive correlation. Besides, much more work needs to be done on the way the scribe lays out his page. Knowledge of $\alpha$ and $\beta$ measurements is in itself insufficient, without attention to relative sizes of page and margins (upper and lower, inside and outside). A rule of thumb would allow the lower margin to be bigger in proportion of 3:2 than the upper margin. But it is usually the margins that have suffered most in our fragments.

The immediate question to be asked is whether parchment codices in turn can be classified into groups according to their formats; if so whether these groups also were favoured by scribes at certain chronologically definable periods, and whether they bear such a relationship to the groupings of papyrus codices that the influence of one class on the other may be postulated. I have therefore next attempted to tabulate codices on parchment according to their dimensions on the same principles as applied to papyrus.

## TABLE 2

### Parchment Codices Classified by Dimensions

(arranged in descending order of breadth)

*I Height 35-40 cm.*

| | | |
|---|---|---|
| 35B x 40H (T. C. S.) | א | Bible, "Sinaiticus," BM Add 43725, iv |
| [34.5 x 42.5] | | Vergilius Augusteus, date? [cf. Nordenfalk, *Die spätant. Zierbuchstaben,* pp. 70ff; A.Petrucci, *Miscellanea Cencetti* (1973), 31-45] |
| 32.5 x 40 | **NT Parch. 7** | Greek lectionary, Vienna G. 2324, vi (E. G. T.) |
| 30.5 x 36.5 | **CL 2** | Dioscorides, Vienna Med. gr. 1, A.D. 510 |
| 29.5 x 38.5 | **NT Parch. 71, 104** | Coptic-Greek Lectionary, *Stud Pal.* xi p. 16, ix |
| 28 x 38 | **509** | St. Cyril, *CQ* (1949), 5, viii |
| 27.7 x 36 | **NT Parch. 41** | Coptic-Greek lectionary, *Stud. Pal.* xi 55, vi? |
| 25 x 36 | **"M"** | Octateuch, Paris gr. Coislinianus 1, vi |

*II Height 35-30 cm.*

| | | |
|---|---|---|
| 28.8 x 34.4 | **NT Parch. 43** | Coptic-Greek Lectionary, Paris + BM + Vienna, *Stud. Pal.* xi p. 10, vi |
| [28.8 x 32.6] (Bianchi-Bandinelli) | **CL 5** | Ilias Ambrosiana, 1019, vi ? |
| 28.8/28.5 x 33.7/33 | **"N"** | Gospels, Purpureus Petropolitanus, vi |
| 27.3 x 32.3 | | Hexateuch, Ambros. A 147, iv/v |
| 27 x 33.3 (some sheets are bigger; trimmed) | | "Wiener Genesis," Vienna theol. gr. 31, vi |
| 27 x 33 | | John Chrysostom, Homilies, Guelferbytanus 75a, vi/vii |
| 26.5 x 32.5 | **OT 137** | Greek-Coptic Lectionary, *Stud. Pal.* xi 83, vi? |
| 26.5 x [33] | **OT 139** | Greek-Coptic Psalter, *Stud. Pal.* ix 17, vi? |
| 26.4/25.6 x 32.5/31.4 | **"C"** | OT, NT, Codex Ephraemi rescr., Paris gr. 9, v (Hatch), vi (Cavallo) |
| 26.4 x 31.6 (T. C. S.) | **"A"** | Bible, "Alexandrinus," BM Royal Ms 1 D V-VIII, v (cut down ?) |
| 26 x 31 | **"Σ"** | Gospels, Rossanensis purpureus, vi |
| 26.3 x [ ] | **168** | Homer, Berlin pap. 6794, vi |
| 26/25 x 30.5 | **OT 37** | Deuteronomy and Joshua, Freer, vi |
| 25 x 30 (Turin leaf) | **"H"** | Pauline Epistles, v/vi |
| 25 x 30 | **"O"** | Gospels, Sinopensis Purpureus, Paris suppl. gr. 1286, vi |
| [24.7 x 34.3] | **"Λ" = OT 53** | Psalms, Freer, vi-vii |
| 23.8 x 30.2 (Pal. Soc.) | **CL 6** | Homer, Cureton rescr., BM Add. 17210, v/vi |

| | | |
|---|---|---|
| 23.4/21.3 x 30.5/28.8 (cut down) | **"R"** | Luke, Nitriensis rescr., BM Add. 17211, late v? |
| [23? x 33] | **NT Parch. 27A** | Mark, *MPER* iv 32, vi |
| 22.9 x 30.5(?) | **CL 1** | Cassius Dio, Vat. gr. 1288, v (cut!) |
| [22.5 x 31/30] (E. G. T.) | **476** | Codex Theodosianus, P. Oxy. xv 1813, v-vi |
| 22 x 32 | **Lat. 1** | St. Augustine, Paris BN Lat. 11641, papyrus and parchment, vii-viii (E. A. Lowe) |
| 22 x 31 | | Dialogues of Pope Gregory, Vat. gr. 1666, A.D. 800 |

*III Large, "Square"*

| | | |
|---|---|---|
| 26 x 28.1 | **CL 7** | Strabo rescr., Vat. gr. 2306, vi |
| 25.4 x 26.7 (Pal. Soc.; 27 x 27, Cavalieri-Lietzmann) | **"B"** | Bible, Vaticanus gr. 1209, iv |
| 23.8/23 x 25/24.3 | **"G"** | Heptateuch, Sarravianus Colbertinus, iv/v |
| 21.5 x 25.8 (cut down!) | **"D"** | Codex Bezae, v |

*IV c.* 23B x 29H

| | | |
|---|---|---|
| [23 x 29] | **39** | Demosthenes, *PSI* ii 129, iv |
| 22.5 x 29.5 | **NT Parch. 31a** | St. Mark, Ibrim ined., v/vi |
| [ x 28/27] | **470** | Virgil, P. Ant. i 30, iv |
| 22 x 27 | **"E"** | Acts, Codex Laudianus gr. 35, vi-vii |
| [22 x 26] | **NT Parch. 101c** | Titus, palimpsest, Tiflis 2123, v |
| [20 x 26] | **20** | Aristophanes, Hermes 35, 602, v to vii |

*V c.* 20/17 x 25/21

| | | |
|---|---|---|
| [20 x 25/24.6] | **"T" = NT Parch. 44** | Gospels, Borghesi Copt. 109. 65, vi? |
| [20 x 25] | **NT Parch. 12** | St. Matthew, P. Oxy. ix 1169, v-vi |
| 19.7 x 24.8 (Pal. Soc.) | **"D$^{p}$"** | Pauline Epistles, Claromontanus Paris gr. 107, v |
| 19.4 x [24] | **456** | Virgil rescr. Copt., *Studi Calderini-Paribeni* ii 453, v |
| [19 x 24] | **254** | Plato, *Parmenides, GRBS* 1971, 539, ii(ed.), iii/iv(E. G. T.) |
| [20 x 16]* | **218** | Isocrates, *MPER* iii 40, v |
| [19 x 19] (E. G. T.; [20 x 20] Zereteli) | **197** | *Odyssey,* P. Ross. Georg. i 7, iv |
| [19? x 22] | **129a** | Homer, P. Ant. iii 157, vi/vii |
| 18 x [ ] | **204** | Lexicon to *Iliad,* P. Amh. ii 19, vii |
| [18 x 22] | **NT Parch. 74** | Acts iii, Moscow Golenischev Copte 55, v |
| 18 x 21.6 | **347** | Life of Alcibiades, P. Oxy. iii 411, v |
| [18/17 x 20] | **NT Parch. 31** | St.Mark, *MPER* iv no.33, v |
| 17.8 x 22 | **44** | Demosthenes, P. Ant. i 27, iii? |
| 17.7 x [25] | **NT Parch. 93** | 2 Corinthians, *MPER* iv 47, vi |
| 17 x 22.7 | **450** | Juvenal(Antinoe), *JEA* 21, 199, v-vi |
| [17 x 21] | **OT 204** | Jeremiah, *MPER* iv 29, vi |
| 17 x 21.2 | **C 5** | Coptic Pistis Sophia, BM OR. Add. 5114, iv or v? |
| [17/16 x 25] | **OT 40** | Deuteronomy, Nachr. Göttingen (1911), 167, v-vi |

*So editor, ?16B x 20H intended.

*VI Proportion Between* 1 : 2 and 3 : 5. About 29 cm. High

| | | |
|---|---|---|
| 18.5 x [28] | **OT 156** | Psalms, codex Climaci rescr., vii? |
| 17.9 x 29.5 | **"Q"** | Prophets, Marchalianus, Vat. gr. 2125, vii/viii |
| 17/16 x [29?] (ed.) | **471** | Gaius, *PSI* xi 1182, iv-vi |

*VII Breadth* 16 cm. *Not Square*

| | | |
|---|---|---|
| 16.5 x 23.5 | **3** | Aeschines, Von Hartel, *Feierlich. Sitz. Akad. Wien* (1886), 44, v |
| 16.5 x 21 | **41** | Demosthenes, Class. Philol. 20, 97, iv |
| 16.5 x 19 | **47** | Demosthenes, P. Lit. Lond. 127 (BM 34473[1]), ii |
| 16 x 20 (?) see 20 x 16 | | |
| [16 x 20] | **118** | Homer, *Iliad* iv, P. Rain. inv. 26744, vi |

*VIII Breadth* 17/16 cm. *"Square"*

| | | |
|---|---|---|
| 16.2 x [ ] | **OT 2** | Genesis, P. Oxy. vii 1007, iii |
| [ ] x 16 | **NT Parch. 83** | Romans, *MPER* iv 43, iv |

*IX Breadth* 15/14 cm. *Not Square*

| | | |
|---|---|---|
| 15 x 20 | **37** | Chariton "Thebanus deperditus," vii? |
| 15 x 19(ed.) | **NT Parch. 109** | Apocalypse, *PSI* x 1166, iv |
| 14.5/13 x 21/20.5 | **NT Parch. 1** | Freer Gospels, v |
| 14 x 22 | **235** | Menander, *PSI* ii 126, iv or v |
| 14 x 21.2 | **OT 69** | Psalms, *Stud. Pal.* ix no.7, vii |
| [14 x 21] | **56** | Demosthenes, P. Ant. ii 80, iv |
| [14 x 19](?) | **NT Parch. 75** | Acts, *ZNTW* xxvi, 110, v (E. G. T.) |

*X Breadth* 15 - 12 cm. *"Square"*

| | | |
|---|---|---|
| 15 x 17 | **178** | Homer deperditus, *SB Leipzig* (1904), 211, iv |
| 15 x 16 | **229** | Menander, *SB Leipzig* 1908, 145, iii? |
| [14.7 x 16] | **188** | Homer, P. Amh. ii 23, iii/iv (E. G. T.) |
| 14.6 x 16.2 | **NT Parch. 56** | St. John, P. Oxy. vi 847, iv |
| 14.5 x 16.3 | **NT Parch. 66** | St. John, *ZNTW* xxvi, 104, vi/vii (E. G. T.) |
| [14.5] x 15.5 | **OT 80** | Psalms xxv 7- , *BKT* viii 6, v? |
| [14 x 17.8] | **278** | Thucydides, *Wien. Stud.* (1885), 116, v-vi |
| [14 x 17] | **94a** | Hesiod Catalogue, *PSI* xiv 1383, ii/iii (E. G. T.) |
| 14 x [16.5] | **18** | Aristophanes, *PSI* x 1171, iii |
| 14 x [14+] | **OT 141** | Psalms 103, *BKT* viii 14, v |
| [14 x 14] | **NT Parch. 89** | 1 Corinthians, P. Lit. Lond. 216, v |
| 13.9 x [13] (N. B.!) | **OT 185** | Tobit, P. Oxy. viii 1076, vi |
| 13.6 x 15.3 | **NT Parch. 46** | St. Luke, *Stud. Pal.* xii 185, iv/v |
| [13+] x 14.5 | **449** | Cicero, *Mélanges Chatelain* 42, v |
| 13 x 16.8 | **184** | Homer, P. Ryl. i 53, iii/iv |
| [13 x 16.5] | **OT 14** | Genesis, *MPER* iv 1, v |
| [12.7 x 15](ed.) | **NT Parch. 82** | Romans iv, v, *HTR* 45, 81, iii? |
| 12.5 x 15[+?] | **OT 47** | 1 Kings, *Anz. öst. Akad.* 1956, 189, iv |

| | | |
|---|---|---|
| 12 x 15 | **OT 221** | Enoch, *MIFAO* ix 1 (1893), vi (E. G. T.) |
| [12 x 15] | **NT Parch. 51** | St. Luke, *PSI* i 2 + ii 124, iii/iv (E. G. T.) |
| [12/11 x 15/14] | **277** | Thucydides, P. Ant. i 25, iii |
| [12 x 14] | **NT Parch. 65** | St. John, *ZNTW* xxvi, 102, v-vi |
| [12 x 13] | **OT 73** | Psalter, *MPER* iv 6, vi |

*XI Breadth* 11/10 cm. *"Square"*

| | | |
|---|---|---|
| 11.9 x 14.8 (Willis) | **C4** | Coptic Jeremiah, Mississippi Coptic II + P. Bodmer XXII, iv-v? |
| [11.8] x 14.3 | **273** | Thucydides, P. Lit. Lond. 106, iv |
| 11.5 x 14.5 | **80** | Berlin "Cretans," c. A.D. 200 (E. G. T.) |
| 11.4 x [16.2] | **98** | Hippocrates, P. Ant. i 28, iii? |
| [11 x 15/14] (ed.) | **NT Parch. 34** | St. Mark, *Stud. Pal.* xii 186 + *MPER* iv 34, iv/v |
| 11 x 13.6 | **OT 116** | Psalms, P. Lit. Lond. 208, vi-vii |
| [10.5 x 14.3] (E. G. T.) | **40** | Demosthenes, P. Amh. ii 24, iv |
| 10.5 x 13.1 | **OT 121** | Psalms, P. Oxy. xi 1352, iii/iv (E. G. T.) |
| 10.1 x 13.5 | **NT Parch. 105** | 1 Peter (+?), P. Oxy. xi 1354, iv |
| 10 x 11.5 | **C18** | Coptic Acts, Pierpont Morgan Glazier G 67, iv or v |

*XII Breadth* 13 - 10 cm. *Not Square*

| | | |
|---|---|---|
| [13 x 19/18] | **OT 74** | Psalms, *MPER* iv. 7, vii-viii |
| [13 x 18] (ed.) | **OT 169** | Proverbs, *MPER* iv 26, v |
| [13/12 x 18/17] | **221** | Isocrates, P. Ant. ii 83, iv |
| [12 x 19] (ed.) | **NT Parch. 60** | St. John, *MPER* iv 36, v |
| [12 x 17] (ed.) | **NT Parch. 77** | Acts, *PSI* ii 127, v |
| [12/11 x 18] | **256** | [Plato] *Eryxias, Wien, Stud.* 74, 40, iv |
| 11.5 x 19 | **342** | Astrological fragm., München cod. gr. 610, iii |
| 11.5 x 18 (ed.) | **NT Parch. 76** | Acts, *ZNTW* xxvi, 116, iv |
| 10.5 x [18] | **OT 6A** | Genesis xiii, *BKT* viii 2, iv-v |
| [10.5 x 15] | **NT Parch. 80** | Romans, *PSI* i 4, v |

*XIII Breadth Less Than* 10 cm., *Height* = 2B

| | | |
|---|---|---|
| 8.5 x 17.5 | **42** | Demosthenes, *Symmories,* etc., v? |
| [7.5 x 17] | **413** | [Lucian], *Asinus,* Lenaerts *C d É* 1974 115, iv |

*XIV Miniature (Breadth Less Than* 10 cm.)

| | | |
|---|---|---|
| 9.3 x [13/12] | **527** | Hermas Pastor, P. Oxy. xv 1783, iv |
| 9 x 13.5 | | Latin St. John, "Stonyhurst Gospel," vii? |
| [9 x 13] | **NT Parch. 61** | St. John, *MPER* iv 37, v |
| [9 x 13] (E. G. T.) | **OT 42** | Joshua, P. Oxy. ix 1168, iv |
| [ ] x 12.6 | **OT 213** | Bel, Bodl. gr. bib. d2(P), iv-v |
| [9 x 12](?) | **NT Parch. 90** | 2 Corinthians, *MPER* iv 45, vi |
| 9 x [11.5] (E. G. T.) | **NT Parch. 110** | Revelation, P. Oxy. vi 848, v |
| [9] x 10 (E. G. T.) | **217** | Isocrates, P. Oxy. viii 1096, iv |
| [9 x 10] (E. G. T.) | **NT Parch. 107** | 2 John, P. Ant. i 12, iii or iv? |
| 9 x 9 | **NT Apocryph. 13** | Acts of Peter, P. Oxy. vi 849, iii (iv ed.) |
| [8.8 x 10] | **216** | Isocrates, P. Ant. ii 84, iii/iv (E. G. T.) |

| | | |
|---|---|---|
| [8.5 x 8.5] (or 8 x 8?) | **OT 186** | Tobit, P. Oxy. xiii 1594, late iii |
| 8.2 x 9.8 | | Coptic i Samuel, BM Coptic 936, ? |
| 8 x 10 | | Coptic church calendar, *ZNTW* xxxvii p. 23, ? |
| [8/7.5 x 10](?) | **NT Parch. 59** | Latin St. John, P. Aberdeen 1, iv? |
| 7.8 x 9.5 | **NT Parch. 108** | Revelation, P. Oxy. vii 1080, iv |
| 7.8 x 9 | **OT 23A** | Exodus, *Archiv* xx, p. 47, iv |
| 7.7 x 9.7 | **172** | *Iliad, BKT* V, 1, 3 (letter from Wolfgang Müller), iv |
| [7.5 x 10] (ed.) | **NT Parch. 54B** | St. John, *Archiv* xxi, p. 83, vi/vii |
| [7.5 x 10] (ed.) | **OT 175A** | Canticles, *Archiv* xx, p. 57, iv |
| 7.5 x 9.3 | | Coptic Psalter, BM Coptic 941, ? |
| 7.4 x 8.8 | **NT Apocryph. 3** | Apocryphal Gospel, P. Oxy. v 840, iv |
| 7.4 x [7.4] | **OT 29A** | Exodus, *Archiv* xx, p. 51, iv |
| 7.2 x [9.0] | **NT Apocryph. 12** | Acts of Paul and Thecla, P. Ant. i 13, iv/v |
| 7.2 x 8.2 | | Coptic Psalter, BM Coptic 943, ? |
| 7.2 x 7.5 | | Coptic Psalter, BM Coptic 947, ? |
| [7 x 12] (ed.) | **NT Parch. 95** | Galatians, *PSI* iii 251, v |
| 7 x [8.8+] | **OT 23** | Exodus, *Bala'izah* i p. 297, v |
| 7 x 8 | | Freer Coptic Psalter (quoted *ZPE* V, 100, n. 2) |
| 6.5 x [7.5] | **C27** | Coptic 1 Peter, Studies B. L. Ullmann, 265, v |
| 6.5 x 6.75 | | Coptic Proverbs, P. Ryl. Copt. 7, ? |
| 6.5 x 9.5 (E. G. T.) | **NT Apocryph. 17** | Protevangelium, P. Grenf. i 8, v or vi |
| 6.3 x 8.0 (E. G. T.) | **OT 192** | Zachariah, P. Grenf. i 6, iv to v |
| [6 x 10] (ed.) | **416** | Schoolbook, *Ét. Pap.* 7, 93, 'Byz.' |
| 6 x 8.5 | **NT Parch. 58A** | Hermeneia, *Biblica* XXXIV, 17, vii |
| 6 x 7.8 | **NT Parch. 106** | 1 James, *PSI* i 5, iv (E. G. T.) |
| 5.6 x 8.4 | **NT Apocryph. 16** | vi Ezra, P. Oxy. vii 1010, iv |
| 5.5 x 6 | **OT 190** | Jonah, PSI x 1164 + P. Berlin (*HTR* xxxviii, 195), iv/v |
| 5.3 x 6.5 (+?) | **C28** | Coptic St. John, Worrell, *Coptic Texts in Univ. of Michigan,* 1942, 7, date ? |
| 5 x 7.5? | **OT 60A** | Psalms, P. Mich. iii 132, v? |
| 5 x 5.8 | **511** | Didache, P. Oxy. xv 1782, iv or v |
| 4.5 x 6.8 | **OT 154A** | Psalms (amulet), P. Lit. Lond. 239, vi or vii |
| 3.5 x 5 | **OT 13** | Genesis, *BKT* viii 3, vi-vii |
| 3.5 x 4.5 | **Misc. 4** | Cologne Mani, *ZPE* v, 97, iv or iv/v |
| 2.85 x 4 | **OT 131** | Psalm 90 (amulet), P. Oxy. xvii 2065, v or vi. [*Not* a codex.] |

It is probably a fair assumption that the numbers of both papyrus and parchment codices listed in the preceding tables of dimensions are large enough to be a representative sample (about 250 papyrus examples, 165 parchment out of a total of, say, 1200 of both kinds). With the exception of Latin parchment codices, everything that was certain enough to be included has been included. The finds of even fragmentary parchment codices associated with papyrus discoveries have undoubtedly widened the range of available specimens. Few of the well-known "uncial" parchment codices preserved in the world's great libraries belong to the formative period of the codex (mostly they date to v or vi A.D.), and they are usually of large or very large size.

The new discoveries have produced earlier examples (as early as ii A.D.), and also many specimens of intermediate and even small sizes. The wealth of examples of small sizes is very welcome. They are a good counterpart to papyrus sizes Group 9; and as already indicated, a very large number of parchment codices (compared with papyrus) have a breadth of less than 10 cm.

The first impression, however, that is made by a comparison between the two tables is of the striking absence from parchment codices of any equivalent to the papyrus codices of Group 8 (14/12B x 30/25H) in which H = 2B. I have found only one example among parchment codices, a parchment leaf of Demosthenes *Symmories* (**42**) now in Cairo,[9] the height of which is given by Schubart as 8B x 17.5H (Plate 8). This is an eccentric dimension even for parchment, and one that is without parallel among papyrus codices. Also striking is the poor representation among the parchment codices of the large papyrus Group 5 (18 x 30). There are only three approximations to this size, the Marchalianus (17.9 x 29.5) of very late date (vii/viii), the codex Climaci rescriptus (18.5 x [28]), also late, and the Florentine Gaius, *PSI* xi 1182, of uncertain reconstruction and dimensions (16/17 x 29, according to the editors).

When, with these results in mind, one looks more closely at the list of parchment codices, it appears that throughout the table the breadth of a parchment codex is closer to its height than is the case with papyrus codices—i.e., a parchment codex is rarely of narrow format. A favorite proportion is 6:7, rarely is the difference as much as 5:7 (i.e., a little over 3:4). The numbers which reach or surpass a difference of B4, H5 are the following: 5 in the first group of very large manuscripts ([34.5 x 42.5]; 32.5 x 40; 29.5 x 38.5; 27.7 x 36; 25 x 36); about 15 in the next three groups (the greatest disproportion being 22 x 32); the 3 already listed as approximately equivalent to papyrus codices of Group 5; then the Aeschines, 16.5 x 23.5; 5 in Group VII "Breadth 16 cm., not square," 7 in Group IX and 10 more in Group XII. Add in the Cairo example 8 x 17.5, and only 42 out of 165 instances are further from square than the proportion B4, H5. Among papyrus codices tabulated, about 180 out of 250 have, for a figure 5 for H, a figure of less than 4 for B.

One will therefore expect to find many more 'square' types (square on Schubart's definition, which will admit a proportion B:H :: 7:8) among the parchment examples. And indeed there are such, in a great variety of sizes, viz.:

| | |
|---|---|
| 35 x 40 | 15 x 17 |
| 30.5 x 36.5 | 14 x 16 |
| 26 x 28 (27 x 27) | 13 x 15 |
| 23 x 25 | 9 x 10 |
| 19 x 22 | 7 x 8 |
| 19 x 19 | |

It follows from these general observations that correspondence of format between papyrus and parchment codices is likely to be closest for those groups of papyrus codices in which breadth and height approximate to each other. This is clearly the case with the large, nearly square papyrus codices of Group 2 (e.g., the Tourah papyri) and the square codices of Group 9 (12/14 x 14/16). It also applies to those examples in Group 2 which measure 27 x 33 and 23 x 29. And it explains why the classes into which parchment codices seem to fall tend to be different from those of papyrus codices. One favored parchment dimension is of 17/18B x 21/23H. Some of the aberrants of papyrus Group 5 fall inside these limits, for instance P. Ryl. Gk. 457 (**P 52**) (18 x 21), and Ch. B. V Genesis 962 (**OT 11**) (17 x 21), both sizes calculated by me; so does P. Ant. inv. 1 (**421**), shorthand manual, 18.5 x 20.5.

The absence of correspondence between parchment and papyrus formats is particularly striking in the case of the supposed earliest extant parchment leaves, those of the Berlin *Cretans*[10] and the British Museum Demosthenes, *de Fals. Leg.*[11] The leaf of the *Cretans* measures 11.5B x 14.5H. A similar size is found in other parchment codices; P. Amh. II 24 (**40**), also a manuscript of Demosthenes (*Phil.* II) written in two columns (I estimate it at 10.5B x 14.3H); P. Oxy. xiii 1621 (**273**), Thucydides, two columns, [11.8] x 14.3; P. Ant. i 28 (**98**), Hippocrates, one column, 11.4 x [16.2]. The BM Demosthenes (**47**), in two columns, measures 16.5B x 19H. Neither of these parchment sizes has any counterpart among papyrus codices of that date. Another format which is practically restricted to parchment is that of 9/10B x 9/12H. The table shows a number of examples of this format among parchment manuscripts, among them some of the relatively few instances of parchment codices of iii A.D.

Some of the later and larger examples of papyrus codex are of much the same grandiose size as later parchment codices. The enormously broad page of the Callimachus P. Oxy. 2258 (**28**), 37/38 cm., rivals the original page of the Codex Sinaiticus, 35B x 40H;[12] the Berlin Nonnus (**236**), 28 x 40,[13] and the Virgil from Antinoe (**457**) [27.5 x 41],[14] are less broad but taller; a Virgil glossary (**465**)[15] 30 x [36?] is of roughly the same dimensions as the Vienna Dioscorides[16] 30.5 x 36.5; a Berlin Aristophanes codex (**10**)[17] is of practically the same dimensions, 25B x 37H (Schubart, *Das Buch* ², p. 187, gives the height as actually 36 cm.), as the parchment Coislinianus M (Paris Bibl. Nat. 1) of the Octateuch (25 x 36). At the size 22 x 32, sheets of papyrus (as the inner sheets) and parchment (the outer sheet or sheets) are found in the same quire in the seventh century St. Augustine, BN Lat. 11641 (**Lat. 1**) The taxation register made up as a single-quire codex of papyrus, P. Lond. IV 1419 (**Misc. 1**), of the seventh century, is 26 x 33.8 cm. A number of papyrus codices in Group 2 of 23.5B x 29H (e.g., Homer, *PSI* 1298 = **148**) are of a size common in parchment.

It is quite possible that these huge papyrus pages were deliberately created to rival the similar sizes in parchment. But there is not in fact any firm evidence to show that this is the direction in which the influence was exerted, and the opposite view, that parchment books grew in size in order to compete with papyrus, can be maintained with more reason, as will be seen in a moment.

## APPENDIX

### Note on the evidence of Latin codices written on parchment

The tables in this chapter are founded principally on finds of manuscripts made in Egypt, except for a very few selected Latin papyrus codices from the Latin west (**Lat. 1–8**). To test the results obtained it seemed worthwhile to examine the Latin parchment codices illustrated and described in *Codices Latini Antiquiores.* I have worked through the magnificent manuscripts in this collection, with feelings of envy for the much better state of preservation of this material, and consequently much greater sureness in drawing deductions about formats. In doing so I have noted details of all manuscripts or parts of manuscripts down to the end of the sixth century after Christ (in practice this meant inclusion of manuscripts dated by E. A. Lowe to vi–vii). The serial numbers I assigned to such manuscripts (very many of them manuscripts of many gatherings) came to 278. But the true number is higher than that, probably about 290, since I sometimes used a single serial number to cover leaves palimpsested from different sources and eventually united in a single codex. The figure of 290 is, of course, to be added to the fragments already listed under nos. **444–500,** which are derived from Pack² and are in the main of Egyptian provenance.

I have not set out the formats of these 290-odd Latin manuscripts in tabular form. It would take a lot of space to do so. Moreover, questions would be raised which are beyond my competence to answer, and which also go beyond my own immediate enquiry. But it may be noted that the characteristic difference remarked on p. 31 between formats in parchments and in papyrus is sustained. The respective figures there given, based principally on finds from Egypt were:

Parchment codices in which for a figure 5 for H, the figure for B is less than 4 26%
Papyrus codices in which for a figure 5 for H, the figure for B is less than 4 74%

The number of Latin parchment codices falling into this category is 101 out of 290, say about 35 percent. This number includes some cases of manuscripts certainly cut down, and therefore of dubious relevance. The figure is significantly higher than the 26 percent recorded for parchment codices in Greek. But it is still less than half the 74 percent recorded for papyrus codices.

Only 1 of the 101 cases can be regarded as meeting the conditions for inclusion in papyrus group 8, that is having a height double their breadth.[18] This manuscript is:

*CLA* viii 1196 (New Testament) Fulda Bonifatianus 1 (14 x 28.8) A.D. 546/7

This examination may then in general be regarded as confirming the difference in parchment and papyrus formats already noted.

Some detailed observations on Latin practice in such matters as make-up and signatures will be set out in their proper places in this study. But it is worthwhile to comment on one particular difference between Greek and Latin manuscripts. By the time he was editing volume 3 of *CLA*, E. A. Lowe was beginning to draw attention to the value of a "square written area" as a dating feature (see the remarks on *CLA* iii 345, 363, 392,[19] 399). This feature is thereafter emphasized by such words as "square written area, a mark of antiquity." This note is sometimes put against manuscripts which Lowe himself assigned to vi–vii A.D. (e.g., *CLA* x 1481), and sometimes a stretch of imagination is required to define the area as square (e.g., in *CLA* iv 499, the Verona Livy palimpsest, stated to be 16/18 cm.B x 19.5H). A total of some thirty-five examples of the feature is to be found in the twelve volumes of *CLA*. It is clear therefore that a goodly number of Latin parchment codices of high antiquity do display this peculiarity. But not all do. Among the nineteen codices assigned by Lowe to c. iv or iv–v, the following two exceptions are to be noted:

Lucan *CLA* iii 392 iv *EAL* " β measurement" 18B x 23H; Gospels of St. Eusebius *CLA* iv 467 iv² *EAL* " β measurement" 10.5 x 17.

I note one exception from c. v:

Augustine *CLA* iv 491 v¹ " β measurement" 12/13B x 19.5/20.5H

## NOTES

[1]In *The Oxyrhynchus Papyri,* Grenfell and Hunt consistently put H(eight) first, B(readth) second. But after Part 17 the order is often, *but not regularly,* reversed. In *PSI* the order is usually HB; but the order BH is used sufficiently often to cause the user a great deal of trouble.

[2]A certain example of paring down of a papyrus codex is offered by P. Bodmer II. See p. 70.

[3]*Recherches de Science réligieuse* xliii (1955): 163.

[4]The validity of an assumption that the chronological limits fixed by palaeographical criteria for any group are exact and correspond to the period in which that form was used has still to be demonstrated. It is, indeed, improbable that it can be demonstrated. As regards a given format it is possible to imagine that once it was established it might be reproduced over several centuries; and it might be accidental that no early example of it survived. See Chapter Seven, p. 96.

[5]See the list in Chapter Seven, p. 96.

[6]As a matter of speculation might a format of about 12 x 17 represent that of parchment *membranae*?

[7]Codices which are broader than high are very rare indeed. Apart from the two just noted, I can list only P. Oxy. xx 2258, **28**, Callimachus (very big), and a conjugation table, P. Ryl, iii 534, **361**, in which the need for a number of parallel columns perhaps dictated the shape.

[8]*Das Buch*[2], p. 133. Cf. Chapter One, n. 11.

[9]*Das Buch*[2], p. 125 and plate. The papyrus is 'published' inaccessibly (see p. 69 n. 10) but I myself inspected the original in Cairo and Schubart's 8B x 17.5H is correct. The uniqueness of this format was bound to remain concealed so long as searchers were content to record proportions between breadth and height. (Addendum April 1975: J. Lenaerts, *C d'E* (1974), 115ff. has identified P. Lit. Lond. 194 (**413**) as [Lucian] *Lucius sive Asinus.* Its size can now be calculated, namely 7.5 x 17 cm. This provides a second example of this format, and the Demosthenes (**42**) is no longer unique.)

[10]Pap. Berol. 13217, *BKT* v 2, pp. 73–79 (**80**). Schubart originally dated to i A.D. A. S. Hunt disagreed sharply (P. Oxy. vii 1007 introd.), dating to iii A.D. I am not sure that Hunt's instinct is not sound. The matter will be discussed later (p. 38 below) and note at the end of Chapter Three, p. 41.

[11]BM Add. Ms 34473(1) (**47**), ii A.D. There is one single papyrus codex of this size, 16 x 19, namely P. Egerton 5 (**Lit. 4**), of iv-v.

[12]T. C. Skeat, *Cambridge History of the Bible,* 2: 78 for this estimate.

[13]*BKT* v 1.

[14]P. Ant. i 29.

[15]*PSI* vii 756.

[16]Vindob. Med. gr. 1.

[17]*BKT* v 2, pp. 99–108.

[18]*CLA* viii 1075, Breslau Univ. - Bibl. I Fol 120a, a fragment of Hieronymus, Chronicon assigned to c. v, the present dimensions of which are given by E. A. Lowe as 12.3 x 22.5 (13.2 x 21.5), is clearly incomplete.

[19]In *CLA* iii 392 it is the complete page (i.e., my $\alpha$ measurement) which attracts this comment.

CHAPTER

# 3

# The Priority of Parchment or Papyrus?

The comparison of codices of papyrus and parchment initiated in the last chapter has now outdistanced a simple confrontation of sizes and formats. It has raised the question of which material imitated which in the development of the codex. Most scholars have been brought up to believe that the new form of book did not make a beginning with examples made of papyrus, but from parchment because parchment is more suitable for folding and gathering.[1] But a number of considerations will emerge in this chapter to suggest that this belief can no longer be taken as a matter of course.

First, a clear-cut difference between parchment and papyrus codices may be touched on. The scheme of two columns to the page is used somewhat rarely in papyrus codices. Excluding lexica, scholia, glossaries, shorthand manuals, Latin, and Coptic texts with parallel translations, and arithmetical tabulations, I count a total of twenty-one instances (including one of dubious validity). (See Plate 2 and Table 3).

It is interesting to note that the dates assigned are principally ii–iv, even if the latest is vii. The Berlin Genesis codex is specially interesting. Its first eighteen pages are in double column, thereafter the scribe writes long lines in a single column. By contrast, the double column was a favored format for the parchment codex. It is first exemplified in the British Museum Demosthenes (BM 34473[1] = **47**, of ii A.D.). (Plate 3). Thereafter there are 3 instances in iii, 31 in iv alone, and some 60 more between iv and vii, and the incidence of Greek literature in this format is quite high. In neither papyrus nor parchment are there any certain examples of verse books being writen in double column (cf. p. 10). P. Ant. ii 55 (**291**), Menander, which its editor considered was written in that format, is unique and therefore suspect.

It is not clear how one should interpret the relative infrequency of double column in papyrus codices (an infrequency that stands out more sharply when it is borne in mind that there are perhaps two or three times as many examples in total of papyrus than of parchment codices). I think myself that there may be an explanation of a utilitarian character (below Chapter Six, p. 86). F. G. Kenyon supposed simply that the presence of two or more columns indicated an early date: the practice of the papyrus

**TABLE 3**

**Papyrus Codices Written in Two Columns**

| | | | |
|---|---|---|---|
| *Greek literature* | | | |
| (1) Chariton | **2** | ii or ii/iii | *SIFC* (1938), 121 (the two-column arrangement is uncertain) |
| (2) Thucydides | **275** | ii/iii | *Soc. Scient. Fenn.* (1927), 111 |
| (3) Thucydides | **279a*** | iii | (Oxy. ined.) |
| (4) Thucydides | **272** | iii | P. Gen. 2 + P. Ryl. iii 548 |
| (5) Philo (Paris B.N.) | **244** | iii | *MIFAO* (1893) |
| (6) Lysias | **224** | iii/iv | P. Lond. inv. 2852 + P. Ryl. iii 489 |
| (7) Table of Conjugations | **361** | iii/iv | P. Ryl. iii 534 |
| (8) Indeterminate prose | **436** | iv/v | *MPER* iv 47 |
| (9) Declamation | **400** | v | *Et. Pap.* 3, 79 |
| (10) Magico-medical recipes | **393b** | v | P. Ant. ii 66 |
| (11) Rhetorical catechism | **383** | v-vi | *Wien. Stud.* (1937), 68 |
| *"Christian"* | | | |
| (1) St. Matthew | **P 64 + 67** | ii | |
| (2) St. Luke | **P 4** | iii or iii/iv | |
| (3) P. Baden iv 56 Exodus | **OT 24** | ii | |
| (4) Ch. B. VI Numbers etc. | **OT 36** | ii/iii | |
| (5) Origen? | **553** | iii | BM Egerton 3 |
| (6) Berlin Genesis (first 18 pp.) | **OT 1** | iii/iv | |
| (7) Coptic, Mississippi Crosby 1 (composite) | **C 3** | iii or iv | |
| (8) Ch. B. IV Genesis | **OT 5** | iv | |
| (9) Homily, P. Ant. iii 111 | **539** | vi-vii | |
| (10) Louvre St. Ephraem | **520** | vii | |

*[Addendum April 1975: Adam Bülow-Jacobsen will in his publication present a case for regarding **279a** and **272** as parts of one and the same papyrus manuscript. The total number of two-column manuscripts will therefore be ten.]

roll had not been sloughed off. The view has been rightly contested: double columns were used down to the end of antiquity by scribes in writing vellum, and there are double-column papyrus codices dated to iv/v and later; negatively, many undoubtedly early codices are written in a single column. Kenyon, however, in drawing attention to the conservatism of scribes, was quite correct, but gave the wrong emphasis to his inference. It seems to me that the double-column scheme reproduced in many parchment codices *is* an old-fashioned one. When there are two (or more) columns to a page the length of line used is short and the columns are narrow. Now a really high-class roll of Greek prose literature was written in tall narrow columns (cf. *GMAW*, nos. 54, 55, 56, 62, 67). Therefore one might wager that a scribe would suppose a high-class codex should also have tall narrow columns for prose literature. Verse, however, will be given its natural line length, which will almost always be much longer than the lines of prose texts—hence the return to long lines for writing the "poetical" books in the great biblical codices (Sinaiticus has only 2 columns to the page in the Psalms against 4 elsewhere). I have found no other instance of a psalter being written in 2 columns. This view of the matter will certainly adequately explain the choice of the double column scheme in "calligraphic" parchment codices. It would seem to follow from it that scribes who copied on a codex of papyrus in single column were aware that they were writing a second-class book.

Now it may be readily admitted that it is not easy to find examples of calligraphy among papyrus codices of the second or third centuries. Their handwriting is in fact often of an informal and workaday type, fairly quickly written, serviceable rather than beautiful, of value to a man interested in the content of what he is reading rather than its presentation. One thinks of the Oxyrhynchus Xenophon *Cyropaedia*, P. Oxy. iv 697 (**280**), or the Oxyrhynchus Philo, P. Oxy. ix 1173, etc. (**243**), of the astronomical treatise *PSI* iii 158 (**341**) (Plate 1), the Michigan Shepherd of Hermas (**529**) or the majority of the Chester Beatty codices. These give the impression of being "utility" books; margins are small, lines usually long. But the standard by which they are measured and condemned to second-class status is not the contemporary codex of parchment, but the contemporary papyrus roll (a roll such as *GMAW*, nos. 11 or 56).

**TABLE 4**

**Summary Table of Totals**

(details in Chapter Seven, p. 89)

| | | | |
|---|---|---|---|
| Papyrus codices | c. ii | Greek Lit. | 9? |
| | | Chr. | 5 + |
| | ii/iii | Greek Lit. | 16 |
| | | Chr. | 7 |
| | iii | Greek Lit. | 82 |
| | | Christian misc. | 7 |
| | | NT | 18 |
| | | OT | 18 |
| | iii/iv | Greek Lit. | 26 |
| | | Christian misc. | 6 |
| | | NT | 7 |
| | | OT | 13 |

In any case we still know very little indeed about the early parchment codex. Only three extant examples have a claim to be regarded as of the second century; one can be classed as ii/iii; my list shows a further 15 as c. iii examples, and 10 more as belonging to the overlap between iii/iv. They are tabulated below in Table 5, p. 39, and also in Chapter Seven, p. 93. There are, then, fewer than a score of examples in parchment before the fourth century. Within the same span of time my lists show some 160 codices of papyrus, whose time distribution is shown in Table 4. It is not till the fourth century that the parchment codex begins to be at all common in Egypt. It may be objected that parchment codices are not to be expected among finds preserved in Egypt, and that no generalizations should be based on the argument from silence. However, a letter in the Petaus archive, P. Pet. 30 shows that *membranae* were offered for sale in second-century Egypt. (In a private letter from Oxyrhynchus assigned to ii/iii T. C. Skeat has corrected to "two mattresses" the translation "two parchment quaternions," δύο τετραδέρματα, P. Oxy. x 1294, 4). Outside Egypt *SHA* Maximini 30, 4 records that the emperor Maximinus possessed a codex of Homer written on purple vellum in gold letters. The large number of parchment codices of c. iv and later (recorded as found in Egypt) is in striking contrast to their earlier rarity there. The contrast also lends support to the evidence of the Roman lawyers, first properly appreciated by C. H. Roberts, that in legal terminology down to the middle of the third century, a "book" is a roll, not a codex; and also to T. C. Skeat's conjecture[2] that the codices described in Martial's epigrams were novelties which did not catch on.[3]

Of the parchment codices assigned to the second century, one in Latin (P. Oxy, i 30 [**497**], acceptably dated to early in the century by J. Mallon, *Emerita* 17 [1949]: 1) tells us almost nothing about its format. But it does not seem to be an experimental type of book, and its mere existence is evidence that this book form had a prehistory. The fact that it is an isolated example also suggests that the early experiments with this form of parchment book may well have taken place outside Egypt. They have plausibly been connected both with Martial's epigrams about parchment books, whether these are normal books or not,[4] and by C. H. Roberts with the merchants' parchment note book *(membranae).* These are the pieces of evidence usually advanced to support the assumption that the impulse to the creation of the codex came from the availability of a different material than papyrus.

Of the other two parchment codices, of c. ii, the British Museum Demosthenes (**47**) is hardly calligraphic, in spite of its double column (Plate 3). The hand is of a sober everyday type, not graceful; the dimensions are idiosyncratic. If the allocation to a date in c. ii is right, the codex is not more handsome than contemporary papyrus codices. The other example, the Berlin *Cretans* (**80**) (Plate 4a), is quite different, for it is a beautiful piece of calligraphy. But is it justly dated to the second century? In a note at the end of this chapter I have given reasons for putting it at least late in the century, and perhaps as late as A.D. 200. If that is right, then we lack evidence that the parchment codex was necessarily prized for elegance from the beginning; that it could be made elegant might have been a gradual discovery of scribes.

It has been demonstrated that the format (defined by its dimensions) of the codex is of a characteristically different shape when it is made of papyrus than when it is made of parchment. In a succeeding chapter another possible physical difference between the use of the two materials will be illustrated—namely that till at least c. iv little effort was made at the make-up stage of gatherings of papyrus to match like page with like page (Chapter Five, p. 65). The discovery that the physical form the codex takes when it is made of papyrus is distinct from the form taken in parchment cannot but lead to a questioning of the assumption underlying much recent discussion of the origin of the codex. Can the assumption that parchment is prior still be made?

We may rule out as unimportant because due to the hazard of discovery the fact that when there are codices of comparable dimensions in the two materials the papyrus example is often earlier in date. P. Ryl. Grk. 457 (**P 52**) is c. ii, the parchment format of 17/18 x 21/23 is not attested before the third century at the earliest (P. Ant. i 27, dubiously iii). Paris, Bibl. Nat. 1 is dated to c. vii by G. Cavallo, while the Berlin Aristophanes is commonly held to be of c. vi. The papyrus codices of Group 5 (18 x 30), such as the Cairo Menander (**227**) or the Oxyrhynchus Callimachus (**34**), are probably not later than c. v., and may be c. iv; but the Florentine Gaius (**471**) is far from certainly dated (E. A. Lowe says v-vi, the original editors, iv-vi) and the Codex Marchalianus is usually put in c. vii/viii. Similarly, the quantitative predominance of papyrus codices of c. ii and iii over parchment may be an accident of survival. The occurrence, however, of papyrus codices of big format in both breadth and height at an early date (see p. 23 above) is not so easily dismissed.

This point acquires a special significance when it is set alongside the fact that among the twenty-nine parchment codices dated between c. ii and c. iii/iv (i.e., early c. iv at the latest) (see Table 5 below) the largest dimensions recorded are [19 x 24], 17.8 x 22, 16.2 x [ ] and 16 x 19; and the greatest number of lines per column is 36, found indeed in the BM Demosthenes Add. Ms 34473(1) (**47**) already discussed and assigned to c. ii, but no bigger in size than 16.5 x 19. In the table of papyrus codices containing

**TABLE 5**

**Detailed List of Early Parchment Codices**

| | | | *α size* | *β size* | *No. of lines* |
|---|---|---|---|---|---|
| ii | Demosthenes | **47** | 16.5 x 19 | 11 x 14 | 36 |
| | Eur. *Cretans* | **80** | 11.5 x 14.5 | 7.5 x 10/10.5 | 26 |
| | Latin *de bellis* | **497** | small? | | |
| ii/iii | Hesiod | **94 a** | [14 x 17] | [11 x 13] | [25] |
| iii | Aristophanes | **18** | [13] x 16.5 | 10 x 11.5 | 30 |
| | Demosthenes | **44** | 17.8 x 22 | 10.6 x 14.4 | 28 |
| | Demosthenes | **58** | — | — | — |
| | Hippocrates | **98** | 11.4 x [16.2] | ? | [30, 32] |
| | Homer | **113** | — | — | — |
| | Menander | **226** | — | — | [29] |
| | Menander | **229** | 15 x 16 | — | 30, 31 |
| | Pindar | **248** | — | — | — |
| | Thucydides | **277** | [11/12 x 14/15] | [9 x 11] | 32 |
| | Astrological | **342** | 11.5 x 19 | — | 26–28 |
| | Romans | **NT Parch 82** | [12.7 x 15] | [8.5 x 11.7] | 24 |
| | 2 John | **NT Parch 107** | 9 x [10] | 6.9 x [7.9] | 20 |
| | Acts of Peter | **NT Apocrypha 13** | 9.1 x 9 | 6 x 7.3 | 14 |
| | Genesis | **OT 2** | [16.2 x ] | — | [33] |
| | Tobit | **OT 186** | [8.5 x 8.5] | 6.7 x [5.0] | 11? |
| iii/iv | Homer | **119** | — | — | 30 |
| | Homer | **184** | 13 x 16.8 | 11.3 x 13.5 | 28–34 |
| | Homer | **188** | [14.7 x 16] | — | 29 |
| | Homer | **190** | — | — | 33–34 |
| | Isocrates | **216** | [8.8 x 10] | [5.2 x 6.9] | 18 |
| | Parthenios | **241** | — | — | — |
| | Plato (Duke Univ.) | **254** | [19 x 24] | — | [29] |
| | Luke | **NT Parch 51** | [12 x 15] | — | [23–24] |
| | Exodus | **OT 29B** | ? | [ ] x 10.5 | [20] |
| | Psalms | **OT 121** | 10.5 x 13.1 | 8.2 x 10.5 | 21, 22 |

50 lines or more per page or column given in Chapter Seven, Table 14, twenty items are listed which are dated between c. ii and iii/iv; for the same period *no* such parchment codices are listed. Once again, no doubt, one must beware the dangers of the argument *e silentio.* But after all, in Table 5 itself there are twenty-nine parchment codices of the period ii to iii/iv; the sample is not entirely contemptible. The inference I draw is that the large-sized parchment codex with up to 50 lines in a column which begins to appear in c. iv is consciously modeled on the already existing large-sized papyrus codex, but is intended to surpass it in excellence (durability, beauty, lay-out).

A further point to which significance must be attached is the large number of certainly third century examples of papyrus format Group 8 which have no counterpart among parchment manuscripts. If the papyrus codex is confessedly modeled on the parchment codex, why should it at an early date have developed idiosyncratic forms (idiosyncracies which, as a succeeding enquiry will show, may also have extended to its make-up)?

Points in favor of the priority of parchment are no doubt the Latin term *membranae* applied to parchment notebooks used for business purposes, as C. H. Roberts has shown, and then perhaps extended;[5] and the references in Martial to what seem to be early parchment codices (such as the "Livius in membranis").[6] A stronger argument than any of these may be the consideration that in Egyptian book technique the papyrus roll was so firmly entrenched that a major shock was needed to prompt the experiments that resulted in its eventually being supplanted by the codex. Such a shock, it has usually been thought, was applied by the development of parchment, and its effective utilization in codex form as a menacing competitor to the use of papyrus. Yet reflection will show that the mere existence of parchment (known after all since the second millenium B.C.) could not have been sufficient to accomplish this revolution. There must also have been a powerful motive for using the codex form. One can imagine a number of coinciding and contributory reasons. For Christians, the desire to publicize the Gospel in a format clearly distinguished from the Jewish roll (the hypothesis of C. H. Roberts) was a motive of adequate power, and for them it was a matter of indifference whether the writing material was treated skin or papyrus. For non-Christians (the writer of P. Oxy. i 30 = **497**, for instance) convenience, utility and the use of both sides of the material may have been the decisive factor.

I am not here trying at all costs to assert the priority of papyrus over parchment in the development of the codex, but I am arguing that the automatic assumption of the contrary needs a new justification.[7] At the moment only one other corollary needs to be drawn from the sceptical attitude here adopted. It is that there can be no automatic presumption that the codex of papyrus is restricted to Egypt. Even if the codex of papyrus developed only in parallel with rather than preceded the codex of parchment, the lead in such a development of the best known writing material of the ancient world may have been taken outside Egypt, both in its early and its later stages. The evidence for the early stages is missing; but there is good evidence that papyrus continued to hold its own against parchment in the early medieval world. We know that important and still surviving papyrus codices of the sixth century (e.g., the Paris Avitus [Plate 7], the Vienna St. Hilary) were written in southern France, with which Egypt still maintained a flourishing commerce of papyrus. The argument from use of papyrus for a manuscript to Egyptian origin for that manuscript must be used with great care. Of course it is probable that a codex of papyrus found in Egypt which is written in a routine fashion would have been written there, since it would not have been worth anyone's while to bear the cost of transporting cheap written products. But a better quality codex might have been imported. And we are not entitled to assume that in centers outside Egypt—Antioch, Athens, Rome, Constantinople—experiments with the codex form were made only with parchment. Letters from these places of the third to the sixth centuries show that papyrus continued to be readily available in them. Books in roll form continued to be copied. As we shall see in the next chapter, a papyrus codex was very frequently made up out of a new papyrus roll; and this method would have been available to the scriptoria of Rome as easily as to those of Alexandria.

## APPENDIX

### The date of the Berlin *Cretans* (Plate 4)

Discussion of the date of this manuscript is desirable, since it is usually given as a standard example of an early parchment codex, and in some expositions considerable weight has been placed on it. The fact that it is in single-column format tells neither in favor of late or early date, since the contents are in verse. The arguments in favor of an early date are two. One is based on the format, 11.5B x 14.5H, written area 7.5 x 10 (10.5). This shape is considered to correspond to the adjective *pugillaris,* "the size of a fist," transferred from tablets of wood to parchment codices by Martial. It has been felt that this leaf might well be an example of the kind of manuscript Martial was alluding to. Secondly, the handwriting is assigned by scholars to the second century on the basis of morphological analysis. It is characterized by Schubart as an example of his "decorated style" (*Zierstil*) because of its dotted finials and serifs (*Das Buch*[2], p. 117, where he offers the date as second century; later in his *Gr. Paläographie,* p. 130, he confessed himself completely baffled. Cf. Chapter Two p. 34 n. 10).

Against these arguments it may be urged: (1) as regards format, there is no cogency in identifying this shape as that of a "codex *pugillaris*" and using that identification as evidence of an early date. It has already been pointed out that 11.5 x 14.5 is a dimension found in other parchment codices, mostly of later date, viz:

| | | | | |
|---|---|---|---|---|
| [11/12 x 14/15] | **277** | Thucydides | iii | P. Ant. i 25 |
| [12 x 15] | **NT Parch. 51** | St.Luke | iii/iv | *PSI* i 2 + ii 124 |
| [11.8] x 14.3 | **273** | Thucydides | iv | P. Lit. Lond. 106 |
| [11 x 15] | **NT Parch. 34** | St. Mark | iv | *MPER* iv 34 |
| [10.5 x 14.3] | **40** | Demosthenes | iv | P. Amh. ii 24 |

This comparison is not, of course, decisive for the dating of the *Cretans.* But it is a warning against too hasty an identification with Martial's codices.

(2) In the light of morphological analysis I should urge the case for a later date than Schubart's first thoughts. The hand of the *Cretans* is tiny in scale, a beautifully and regularly executed example of the "mixed" style (*GMAW,* p. 26) in which there is a contrast between the broad letters ( $\delta, \eta, \kappa, \pi, \tau, \omega$ ) and the narrow letters (not only $\epsilon, \theta, o, \sigma$ but also $\beta, \rho, \upsilon$). The hand slopes slightly to the right; certain forms such as the normally triangular $\alpha$, the $\delta$ with long downward oblique starting from a high dot, and the triangular "loop" to $\phi$ are strongly stylized. There are certainly tiny hands of

relatively early date which are superficially similar: e.g., P. Oxy. xxxi 2535 (*GMAW*, no. 38) which I have myself assigned to late i A.D., and which has decorations on the extremities of letters; P. Oxy. xvii 2078 (*GMAW*, no. 33), a plain nondescript hand I have assigned to c. ii A.D. But stylistically the resemblances are not strong: the former is essentially a rounded hand, the latter is of a plain style. A closer papyrus parallel is a fragment of Thucydides on a roll, probably of the early second century (P. Oxy. xiii 1622; on the back of the roll is a document dated to A.D. 148). The contrast between broad and narrow letters is not so marked, and the stylistic peculiarites (e.g., in $\phi$) are not so exaggerated as in the *Cretans*. The contrast in this latter of broad and narrow letters seems to me to be of capital importance, and (*GMAW*, p. 27) I have given reasons against dating the appearance in Egypt of this feature before the middle of the second century. If then the *Cretans was written in Egypt* (possibly a riskier hypothesis than usual, seeing the material is parchment), its date should not be earlier than that. The stylized $\alpha$, $\delta$, $\phi$ seem also to point the same way. The handwriting has marked similarities to three other handwritings on parchment, which their editors have assigned to this or a later date. They are: 1) *PSI* xiv 1383 (**94a**), a finely executed Hesiod in a small handwriting, dated by its editor to c. iii; 2) P. Ant. i 27 (**44**), a Demosthenes less well executed, the letters of which are taller and admit irregularities of form, again dated by its editor to c. iii; 3) P. Ant. i 26, a parchment roll of Xenophon, which is written on larger scale and has taller letters than the *Cretans*, but is stylistically reminiscent of it (note its $\alpha$, $\delta$ and peculiar $\upsilon$). Its editor has analyzed it scrupulously and assigned it tentatively to the second half of the second century. He considers that it was written outside Egypt. In the light of these parallels I am inclined to date the *Cretans* to the latter half of c. ii A.D. (c. A.D. 150–200). If its date is as late as this it can hardly be regarded as the prototype of the parchment codex, and the purpose of this note has been to give reasons why I do not so regard it.

## NOTES

[1]E.g., H. Hunger, *Forschungen & Fortschritte* Band 35, Heft 1 (January 1961): 23, "Als sicher kann es gelten, dass die neue Form des Buches nicht von Papyrusexemplaren ihren Ausgang nahm, sondern von dem für Faltung and Heftung viel geeigneter Pergament."

[2]*Cambridge History of the Bible*, 2: 68ff.

[3]See the passages collected and discussed by F. G. Kenyon, *Books and Readers*[2] (Oxford, 1951), pp. 133–34.

[4]*The Codex*, p. 174; and the attestation in Egypt of written *membranae* apparently offered for sale in c. ii A.D. in P. Petaus 30 (cf. E. G. Turner in *Greek, Roman and Byzantine Monographs*, Suppl, vi [1937]: 38) has already been referred to. Are there any details available on the physical size of such *membranae*?

[5]See n. 3 above.

[6]See the passages referred to n. 3 above.

[7]I have not in these pages discussed the relative suitability as material of papyrus and parchment for forming a codex, nor do I intend to do so. But one particular point made by H. C. Youtie (*A. J. Phil.* lvii [1936]: 217ff. = *Scriptiunculae* ii [1974]: 719 and 722) will bear repeating: the greatest disadvantage of papyrus is not fragility or even liability to crack, but its exposure to damage at the fore edge.

CHAPTER

# 4

# Manufacture and Size

One obvious reason why codices of parchment do not seem to occur in sizes that match codices of papyrus is a physical one. There are clearly several ways in which an animal skin can be cut up to form sheets (double leaves) for a parchment book. The size of the skin itself limits the maximum size of sheet. The actual dimensions of smaller sizes are no doubt governed by the most economical way of folding and cutting a skin: the manufacturer asks what size of sheets can be obtained without wastage. Do mechanical considerations also help to determine the size of papyrus codices and govern the distribution into groups which I hope I have convinced you does exist?

The size of a "sheet," whether the codex is of parchment or papyrus, must be twice the B(readth) of a page (leaf). The unit of manufacture must then be a sheet the dimensions of which have the same height but twice the breadth listed in my tabulations; for the sheet has to be folded centrally. The maker of a codex, whether he is the scribe or the stationer, must procure a number of sheets, which are placed above each other and then folded down their center in "gatherings"—in ways which will be explained in a later chapter.

For the benefit of those who are not familiar with papyrus it may be said at once that it will test the skill of the manufacturer of papyrus to make a sheet in one piece, without joins, out of which can be constructed even one of the more modest sizes of codex (say of my Group 8). We are certainly not to think of papyrus being manufactured in huge sheets, as paper is, and then being folded and cut. It is surely an aberration on the part of W. Schubart[1] to suppose that we may account for the way in which in the Cairo Menander (**227**) horizontal fibers are on the right-hand pages of sheets 1 and 3 and vertical fibers are on the right-hand pages of sheets 2 and 4 by the supposition that a sheet four times as large was folded into four and cut. Assuming no damage, a single constituent sheet of this codex must measure 36B x 30H. A sheet four times that size would be 1.44 m. broad and 1.20 m. high and it is a fantasy to suppose that papyrus manufacturers ever made a sheet like that.[2] The idea has come from a supposed analogy with folding the skin of an animal to make a quire in a parchment manuscript (actually it is far from certain that this is the true explanation even of this phenomenon) or with the system of "imposition" practiced by printers (cf. p. 44 n. 1).

It seems desirable to remind ourselves of the way in which the papyrus manufacturer went about his business.[3] The papyrus reed grows to a height of seven feet or more. It has a triangular stem. From one of its triangular faces the coarse rind is trimmed away and long ribands are torn (or cut—but experience shows that tearing produces a more uniform riband). These ribands are laid side by side on a hard, smooth surface, not so close that they overlap, nor so far apart that on drying shrinkage will leave a gap between them; above them a second layer is placed with equal care at right angles. A few blows with a mallet make these two layers coalesce firmly; the natural juices ("polyesters," as the chemist would term them) cause them to adhere without any added gum. The size of sheet this will make (we are speaking now of the manufactured unit) depends on the skill of the craftsman. The largest known is 46 cm. (about 18 in.) high, but it is rare to find one more than about 37 cm. (15 in.) in the Roman period, and about 28-30 cm. (11–11½ in.) is a good height then. The Elder Pliny gives a table of sizes according to breadth (he does not mention height) and their trade names. These sheets were made separately, and then gummed together into rolls—sold at the stationer's in units of twenty, fifty or even seventy sheets.[4] In these rolls, the horizontal fibers are placed on the inside where they are best protected from the constant strain involved in rolling and unrolling. Since the inside of the roll is also most easily protected from damage, it is the side usually chosen to carry the writing—what is in consequence usually called the "recto" of the roll. We should note carefully that we cannot define this "recto" except in relation to the incorporation of a sheet in a roll. The "recto" is not the apparently smoother side. In a well-pasted roll, also, the joins between the sheets will show only on the recto. As a term to describe these joins I shall use the Greek word *kollesis,* to be distinguished from *kollema* which I shall use for the sheet that is joined. These terms are explained in more detail on p. 47.

At once the idea comes up: if it is a codex you wished to make surely the papyrus craftsman provided you with separate sheets, not with sheets already pasted together to form a roll which you then had to cut up again? Yet it seems very doubtful that so simple and obvious a procedure was in fact carried out.

The question just asked seems straightforward enough. But it is not easy to answer just because editors and palaeographers have usually not asked it; and since photographs are usually inadequate to allow an answer, only examination of the originals will provide one. If the description provided by an editor is silent, no answer can be ventured till the original is inspected.

One of the earliest scholars to call attention to the presence of *kolleseis,* which he called *Klebungen,* was G. A. Gerhard [quoted by A. Deissman, *Heidelberger Septuaginta Pap.* (1905), p. 4] in his reconstruction of Heidelberger Septuaginta-kodex 1 (Minor prophets = **OT 191**): "[Kollesis] is on recto (i.e., →) of double leaves XVII–XVIII at beginning of column; that is, a normal *selis* is of c. 20 cm." Since then six scholars have put on record views on the question at issue. The view that in general holds the field today was first conceived by H. Ibscher. W. Schubart in 1921[5] described Ibscher's discovery as follows: "Ibscher has been able to establish, in the case of a Coptic codex,[6] that the leaves all originate from a single roll. This had originally been cut in a horizontal direction into three strips, from which the sheets were

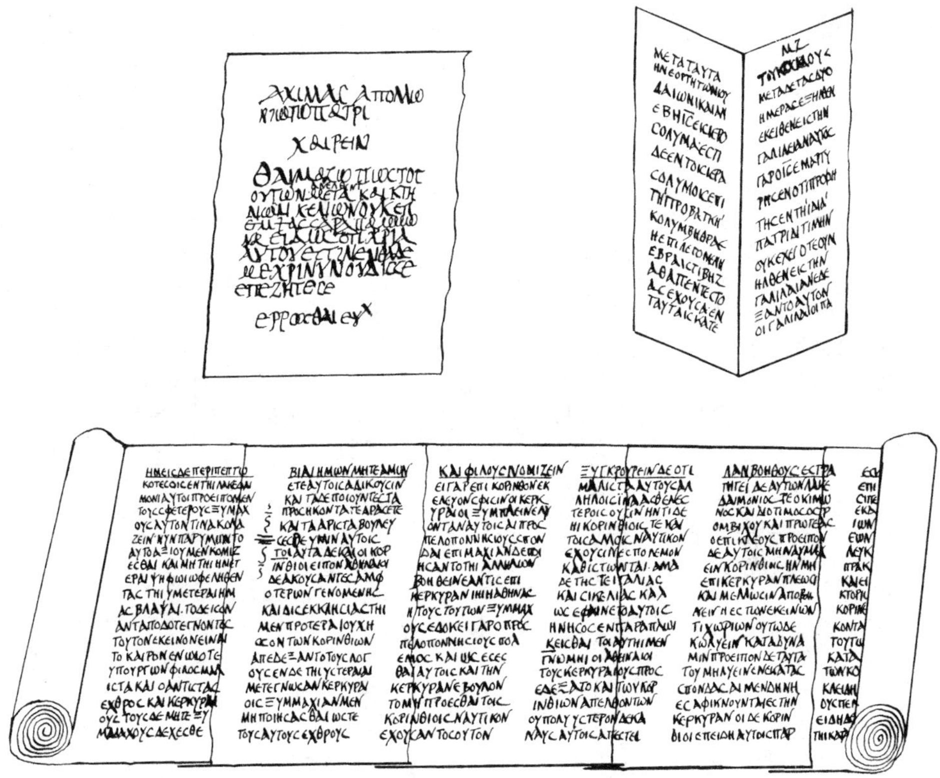

Fig. 1 Above: (a) a single sheet of papyrus used for writing a letter
(b) a single sheet folded vertically down its center (the method used in making a codex)
Below: an open papyrus roll. The wavy lines running from top to bottom indicate the points where one sheet joins the next *(kollesis)*. Writing often crosses them.
Drawn by W. E. H. Cockle

cut. Small pieces at the end which were not big enough to make a sheet were from time to time inserted as single leaves. Single leaves of this kind, which are often found and up till now were hard to explain, now become intelligible. [This account of] the origin of the sheets of a codex is so illuminating that it should probably be treated as a rule."

The answer seemed to be, then, that the manufacturer did not supply special sheets for the construction of codices, but that the scribe simply cannibalized a roll. There the matter rested till the discovery of a number of Coptic Manichaean codices in the early 1930s. In describing them, C. Schmidt and H. J. Polotsky wrote in 1933: "Material for the manufacture of codices was normally taken from papyrus rolls, so that frequently the joins of leaves ran vertically across the sheets. The Manichaean codices, however, do not show the same features as Coptic codices of the fourth century. Contrary to expectation, these leaves are thin as silk, and may be compared with the very best Egyptian papyrus. In fact the material for these sheets was not cut out of rolls but was specially manufactured in sheets size 31.5 x 36 cm. or 27 x 35 cm. (the height of the sheet is given first)."[7] When these scholars asserted that the sheets were specially manufactured, I presume them to be voicing a hypothesis based on the quality of the papyrus and the fact that they have not found any sheet joins. H. Ibscher, writing later (in 1937), stated the same opinion, but gave no reasons. I presume that the observations he made during the conservation work on these codices are the foundation of it; and that it is essentially his opinion that Schmidt and Polotsky voiced in 1933.[8]

A model for the way in which our question could be investigated, and should be described by every editor, was offered by J. Scherer in his publication in 1956 of the codex of Origen, *Contre Celse.*[9] He was able to show that the sheets of this codex had been cut from a roll by tracing the horizontal fiber continuations from one sheet of the codex to the next at the point where the maker of the codex had cut them out of the roll; and he also traced and found the original joins (*kolleseis,* to be discussed shortly) of single sheets in the roll itself. His diagram will make his method clear.

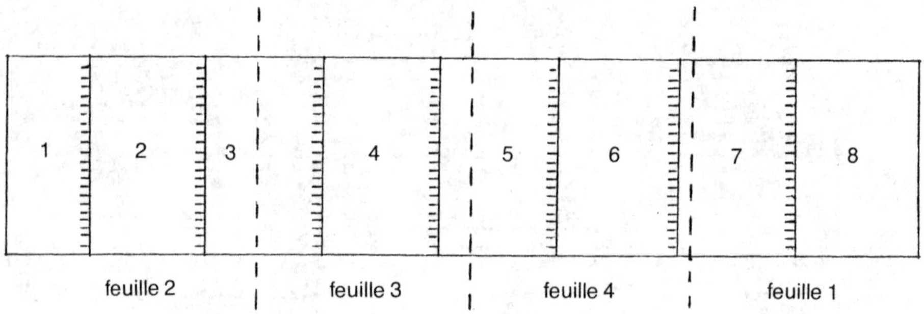


Fig. 2 To show how to identify the original gummed sheets in a papyrus roll cut up to make new 'sheets' for a papyrus codex.
[From J. Scherer, *Extraits des Livres I et II du Contre Celse d'Origène d'après le papyrus inv. 88747 du Musée du Cairo* (**551**). By permission of the author.]

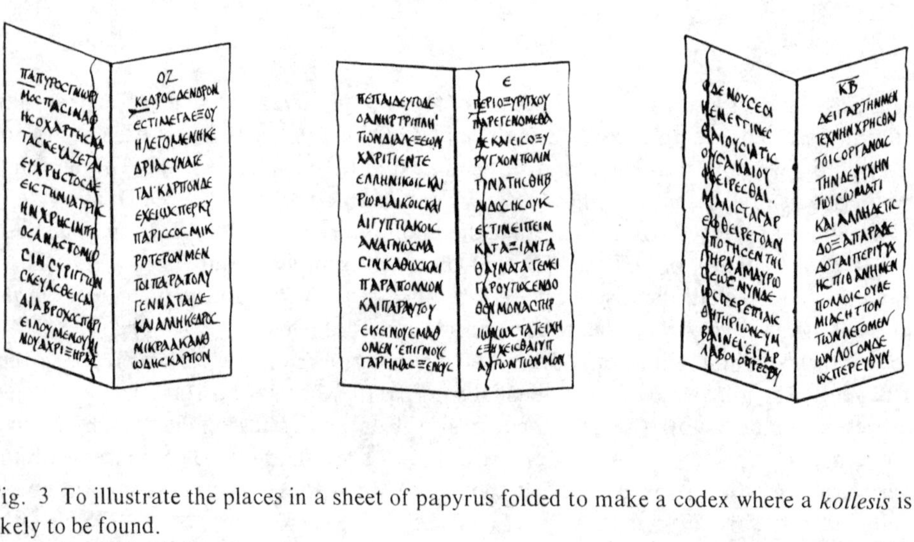

Fig. 3 To illustrate the places in a sheet of papyrus folded to make a codex where a *kollesis* is likely to be found.
Drawn by W. E. H. Cockle

For the sake of completeness I should mention two other scholars who have expressed ideas on this question. Berthe van Regemorter wrote a short description in 1960 of a notebook in the Chester Beatty Library in Dublin.[10] It was made up of several gatherings, each a quaternion, the leaves of which were still uncut at the fore edge ("encore réunis à la gouttière"). From this fact she inferred that to form each quaternion a large sheet of papyrus (size estimated at 52 cm.B x 35 cm.H) had been folded in 8 so as to give 16 pages. This, as she points out, would be the system of "imposition" practiced by present-day printers. Wishing to confirm this interesting information, I applied to Dr. A. Wouters, who is at present engaged in the publication of texts belonging to this collection. Mme van Regemorter gives no catalogue number of the manuscript, and only a vague description ("quadruples listes de mots en grec, ce qu' on appelle communément un dictionnaire"). But the dimensions allow it to be identified with Ch. B. Ac 1499, on which Dr. Wouters is now working. He kindly informs me that the papyrus has now been mounted in separated double-leaves under glass, and in such a way that Mme van Regemorter's description can neither be verified nor rejected.[11]

Professor R. Kasser of Geneva in 1969 made a similar statement about P. Bodmer IV, XXV, XXVI, the Menander Codex of *Samia, Dyskolos* and *Aspis* (**225**). His investigation depended on tracing a continuity of horizontal fibers from one sheet of the codex to an adjoining one, and so on. He calculated that a roll 4.20 m. long was used up in this way. Unfortunately there is a serious difficulty in the way of accepting his account, for he notes only two *kolleseis* ("raccords") in this great length of roll.[12]

A second look at the paradigmatic papyrus roll already illustrated (p. 45) will help us to clarify our ideas, to see what is meant by "joins" and to observe the ambiguity of the term "sheet." This last word, when applied to codices, means the double-leaf, the unit of which the codex is built, a unit which is folded centrally so that four pages are formed by the folding. When applied to the roll the word means the unit manufactured by the papyrus-maker, a unit which is turned into a roll by progressive pasting on of further sheets; and such sheets will, I suppose, be of one of the varieties actually named by the Elder Pliny. It will be convenient to term the single sheets which constitute the roll, *kollemata.* (This is what the ancients called them, and when they formed a dossier by pasting together such *kollemata* or single sheets *after* they had been written on, they would give each *kollema* a number.) The pasting of a roll is done in such a way that the new sheet takes up under the old, and the scribe can write across the join without any resistance to the pen. The join, moreover, is so cleverly made that it can be detected only on that side of the papyrus in a roll in which the papyrus fibers run in a horizontal direction. Let us call the actual joins *kolleseis.*[13] No doubt a clever builder of a papyrus roll will choose sheets of an even breadth. But inspection of a number of rolls found more or less intact shows that from time to time the maker slipped in a sheet of less than normal dimensions. In the Hawara Homer, working backwards from the intact end of the roll, I have measured sheet sizes (that is, intervals between *kolleseis*) as (12)cm./26.5/26.5/26.5/26.8/26/24/25/18/27. (This brings us only to verse 660, after which calculation replaces measurement.) In the British Museum Hyperides roll I have measured the following series: 21.5/20/16.5/22.3/24.7/28/19/21.5/14/15.2/14/15.2/14/15.2/21.5/24/26/25.5 cm. In the BM Bacchylides, Pap. 733, the following series occurs in frame 1 (cols. i–xii): 22/22/20.5/21.5/20.5/22.5/10+. The Berlin Timotheus has *kollemata* of 22 cm., and the Vienna "Curse of Artemisia" one *kollema* of 29.5 cm, (both c. iv B.C., figures from U.

Wilcken, *UPZ* 1: 98, who describes these dimensions as "ungewöhnlich gross"). In the *livre d'ecolier* (c. iii B.C.) *x*/16.5/16/13/14[+]/11.5/16/16/16.5/16/13/10/17/15/17/17. In the *Diegeseis,* from right-hand of roll, c. 10 cm./12.5/lost—/12.5/12.5?/18/lost/11/1[ ]. The Jena Irenaeus, a papyrus roll of iii/iv A.D., has *kollemata* of about 17–18 cm. (F. Uebel, *Eirene* 3 (1964): p. 65 and n. 39). The Paschal letter Berlin P. 10677 (BKT VI, p. 55) is a roll of twenty sheets 25 cm.B x 45 cm.H. Each sheet overlaps the succeeding ones by 2 cm., so that the intervals between *kolleseis* are reduced to 23 cm.

Documents: P. Leiden G, i B.C.: 14.5/14.5/16
P. Hauswaldt (Demotic) 1, 265 B.C.: 16.5/11/16/6/14.5/14
P. Mich. 121, A.D. 42: dimensions vary between 15.5 and 17.7
P. Bouriant 20, ii/iii A.D.: average is 18 cm.
P. Merton II 88, A.D. 298–301: average 18/19 cm.
P. Graec. Vindob. 19996 (*MPER* i [1932], 1): average 13 cm.
P. Graec. Vindob. 19853 (Gerstinger, *Anz. Öst. Akad.* 1950, 20) A.D. 319:19/18/15
P. Oxy. ined. (*parachoresis* and sale of A.D. 139): four *kollemata* of 22–23 cm. each
P. Oxy. xliv 3197 (slave diaeresis, Hadrian): two *kolleseis* 22.5 cm. apart

I have given these figures in some detail, since they are not to be found in the handbooks, and I have had to discover them for myself by doing my own measuring. The widest *kollema* I have noted is 32.5 cm. in a well-written, luxury copy of Old Comedy (Cratinus?) originating from Oxyrhynchus (P. Oxy. xxxvii 2806, ii A.D.). Note that the full width of the sheet is likely to have been more than 32.5 cm., since 2 cm. or so has to be allowed for overlap at the point of pasting. This figure is perhaps as near as we shall get to Pliny's widest sheet size named *cubitalis macrocolis,* which if calculated at 18 *digiti* of 1.85 cm. each gives a breadth of 33.3 cm.

We may therefore say of the papyrus roll: (1) that no roll (whether intended to carry literature or documents) is without joins, *kolleseis;* (2) that the joins, *kolleseis,* tend to be fairly close—18 or 16 cm. is a much more usual distance than the 27 cm. which is the more commonly found distance in the avowedly calligraphic Hawara Homer; (3) the distances apart of the joins (alternatively put, the widths of the sheets) may be irregular in one and the same roll.[14]

Let us now postulate that the sheets needed to construct a codex are too broad to have been made without a join (*kollesis*)—whether they were specially made for that codex or cut from a roll. Whereabouts in the sheets of this codex could the *kolleseis* occur? Not, of course, at the very center of the sheet, because folding would then very quickly break the back of the sheet and the book. They could be allowed at one side or other of the central fold; in the middle of either page; or toward the outside edge of either page. If they were in this last named position it is quite possible that with the passage of time the papyrus edge might have broken away and carried the *kollesis* with it so as to render the *kollesis* no longer observable. For a similar reason small fragments of a papyrus codex may have lost a *kollesis.*

Bearing these points in mind I have myself done some further inspection of codices to try to clarify our original problem. The results may be set out as follows in three paragraphs:

(1) Codices in which there are no apparent sheet joins:

(a) The Manichaean codices already reported by Schmidt/Polotsky/Ibscher.

(b) P. Oxy. 2258 (**28**), a codex of Callimachus, c. vi–vii, which has a page 37 cm. Broad. Two consecutive and conjugate leaves of this codex survive. It is not certain whether the physical point of junction between them is preserved. But an isolated leaf of 37 cm. Breadth is broader than the widest sheet we have as yet noticed (32.5 cm.). Somehow this size will have to be accounted for.

(c) I cannot see any *kolleseis* in the facsimile reproductions of P. Bodmer II St. John (**P 66**), sheet size 28.4B x 16.2H, c. iii; or in P. Bodmer XX (**OT 87a**) (a composite codex), sheet size 28.4B x 15.5H, c. iv. In November 1971 I could not see any *kolleseis* in P. Bodmer V and XIII (Table 12, parts of the composite Bodmer codices), and since the fibers run continuously from left edge to right edge, one can be confident that there were none.

(d) The Oxyrhynchus-Copenhagen etc. Philo codex (P. Oxy. 1173 + ) (**243**). The Oxford portions contain two conjugate leaves, and I have seen a good photograph of a similar leaf in Copenhagen. Since in this manuscript the codex sheet is 30 cm.B. before folding, while the H is only 17.5 cm., it would be possible for these sheets to have been cut from a roll 30 cm.H to a width of 17.5 cm., and then turned through 90°.

(e) Paris St. Cyril **507** (Louvre E. 10295 + ). Several complete folded sheets survive, B = 43/43.5 cm., *no kollesis*.

(f) See Appendix to this chapter on those Nag Hammadi codices without apparent sheet joins.

(2) Codices in which at least one *kollesis,* and sometimes two *kolleseis,* are visible on every sheet:

(a) The codex "Q" of St. John in Coptic (**C 2**), sheet size 25B x 25H, c. iv.

(b) The codex of Hilarius, de Trinitate (Vienna 2160) (**Lat. 5**), sheet size 40B x 27H, usually dated to c. vi. (Dr. W. E. H. Cockle has lent me a collation of the complete codex.)

(c) Tourah Codex II (**551**), Origen, *Contra Celsum.*[15]

(d) Pindar, P. Oxy, 1614 (**247**), sheet size 42B x 37H, v or vi.

(e) Chester Beatty schoolbook, *Ancient Society* I: 201–35 (**416a**), c. iv.

(f) Pierpont Morgan *Iliad* (**140**), sheet size 25/28B x 27H, c. iv.

(3) More often I have succeeded in observing *kolleseis* only occasionally, or have information enough to say only that they appear occasionally. I can see them occasionally in the reproductions of Ch. B. codex II (**P 46**), Pauline Epp., sheet size 30B x 27.0H, c. iii?; Ch. Beatty codices IX/X (**OT 183**) Ezekiel, Esther, Daniel etc., sheet size 25.4B x 34.4H, iii? (a number of *kolleseis* I have verified on the portions preserved in Princeton [Plate 6]) and Campbell Bonner reports two examples in the Michigan leaves of Ch. B. XII (**OT 222**) (*The Last Chapters of Enoch in Greek,* p. 6); P. Bodmer IV, XXV, XXVI (**225**) Menander, sheet size 26B x 27.5H, iv; P. Bodmer XIV/XV (**P 75**), St. Luke and St. John, sheet size 26B x 26H, iii. I have observed *kolleseis* on a few pages of the Freer Codex of the Minor Prophets (**OT 187**), sheet size 29/28 x [32], iv; and in the Paris Avitus, BN Lat. 8913, vi (**Lat. 2**), on the very edge of the page. In the Heidelberg Septuagint codex (**OT 191**) Gerhard reports that in one instance the distance apart is 18 cm.; as the page is c. 17.5 cm.B, the sheet was presumably 35 cm.B.

*Kolleseis* are reported by R. Roca-Puig on two out of five leaves of the *Psalmus Responsorius* (**446a**).

I have scrutinized with special care BM Ms Or. 7594 (**C 1**), Deuteronomy, Jonah and Acts in Coptic, sheet size 33B x 29.3H, iv, which is a well-made and written manuscript, and specially interesting since the finding of Greek documents in its binding and the form of its colophon give more than usual confidence in the date (mid iv A.D.) assigned to it. In each of two separate gatherings which I examined (the gatherings in this manuscript are fives, quinions) a *kollesis* was visible in only one out of the five sheets. On the other four sheets of each gathering the fibers could be seen to run continuously from left edge of left-hand page to right edge of right-hand page. I looked for evidence of these fibers continuing on to adjacent sheets, but could not convince myself that I found any. We must then reckon with the possibility that there were no such continuations and that the man who constructed the codex—from a roll, as one *kollesis* on every fifth sheet suggests—deliberately cut them out. A craftsman who took pride in the look of his book might well want to cut them out. In doing so he would of course waste a certain quantity of the roll. But we shall also note that the distance apart of the *kolleseis* in that roll is at least 33 cm., equal to the greatest distance apart ever actually found in a roll.

To sum up, then: the facts (hard to come by, as we have seen) are complex. There are a very few authenticated cases of sheets of codices which show no *kolleseis,* joins, over a breadth of such size that joins would certainly be expected. There are a number of well-authenticated instances of codices which show at least one such join on each sheet; and there are several codices in which such joins are found, but not on every sheet. The economical hypothesis to cover all these facts is that normally a codex was made by cutting up a roll into lengths of the right size to form the constituent sheets of that codex; that sometimes care was taken to cut out the *kolleseis* found in the original roll; and that special reasons (e.g., the great care lavished on the physical form of their books by the Manichaeans) must be invoked to account for the few exceptions to this norm.

Was it not possible, it may however be asked, for specially pasted double or treble sheets of papyrus to have been made for the benefit of the writers of codices? Where fiber continuations from one codex sheet to the next have not been specifically noted such a procedure is presumably conceivable. But against such a theory stand the observed facts that some codices were certainly cut from rolls; that rolls continued to be manufactured for documentary use till the sixth and seventh centuries; and that we know moreover of rolls already written which were converted into codices. Tourah Codex VI (Didymus ad Zacchariam) (**515**) and III (ad Ecclesiasticum) (**512**) were cut out from documentary rolls, in which the original writing was not uniformly spaced out.[16] P. Ch. B. Panopolis 1 and 2 consist of large pieces of papyrus cut from rolls of administrative letters. The written faces of these rolls were pasted together to make sheets for use in a crude codex that in consequence had sheets of double thickness. A similar procedure was used in fabricating P. Bouriant 3. In this case it is interesting to note that the adaptor of the rolls cut out those parts which contained the joins, *kolleseis.*[17]

Important consequences flow from acceptance of the hypothesis that codices are usually cut from rolls. The height of the sheet will be governed by the material available—that is to say, the height cannot be greater than the height of the roll, though it may be less if the roll is cut into strips lengthways. But the breadth of the sheet is not so governed. It is variable at will. The maker's choice may be dictated by fashion, by the practice of a particular scriptorium, or the needs of the text he is copying. This is the point of importance that emerges from our listing dimensions with breadth first, height second. We may postulate rolls of certain groups of heights—e.g., (a series which is quite arbitrary) 41–37 cm., 37–34 cm., 34–32 cm., 32–30 cm., 30–28 cm., 28–26 cm., 26–24 cm., 24–22 cm. If rolls of about these heights were available from the manufacturer, all the sizes shown in my tabulations could easily be constructed.

There is, however, one important limitation on the free choice of breadth of page when a codex is constructed out of double leaves of papyrus cut from rolls. The breadth cannot be wider than half the breadth of the sheet as produced by the manufacturer, unless the maker of the book is prepared to tolerate a pasted join (*kollesis*) running from top to bottom of one of the pages formed by folding the double leaf; or in the case of very wide codices, on each of these pages. Since the breadth of sheet produced by the manufacturer is not more than 33/34 cm. (except for two phenomenal and unexplained examples), and normally averages about 20 cm. or less, the desire to avoid pasted joins, or at least to restrict them to not more than one to a double leaf, may have been an important factor contributing to determine the relative narrowness already noted as a characteristic of codices made from papyrus when compared with the relatively square format favored in codices of parchment.

Whatever norms we choose as heights of the roll, it is unlikely that the manufactured product will be precisely constant. It is not being manufactured by machine, but by hand; the materials (the quality and length of reed available) will differ from one day to another; it is unlikely that the craftsmen concerned used precise measuring tools, but they will rather have worked by guess-work of eye and the rough and ready measurement provided by "cubit" (the distance from extended middle finger to elbow), "foot" and "finger" (*digitus,* which we translate by "inch"). Moreover there might well have been several centers of production, some of them noted for special sizes (Pliny gives at least one such "manufacturer's name," *Fanniana,* among the sheets whose breadth but not height he enumerates). Changing fashions will also have played a part. The demand at certain periods was probably for certain favored sizes and not for others.

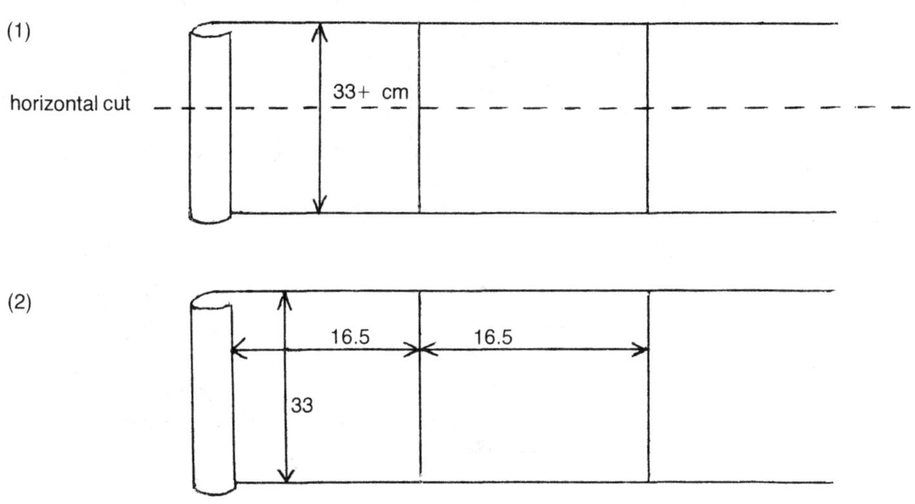


Fig. 4 To illustrate how a papyrus roll could be cut to produce a smaller format.

The way in which standard sizes could be cut may be illustrated diagrammatically. Codices of height 16.5 cm. or smaller could be made by cutting a roll in one of two ways: (1) a roll of 33 + cm. height could be cut into two[18] horizontally, that is down its length; or (2) sheets of the size desired, breadth 33 + cm., height 16.5 cm., could be cut vertically out of a roll in which the *kolleseis* were at least 16.5 cm. apart. These would then be slewed round through 90° before being laid on each other.

That the first method was in fact practiced seems clear from Ibscher's observation of examples that a roll was deliberately cut down. Whether the second method was practiced I do not know. I presume that with luck it might be identified by fiber continuations. But I should like to point out how relatively restricted a number of roll

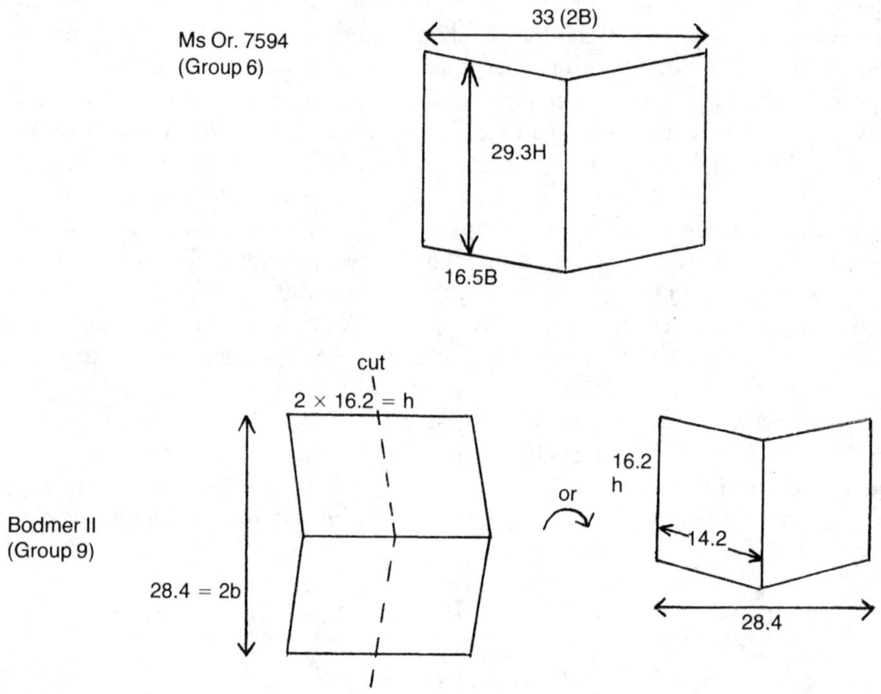


Fig. 5 To illustrate how a given size of sheet of papyrus could be cut to produce a smaller format.

sizes could provide for my smaller groups. A roll which could provide codex sheets without *kolleseis* for codices of Group 6 (and we have seen that in two gatherings of BM Ms Or. 7594 (**C1**) four out of five sheets do not show *kolleseis*) could provide them also, slewed through 90°, for codices of Group 9.

In this mode of construction, the H(eight) of the larger format is twice the B(readth) of leaf (page) = width of the sheet of the smaller. If we use B and H to stand for the dimensions in the larger format, and b and h for the dimensions in the smaller, the relationship may be expressed thus:

$$b = \tfrac{1}{2}H, \; h = B$$

Similarly, some of the sizes in Group 5 could result in the sizes in Group 9; the size 14 x 30 taken from Group 8 could give the aberrant Mississippi Crosby codex (**C 3**) of Group 9; and Group 4 could produce Group 11.

Now such an interchangeability in terms of fixed, not relative, dimensions is what I had in mind in challenging Schubart's interpretation in my first chapter (p. 5) of those cases where new formats are created by halving existing pages. Schubart had treated this procedure as confirmation of his view that proportion between dimensions of breadth and height was the crucial point to take account of. Since the interchangeability applies within such rigid limitations of size, the truth seems to me to be the exact opposite.

There is one final point, and it is speculative only. Could the very broad sheets of the exceptional Callimachus codex P. Oxy. 2258 (**28**) also have been cut vertically across a roll and then slewed through 90°? If there really is no *kollesis* at any point in the conjugate leaves, this would indeed involve a height of roll of 56 cm. It may well be judged that such a height involves difficulties of the same order as postulating a sheet specially manufactured to be 28 cm. high but 74 cm. broad.

## APPENDIX

In Chapter Four, pp. 43, 46, 47 and especially notes 1, 2, 6, 12, I have expressed scepticism about the correctness of the identifications of consecutive sheets as cut continuously from a roll, when the acceptance of the identifications produces a roll of a length of about 1.60 m. containing no *kolleseis*. Professor James M. Robinson informs me that close inspection of the Nag Hammadi Coptic codices reveals more than two of them that seem to have been cut from rolls which will have been of a length of more or less 2 m. without *kolleseis*. My scepticism may therefore prove to have been unjustified. If so, however, we should note that the rolls from which these codices were cut were made in a way other than was normal for rolls intended to hold a text copied in roll form. Such rolls show a *kollesis* at short intervals, and no sheet is broader than 32 cm. (Chapter Four, p. 48). A roll without *kolleseis* of a length of about 2 m. would have been constructed using the full height (about seven feet) of the papyrus stem. If such rolls were made, they would appear to be a novelty designed to meet the requirements of codex-makers. It is to be noted that most of these supposed rolls with *kollemata* 2 m. wide are of very coarse, thick papyrus. If they were available it is odd that very many makers of papyrus codices were content, as we have seen, to cannibalize the traditional type of roll made with *kolleseis* at frequent intervals.

## NOTES

[1]*Das Buch*[2], p. 128. See, however, the appendix at the end of this chapter.

[2]I read in H. Ibscher's introduction to *A Manichaean Psalm Book,* (**C33**) p. xii that he had reconstructed the original papyrus out of which Berlin P. 8502 (Coptic Psalms=**C 34**) was constructed as "a single papyrus strip successfully made by an artist in papyrus to the length of over 160 cm." Other explanations of the relative scarcity of *kolleseis* in this manuscript can be put forward (see pp. 50, 52).

[3]See N. Lewis, *Papyrus in Classical Antiquity* (Oxford, 1974), pp. 34ff.

[4]Seventy sheets, P. Oxy. ined. 35 4B/101 J(1-2)(a), Private letter, c. ii A.D. *αγορασον δε μοι κυριε μ̣[ου] πατερ χαρτην ἑβδεμηκοντακολλον* (1. *ἑβδομηκοντα-* )

[5]*Das Buch*[2], p. 129.

[6]This codex is unfortunately not positively identified. Ibid., p. 186; "a Coptic codex in a Prussian state library." It seems probable that it is Berlin Coptic 8502 (**C 34**).

[7]*Sitzungsberichte d. Preuss. Akad.* (Berlin, 1933), pp. 84ff.

[8]H. Ibscher, "Der Kodex," *Jahrbuch d. Einbandkunst* iv (1937): 3–15, esp. pp. 12–13.

[9]Jean Scherer, *Extraits des Libres I et II du Contre Celse d'Origène d'après le papyrus no. 88747 du Musée du Caire* (Inst. fr. d'Arch. Or., Bibliothèque d'étude 28, 1956).

[10]Berthe van Regemorter, *Cd'E* xxxv (1960): 278; A. Wouters, *Anc. Society* 3 (1972): 259–62. J. Irigoin observes (*Lustrum*, 1962/7, p. 23) of the Chester Beatty example that such folding in any case applies only to a manuscript of small format, in this case 13B x 17.25H constituting a student's notebook. (If the manuscript illustrated and described as *CLA Suppl.* 1683 is this same notebook, as seems likely, the dimensions are given as 13.6 x 16.8 cm.) This is probably my **355b.**

[11]Dr. Wouters writes to me (14 July 1974): "I was in Dublin (Chester Beatty Library) for two weeks. I think the problem about the codicological form of *Ac* 1499 (**355b**), on which we corresponded (your letters of 15 May and 15 October 1973), are now resolved. In the strong room of the Chester Beatty Library I happened to find the unwritten folia that were discarded when the codex was put between glass. The description of Madame Van Regemorter can partially be controlled on these unwritten *cahiers*. The whole codex has fifty-two folia (not fifty-one as E. A. Lowe, *CLA Suppl.* no. 1683 mentions)." We shall look forward to Dr. Wouters' investigation.

[12]R. Kasser in P. Bodmer XXV, introd. pp. 11ff. He is of the opinion that the sheets in the center of the codex were cut first. His further idea that the papyrus text of Menander was written by the scribe, both front and back, before the roll was cut up I find frankly incredible.

[13]Professor R. Roca-Puig is one of the few scholars who, in describing a papyrus codex, have reported every place in which they occur. *Psalmus Responsorius* (**446a**), pp. 3, 61, 69.

[14]What has been said here quite shortly shows that it would be worth a scholar's while to collect evidence for sizes of *kollemata* and heights of rolls. Sir Frederic Kenyon's general statement, *Books and Readers*[2], p. 51, requires modification in detail, but is not absolutely in conflict with the evidence just put forward: "It may be taken, therefore, as established by experience that a papyrus sheet intended for a roll on which a work of Greek literature might be inscribed rarely, if ever, exceeded [23B x 33H cm.], while something more like [19B x 25.5H cm.] would be more common for a book of moderate pretensions."

[15]J. Scherer, l.c. n. 9 above and p. 46.

[16]L. Doutreleau, "the original writing sometimes goes right up to the margin, i.e., it was originally written in a roll," L. Doutreleau, *Didyme l'Aveugle* (Paris, 1962), 1: 142–43. Cf. *ZPE* ii (1968): 45, n. 5 and n. 9.

[17]Other examples of this practice which I have noted are:

(1) P. Ryl. I 1, early iv, papyrus then used for a copy of Deuteronomy (**OT 38**).

(2) A Latin fragment in Vienna, v, *CLA* x 1521.

(3) P. Achmim 6–9 (P. Achmim 7 is a republication of P. Bouriant 3/41a).

(4) Coptic Exodus (**C 12**), Lacau, *BIFAO* viii 43ff., 64ff.

(5) Coptic Sirach (**C 13**).

Nos. (3) - (5) were discovered at the White Monastery, i.e., in the Panopolite nome, like P. Ch. B. Panop. and P. Bouriant 3.

[18]To make a sheet only 11 cm. high, such a roll could of course be cut in three horizontally.

CHAPTER

5

# How a Codex Was Made Up

Two other important physical features of the codex have not been touched on. They are: (1) the number of sheets that constitute its "gatherings;" (2) the homogeneity of surface found on facing pages. To make these points clear it will be helpful to recapitulate.

The essential feature of the codex, as we have already seen, is that a sheet or a number of sheets of material of the height but double the width of the page desired is folded centrally. When folded, each sheet will give a sequence of 2 leaves 4 pages. Two sheets laid above each other before folding will give 4 leaves 8 pages, three sheets, 6 leaves 12 pages, four sheets, 8 leaves 16 pages, and so on. The system of 4 sheets 8 leaves 16 pages eventually became the canonical form, and from the Latin word *quaternio,* for a "set of four," was derived the English word "quire," which has come to be used (against its etymology) of a gathering whatever the number of sheets. A convenient division for us at the moment (it need not reflect the historical origin of the form) is between those codices in which all the sheets were laid above each other before folding, and those codices in which a limited number of sheets were laid above each other before folding; the folded sheets were then laid on one side, and a new set of sheets laid one above the other and folded, followed by a repetition of the process. In the former type there is only one "gathering" in the whole book, and it has become common to call this type a "single-quire" codex. In the latter type, each set of folded sheets is "gathered" together and stitched, i.e., the sets form "gatherings." One set of threads holds each gathering together. If the book has a binding, a second set passes horizontally through the first set and unites the gatherings; it is taken then through them across the spine of the book and secured to the front and back binding covers.

It has been supposed, that the second of these two methods of putting together a codex arose from the way in which a skin prepared for writing was folded and cut. If a skin were folded centrally and then folded again it would give a series of two-sheet quires; if it were folded a third time the quires would be four sheets, i.e., *quaterniones.*[1] Once again it must be emphasized that it is quite uncertain whether this supposition corresponds to the actual historical origin of the system of gatherings in a codex. But we note one point about it, which is that it will account for alternation of the two sides

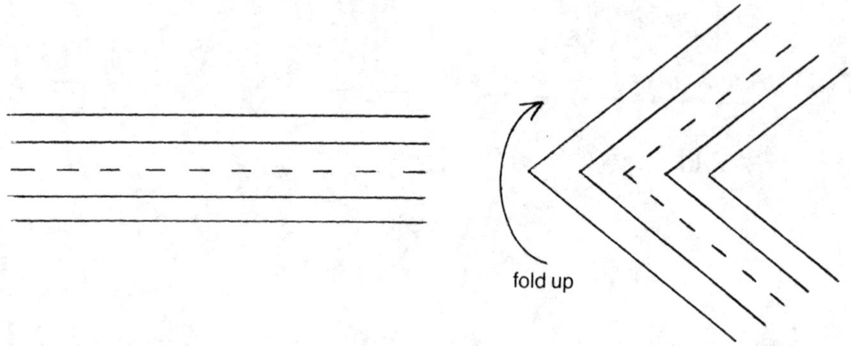


Fig. 6 The method of folding a gathering of sheets in a codex.

of a skin in a made up gathering. There is a difference in a skin between the 'flesh' side which tends to be whiter and more even, and the "hair" side which may be yellower and show little pittings which are the roots of the hair follicles. The difference in quality between the sides will be less obvious to the eye if pages from the same side of the skin confront each other, that is, if hair side is opposite hair side, flesh side opposite flesh side. C. R. Gregory[2] observed that parchment manuscripts written in the East show the flesh side on the outside (i.e., on the initial right-hand page) of a gathering, and on its final left-hand page, and at the central opening; page two will therefore be hair side, and the next sheet will be so arranged that its first right-hand page is hair side, so as to face a page of the same kind; the next pair of openings will both be flesh side. If the gathering has an even number of sheets, flesh side will face flesh side at the central opening[3]. On the other hand, manuscripts written in the Latin West usually have the hair side on the outside right-hand page (and so on).

Now we saw in the last chapter that a piece of papyrus for writing is made of two layers taken from the papyrus reed, arranged so that on one side the fibers run in a horizontal direction, while on the other side they run in a vertical direction. To indicate the fiber-direction I use throughout this book as shorthand the symbols → and ↓, → standing for fibers horizontal in direction, ↓ for fibers vertical in direction.[4] When we come to fold a sheet of papyrus to form a codex we shall find a situation analogous to that of the flesh and hair sides of a parchment codex. A single sheet (equal to four pages) may have its outside right-hand page ↓; then the next page will be →, and if the codex has gatherings of single sheets it will necessarily be followed by →, and the fourth page will be . This may be diagrammatically shown thus:

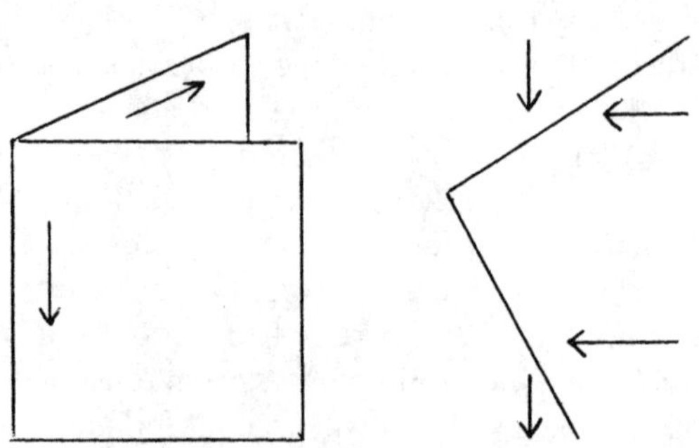

Fig. 7

But if the gathering is of more than single sheets, will → face → (like opposite like, as in parchment) or will they alternate? Actually both systems (alternation, and like facing like) were in use, as we shall see; and the introduction of the system of like facing like offers a useful dating criterion.

There are, then, two variables in any papyrus codex: (1) The gathering system—whether the sheets are put together in one single-quire codex or in a number of gatherings. If the latter, how many sheets are there to a gathering, and is the number uniform? (2) The way in which → and ↓ are arranged: which is on the outside, and do→ and → (or ↓ and ↓) face each other or alternate on the inside?

As an example of a single quire codex we may take the Bodmer codex of Menander (IV *Dyskolos;* XXV *Samia;* XXVI *Aspis*) (**225**). Sixteen sheets were laid on top of each other in a pile, then folded across the center, to give 32 leaves or 64 pages. The sheets were in fact almost square, 26 (or 26.6) cm.B x 27.5 cm.H, giving a folded page size of 13.0B x 27.5H.[5] It is simplest to suppose that the sheets were laid on a surface (ground or table) ↓ side downwards; folding centrally would then bring up the right-hand outside page showing vertical fibers:

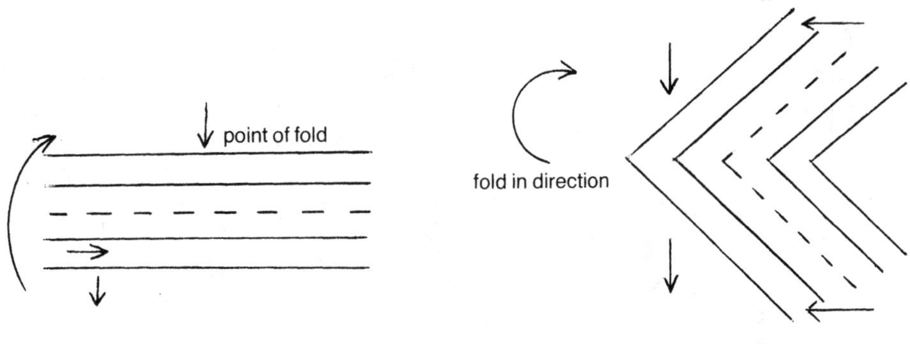


Fig. 8 Method of folding, to illustrate fiber direction in successive sheets of a papyrus codex (cf. Fig. 6).

The codex was not of course found intact like this. Its back was broken and the pages lay separated, in some cases torn, and the fragments loose. There are three reasons for certainty that it is a single-quire codex: (1) The fiber alternations are ↓→↓→ to the middle of the book; then →↓→↓ from the middle to the end. (It will be found that if this alternation pattern can be established it is decisive for the classification of a book as single-quire codex.) (2) Some of the pages have page-numbers (even if these have been altered and the succession tampered with, as R. Kasser thinks); and continuity can in general be checked from continuity of the action in the plays they contain, and in that part of the *Samia* which is also in the Cairo codex by whether or not the text coincides. (3) A certain number of overlaps can be traced between the horizontal fibers of one sheet and the next.[6]

The date of this manuscript can be assessed only on palaeographical grounds. The handwritings to which it seems to me to be closest are dated to the early fourth century.[7] Others, however, have put it in the third century, V. Martin early in that century.

The disadvantages of this method of make-up are obvious. Its size makes it tend to break at the spine. This happened more than once in antiquity to this very manuscript, since R. Kasser has shown that it was twice restitched. Secondly, if the book is to have an even appearance when closed, it must be trimmed at the fore edge, and this will result in the pages in the middle of the book being narrower than those on the outside.[8] This disproportion is not obvious to the eye in this particular manuscript; but it is one that the eye at once remarks in the Pierpont Morgan *Iliad* in which the outer pages are 14 cm. broad, the inner are reduced to 12.5 cm.[9]

A survey of Table 6 which lists papyrus codices in this format (no doubt it is not complete) shows that they are sometimes of considerable bulk. Ch. B. IX-X (**OT 183, 207A**) Ezekiel-Daniel-Esther totals 236 pages; the Milan Coptic codex of the Epistles of St. Paul (**C7**) probably runs to more than 280 (the last surviving page number is 279); another twelve in the list have 100 pages or more.

The most favoured dimension is Group 8 (H = 2B) into which fifteen + examples fall; but the single quire make-up is not restricted to this group. Group 5 has three (four?), Group 5 ab. two (+ two?), Group 6 two, Group 7 nine (?), Group 7 ab. two, Group 8 ab. 1 and 2 four and three respectively, Group 9 three, Group 9 ab. one.

It is noticeable that the dates suggested by palaeographers are almost all iii A.D. or iv A.D. The Milan Coptic letters of Paul is probably v A.D., and it is wise to reckon with the possibility that some of the other Coptic hands could be as late as v. The relatively early character of this make-up is a striking fact. No doubt this relatively early appearance is a support to those who (like H. Ibscher) claim that it is the original form of the papyrus codex—a claim that must be considered later on. That it should continue on into the fifth century is not surprising, given the conservatism latent in all craft traditions in Egypt. It is worth noting that no example of a single-quire codex of parchment has yet been identified.[10]

If the alternative method of making a codex is utilized—namely that of forming separate gatherings of sheets, then the number of sheets constituting such a gathering has been found to vary from one to seven.

## TABLE 6

### List of Single-Quire Codices

*A Greek Literature*

(1) B M Harris Homer (**106**) 9-18-36 ↓ → ↓ → to center, iii.
(2) Pierpont Morgan *Iliad* (**140**) 31-62-124 ↓ → ↓ → to center, iv.
(3) Bodmer Menander (**225**) 16-32-64 ↓ → ↓ → to center, iv.
(4) (Uncertain but probable. Alternative is seniones.) P. Oxy. 2656, Menander, *Misoumenos* (**234a**), iv.

Possible examples:
(5) Scholia on Homer, *PSI* x 1173 (**207**) Fr. 1 on *Odyss.* iii is ↓ →, frs. 2-7 on *Odyss.* xi-xiv are all → ↓. iii. First, then second half of a single-quire codex?
(6) Homer, *Iliad* viii-xvi, P. Ant. iii 158 (**175a**). 7 pieces (of which only 2 are consecutive), all → ↓. Second half of single-quire codex?
(7) Homer, *Iliad* ix, P. Ant. iii 160 (**133a**), iii/iv, 5 leaves always → ↓. Second half of single-quire codex?
(8) Homer, *Iliad* ix-x, P. Ant. iii 161 (**135a**), v (so ed., iv ? E. G. T.). 5 leaves always → ↓. Second half of single-quire codex?
(9) Homer, *Iliad* xviii-xxiii, P. Ant. iii 165 (**162a**), iv. 2 fragments, both → ↓. Second half of a single-quire codex?

(10) Homer, *Iliad* vi-xiii (**128**), iv, *BIFAO* lxi, 151ff. Regular alternation → ↓ in folios 3–36 looks like second half of a single-quire codex.

*B Greek "Christian"* (including Old Testament)

(1) Pauline Epp. Ch. B. II + Michigan [51-102-204] (**P 46**) ↓ → ↓ → ↓ to center. iii.
(2) Ezekiel, Daniel, Susanna, Esther (**OT 183**) Ch. B. IX-X + Princeton + Cologne + Barcelona + Madrid. [59-118-236] ↓ → ↓ → to center. iii.
(3) St. John and St. Luke, P. Bodmer XIV/XV [36-72-144] (**P 75**) ↓ → to center. iii.
(4) St. John, P. Oxy. 208 + 1781 (**P 5**) (cf. D 1) [25-50-100] ↓ → to center. iii.
(5) [Uncertain but likely] Revelation Ch. B. III (**P 47**) [16-32-64?] ? ↓ → to center. iii.
(6) Berlin Genesis (**OT 1**), Rahlfs 911 16-32-64 ? ↓ → to center. iv?
(7) Freer Minor Prophets (**OT 187**)* 19-38-76 ↓ → to center. iv.
(8) Isaiah Ch. B. VII (**OT 195**) [56-112-224] ↓ → to center. iii?
(9) Jeremiah, Ch. B. VIII (**OT 202**) ? ↓ → ↓ → iv (E. G. T.).
(10) Psalms, P. Bodmer XXIV (**OT 75a**), orig. 82 leaves, ↓ → ↓ → to center. iii/iv.

Other theological codices
(11) Hermas (**529**), Univ. of Michigan [43-86-172] *plus* ↓ → to center. iii.
(12) Enoch and Melito, Ch. B. XII (**OT 222**) ↓ → to center? iv.

Possible examples
(13) Genesis, Ch. B. IV (**OT 5**). May have been single quire.
(14) Numbers and Deuteronomy, Ch. B. VI (**OT 36**). May have been single quire. (But see p. 61.)
(15) Proverbs, P. Ant. i 8 (**OT 165**), iii (E. G. T.) ↓ → in 6 consecutive leaves of Proverbs, → ↓ in Eccles.
(16) Genesis, P. Oxy. iv 656 (**OT 9**), ii/iii, ↓ → in first 2 leaves, → ↓ in others.

*C Greek Other*

(1) P. Holm (**M 5**) 7-14-28. Prob. ↓ → to center. iv.
(2) P. Leiden "X" (**M 4**) 10-20-40. Not known. iv.
(3) *PGM* I iv Paris suppl. gr. 574 (**M 1**) 18-36-72 ↓ → to center.iv.
(4) *PGM* I v P. Lond. 46 (**M 2**)** (4-7-14, one leaf now being lost) ↓ → to center. iv.
(5) *PGM* II xiii P. Leiden "W" (**M 3**) 8-16-32. Not known. iv.
(6) Tax register, P. Lond. iv 1419 (**Misc. 1**) ?-33-66(+) viii.
(7) Shorthand Manual: The Commentary, BM Inv. 2561 (**420**), 6-12-24+1, ↓ → to center. iii/iv.

* The last page of the Freer Minor Prophets (**OT187**) bears a note in a different hand, which was read by H. A. Sanders as ϵ δλοκο(ττινοι), "5 holocottinoi", and interpreted by him as the price of writing or of the completed book. The holocottinos was taken to be a silver denarius, and it was therefore argued that the date of the manuscript must be earlier than A. D. 270.

There is no need to comment on this argument, for a more plausible explanation and reading of the note suggests itself. The page has been reconstituted from many fragments, and there is a small piece missing after the first ϵ. The abbreviation stroke above the Kof ολοκ is looped thus ℓ, and more plausibly to be read as λ than as ο. The two words will therefore constitute a part of the common term ϵ̣[ξ] δλοκλ(ήρου) = "complete." Inspection of the original suggests there is adequate space for the lost ξ. The note, on this view, is likely to be that of a subsequent scribe (or perhaps of the librarian of a monastery) "Prophets [and?] . . . (here is a word which neither Sanders nor I succeeded in reading) complete," and offers no information about the date of writing of the codex. In my opinion the date of the hand of this note is in any case very definitely later than that of the main scribe of the manuscript.

**H. I. Bell, *The Library*, n.s. x (1904): 307 described this manuscript as formed of quires of single sheets. The leaves are of course now separated from each other. But the sequence ↓ → ↓ → which reverses to → ↓ → ↓ → ↓ at folio 5 rules out this interpretation; and I believe I can observe fiber connections on → between sheets 4 and 5, 3 and 6, 2 and 7.

(8) Shorthand Manual: The Commentary, BM Inv. 2562 (**419**), 9-18-36, ↓ → to center. iii/iv.

(9) School-book, P. Ch. B. (**416a**), *Anc. Society* I (1970): 201ff. ↓ → ↓ → ↓ → to center. iv.

*D Coptic*

NT (1) St. John (Brit. & Foreign Bible Soc. = 'Q') **C2** 25-50-100 ↓ → ↓ → to center. iv.

(2) Mississippi Crosby I-Melito, 1 Peter, Jonah **C3** 34-68-136 → ↓ for first 8 leaves, then ↓ → ↓ → to center. iv?

(3) P. Milan Vogliano V, Pauline Epistles **C7** [70-140-280] ↓ → to center. v.

OT (4) Achmimic Proverbs, Ms Berol. Or. Oct. 987 **C6** [42-84-168] ↓ → to center. iv.

Other (5) Sahidic Apocalypse, *Texte und Untersuchungen* 1899 **C11**. v?

(6) Gespräche Jesu, Achmimic, *Texte und Unters.*, 1919 **C9** [23-46-92] ? iv?

(7) 1st Ep. of Clement, *Texte und Unters.*, 1908; *SB Berl. Akad.* 1907, 24 **C8** 22-44-88 plus 2. Prob. ↓ → to center. iv?

(8) Heidelberg Acta Pauli.

(9) Elias Apocalypse, Achmimic (plus Apocalypses in Sahidic), Paris and Berlin, *Texte und Untersuchungen* 1899 **C10** iv or v.

| | | | | |
|---|---|---|---|---|
| Nag | (10) Nag Nammadi* I (Krause) | **C41** | [146?] | iv. |
| Hammadi | (11) Nag Hammadi II (Krause) | **C42** | 37-74-148 | iv. |
| | (12) Nag Hammadi III (Krause) | **C43** | 38-76-152 | iv. |
| | (13) Nag Hammadi IV (Krause) | **C44** | - -92 | iv. |
| | (14) Nag Hammadi V (Krause) | **C45** | - -100 | iv. |
| | (15) Nag Hammadi VI (Krause) | **C46** | 20-40-80 | iv. |
| | (16) Nag Hammadi VII (Krause) | **C47** | 33-66-132 | iv. |
| | (17) Nag Hammadi VIII (Krause) | **C48** | 35-70-140 | iv. |
| | (18) Nag Hammadi IX (Krause) | **C49** | 19-38-76 | iv. |
| | (19) Nag Hammadi X (Krause) | **C50** | -84 | iv. |
| | (20) Nag Hammadi XI (Krause) | **C51** | -76 | iv. |
| | (21) Nag Hammadi XII (Krause) | **C52** | -72 | iv. |
| | (22) Nag Hammadi XIII (Krause) | **C53** | -[16] | iv. |
| | (23) New Testament Apocrypha | **C34** | 36-72-144 | v. |

*Information from *ADIK* xviii (1962): 123, corrected from James M. Robinson, *The Facsimile Edition of the Nag Hammadi Codices*, pp. 17-19. Nag Hammadi I and XIII are actually in two gatherings, both very large. They are in fact 2 single-quire codices bound together. In Codex XII → faces →. In every other case the hypothetical order ↓ → ↓ → to center has proved a successful base for restoration.

*Ones* ("uniones") are those gatherings which consist of single sheets centrally folded, 1 sheet = 2 leaves = 4 pages. Examples of this make-up used throughout a codex are very rare indeed.[11]

In view of their early dates codices made up in this way contend with single-quire codices to be regarded as the earliest form of codex (see discussion later p. 99). But there are also late examples of the form. P. Colt 8 and 9 (**352**), a codex containing a Cyril Glossary and "A Chapter on Faith" use this make-up in vii A.D.

Naturally also a quire of a single sheet may appear as a singleton in a codex where the gatherings are normally larger (e.g., at the end of Tourah Codex I, following three quaternions in the as yet unedited "Discours sur la Paque"). Its presence in P. Bodmer IV (**P 66**) is more doubtful. V. Martin postulated a (now lost) single sheet quire in this manuscript.[12] But its presence between a quaternio and a quinio, and not at the end, is doubtful. Moreover, this codex may have been rebound in antiquity.

**TABLE 7**

**List of "Uniones"**

*Papyrus—possible examples:*

(1) Ch. B. I. (**P 45**) Gospels and Acts, iii A. D.?, 120 sheets (identified as *Unio* by occurrence of two successive conjugate leaves)
(2) Possibly Ch. B. VI (**OT 36**) Numbers and Deuteronomy. Cf. p. 59 n. 17.
(3) P. Colt 8-9 (**352**), Cyril Glossary, and Pseudo-Gregory (**524**), 6 single sheets, forming "uniones." A very rough note book. vii.
(4) Documents of c. vii-viii. H. I. Bell writes, "This format is the almost invariable rule in the eighth cent. Aphrodito papyri, composed of papyrus of fine quality and carefully written."* The rule is ↓ → → ↓ except for P. Lond. IV 1419 (**Misc. 1**).
(5) Pauline Epistles (**P 30**), P. Oxy. xv 1598, iii/iv contains two consecutive leaves in order → ↓ ↓ →. But it need not be a unio.

Parchment—none known.

**The Library* ns. X (1909): 307f.

*Twos,* "biniones," 2 sheets, 4 leaves, 8 pages, occur mixed with larger gatherings, as shown in the tabulation. I do not know of any codex composed solely of twos.[13]

| | |
|---|---|
| Papyrus: | P. Bodmer Composite (p. 79 below), iv A.D. |
| | Pamprepius (**240**), *S.B. Wien* (1928), Abh. 3, v/vi (possibly last gathering in the book) |
| Parchment: | Freer Gospels (**"W"**), v, mixed with threes and fours |

*Threes,* "terniones," 3 sheets, 6 leaves, 12 pages, are also usually mixed with other gatherings when they occur, though a regular sequence of threes has been claimed (inconclusively) for some examples.

**TABLE 8**

**List of "Terniones"**

| | |
|---|---|
| Papyrus: | (1) P. Bodmer Composite, iv A.D. (cf. under twos) |
| | (2) Coptic Ms d'Anastasy No. 9 (**C 29**), vi or later, composite.* |
| Parchment: | (1) Freer Gospels (**"W"**), v A.D. (see under twos) |
| | (2) Freer Psalms (**"A"**), vi, mixed with fours |
| | (3) Freer Joshua and Deuteronomy, (**"H"**), vi, mixed with fours |
| | (4) Initial quire of BM Coptic Pistis Sophia (**C5**), Or. Add 5114, iv A.D., is a ternio, the rest being fours |
| | (5) Final quire of P. Bodmer XXII + Mississippi Coptic II (**C4**) is ternio |
| Possible examples: | (6) P. Rainer inv. 26750 (**174**), Homer *Odyss.* i-ii, iv A.D. So H. Gerstinger, *Archiv. Bibl.* I (1926): 91–92, no. 22. His arguments are not cogent. |
| | (7) *PSI* ii 126 (**235**), Menander, iv or v. Could be quaternio. |

*W. Pleyte and P. A. A. Boeser, *Manuscrits Coptes des Pays-Bas* (Leiden, 1897), pp. 449ff.

*Fours,* "quaterniones," 4 sheets, 8 leaves, 16 pages. We have already seen that this number eventually became the standard, and produced the word "quire." Almost all the Latin codices of iv-vi listed in *CLA* are arranged in quaternions. Pre-eminence of this arrangement, however, was only gained through the passage of time. The tabulation below will show that there is no example which can be incontrovertibly dated before c. iv A. D. of a codex consisting only of quaternions.

**TABLE 9**

**List of "Quaterniones"**

Papyrus

(1) Earliest example: *some* of the quires in P. Bodmer II St. John **P 66**. These are mixed among fives. It is possible that they begin ↓→

(1a) Philo Paris BN Suppl. gr. 1120 (**244**), iii, →↓→↓→↓→↓⋮↓→ .

(1b) P. Bodmer Composite (pp. 79–80), iv, mixed with *threes.* Quires begin both →↓|→↓| etc. and ↓→|↓→| etc.

(2) Virgil glossary with Greek rendering, P. Ryl. III 478 + P. Med. I 1 + P. Cairo in *JJP* IV (1950): 239ff. (**459**). Date uncertain, iv ?→↓↓→ →↓↓→⋮→↓ etc.

(3) Hamburg *Praxeis Paulou* (**NT Apocryph. 9**). early iv A.D.? ↓→↓→↓→↓→⋮→↓ etc.

(4) Cairo Menander (**227**), iv/v A.D.? Order of →↓↓→ etc., as in (2).

(5) The Tourah Codices (Origen (**551, 552**), Didymus (**512-517**) in the main (Codex II and Codex IV have fours and fives combined) consist of quaternions following the order of (2). vi A.D.

(6) St. Hilary (**Lat. 5**), Vindob. 2160, v or vi? Similar order to (3).

(7) St. Cyril, De Adoratione (**507**), vi/vii, as in (2).

(8) Heidelberg Minor Prophets (Septuagint 1) (**OT 191**), vii A. D., mixed with fives: (a) quaternio; and ↓→↓→ to center
(b) quinio
(c) quinio
(d) quaternio

(9) *PSI* 1298 (**148**), Homer *Iliad,* v or vi, order similar to (3).

(10) Virgil glossary with Greek rendering, P. Colt 1 (**458**), vi, as in (2)

(11) Coptic Manichaean Homilies, ed. H. J. Polotsky (**C 32**), → faces →, iv or v.

(12) Coptic Isaiah, Pap. Bodmer XXIII, (**C 30**), iv.

Possible

(13) Palmomancy (**350**), P. Ryl. i 28, iv →↓→↓ to center. Possibly this would be better classed as a single-quire book, consisting of 1 quaternio.

(14) Astronomical Tables, c. iv (**334**), P. Heidelb. inv. 34. Perhaps more sheets than 4. Order is →↓ . . . →↓

Parchment

(1) P. Ryl. i 53 (**184**), Homer *Odyss.* iii/iv. Flesh/hair hair/flesh etc.

(2) Codex Sinaiticus (in the main), iv.

(3) B M Coptic Pistis Sophia (Or. Add. 5114) (**C 5**), iv? (the first gathering is a three).

(4) Codex Alexandrinus (in the original form).

(5) Codex Bezae (in the main), v?

(6) Vienna Dioscorides, vi.

(7) Coptic Prophets, Mississippi Coptic II + P. Bodmer XXII (**C 4**), iv. One gathering is a three.

(8) P. Berlin 13274 A and B = P. Cairo 274 A and B (**42**) (note 10 above) Demosthenes XIV, XVI, XV, v?

The early parchment Demosthenes *BM* 34473(1) (**47**) was claimed by its editor as a quaternio. But the evidence falls short of proof. What survives is a double leaf, and on the left-hand top corner of its last page is the pagination number (or gathering number) ς (6). Sir Frederic Kenyon described this manuscript (*Journal of Philology* xxii (1894): 247; the description is repeated by H. J. M. Milne, P. Lond. Lit., no. 127) as forming "the two inside leaves of a quaterion. This quaternion was the first in the entire Ms., and its first page held the beginning of the oration." There is something wrong with the arithmetic here. The text of the oration will have begun fairly exactly 4 columns, i.e., 2 pages 1 leaf, before the first column of the surviving double-leaf. If the make-up is in quaternions, two leaves will then have been empty before this oration started.

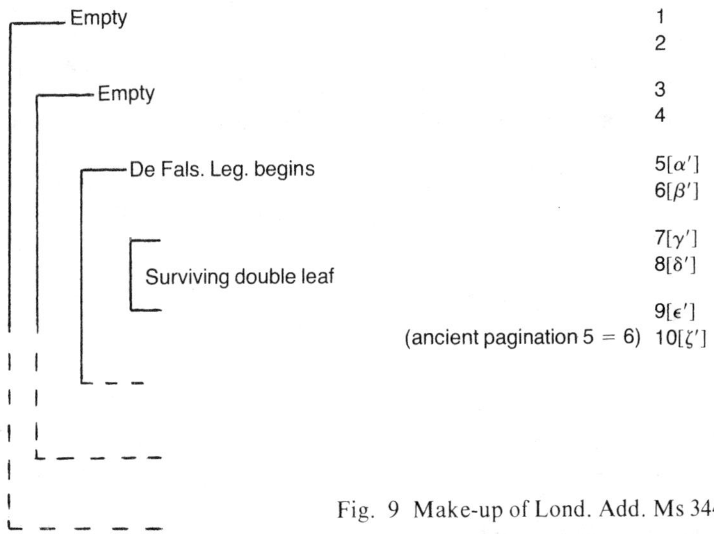


Fig. 9 Make-up of Lond. Add. Ms 34473 (1) = **47**

The argument for make-up by quaternions loses its cogency now that we see that the oration began on page 5 of this gathering. It is, of course, a possible arrangement to suppose two empty leaves; or the manuscript may have held other speeches, and pagination may have restarted at this speech (cf. Chapter Six, p. 76). But it would be better to admit ignorance. Several other arrangements are possible.

*Fives,* "quiniones," 5 sheets, 10 leaves, 20 pages, are in the early period a strong rival to fours. See Table 10, p. 64.

*Sixes,* "seniones," 6 sheets, 12 leaves, 24 pages, are first attested in iii A. D.[14]

Papyrus (1) Philo (**243**)[14], P. Oxy. 1173 + etc. (**243**) iii,
(2) Coptic Manichaean Psalm Book (**C 33**), iv (or v?).
(3) Coptic BM Ms Or. 7594 (**C 1**), mixed with *fives* (q.v.).
(4) Greek P. Bodmer II St. John (**P 66**), mixed with other formations. See p. 70.
(5) P. Amh. i 1 (**OT 223**), Ascension of Isaiah, v.

Parchment (1) The "butterfly" Mani Codex in Cologne (P. Colon. inv. 4780), (**Misc. 4**), 3.5 × 4.5 cm., iv or v.

*Sevens,* "septeniones," 7 sheets, 14 leaves, 28 pages, may occur in the Bodleian papyrus codex of Callimachus, P. Oxy. 1011 (**34**), A. D. iv or v. This arrangement has been argued for by R. Pfeiffer (*Callimachus* ii, p. xxii) for at least one gathering, but not for the whole manuscript.[15]

*Eights,* "octoniones", 8 sheets, 16 leaves, 32 pages. The largest plausibly suggested gathering. But no indisputable example has been put forward.

Papyrus: (1) Origen, MPER iv no. 51 (**548**) iii/iv: "fol. 1 has foliation number ο = 70, conjugate fol. 16 has number πϵ = 85" (ed.). Page numbers? If so, quaternio.
(2) Possibly P. Bodmer II St. John (**P 66**) (cf. p. 70 n. 12). V. Martin argued for an eight, R. Kasser for a nine among smaller gatherings.

Parchment: none.

**TABLE 10**

**List of "Quiniones"**

Papyrus
(1) Ch. B. V 962 (**OT 11**), Genesis, iii/iv A. D. Began with a binio (?), then fives, ↓→ to center.
(2) Possibly Ch. B. IV 961 (**OT 5**), Genesis, iv. Sequence is either ↓→→↓ or →↓↓→.
(3) Possibly Ch. B. III (**P 47**), Revelation, iii/iv (mixed with a six? But it may be a single-quire codex).
(4) BM Coptic Ms Or. 7594 (**C 1**), Deuteronomy, Jonah, Acts, iv, with an admixture of sixes. Sequence →↓ to center.
(5) Heidelberg Minor Prophets (Septuagint 1) (**OT 191**), mixed with fours, vii. See p. 000.
(6) Josephus, Milan Ambros. Cimelio Ms i (**Lat. 6**), vi A. D. Begins →↓.
(7) P. Bodmer II St. John (**P 66**), mixed with other formations. See p. 62 and 70.
(8) Antinoe Theocritus (**266**), v/vi, begins ↓→.

Parchment
(1) Gaius (**471**), Florence, *PSI* 1182, iv-vi.
(2) Vaticanus, Vat. gr. 1209, (**Bible 'B'**) iv.
(3) Terence, Bembinus (Vat. lat. 3226).

*Nines*, "noniones," 9 sheets, 18 leaves, 36 pages: one single such gathering in a papyrus codex is postulated by R. Kasser in his revised organization of the original make-up of P. Bodmer II, see p. 70 n. 12. There is no known example on parchment.

It should be noted that a single leaf (two pages, *not* a sheet) has sometimes been added by a scribe when he believed he was likely to run out of writing material. This is said to occur in the Coptic 1st Epistle of Clement (**C 8**), and at several points in the Tourah codices (L. Doutreleau, *Rev. Sciences rel.* xliii [1955]: 163). Cf. p. 73.

It is now desirable to return to the second *variable* found in the make-up of papyrus codices (p. 57 above), namely the succession of ↓ and → in the various types of gathering just discussed. As we have seen, in each sheet of papyrus used to form a larger whole, whether roll or codex, one side has its fibers travelling in a horizontal direction (→), the other side in a vertical direction. In the case of a sheet forming part of a codex, the matter may be diagrammatically illustrated:

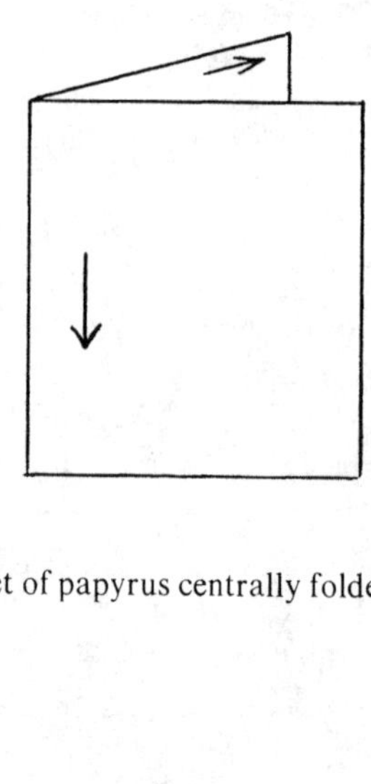

Fig. 10. Fiber direction in a sheet of papyrus centrally folded.

The folded sheet has been illustrated with vertical fibers (↓) on its outside, i.e., its first right-hand page, since that is the formation found in all except one of the single quire codices listed on pp. 58ff. about which information concerning fiber direction is available to me. The exception is the Mississippi Crosby codex **C 3**, which has → ↓ for the first eight leaves, then reverses to ↓ → ↓ → up to the center of the book. There are two other possible exceptions among what may be single quire codices (not listed on pp. 58ff): 1) a miniature codex in Oslo (*Symbolae Osloenses* XXIV (1925): 126, **P 62**), in which the fibers of what is thought to be the central sheet lie vertically when they would have been expected to lie horizontally; 2) P. Ryl. i 28 (**350**), iv, a miniature codex, which begins → ↓ and continues similarly to its center. But there are at least twenty certain instances of what I have called the normal order, ↓ → ↓ → to the center, and some of these are definitely to be dated to the third century after Christ.

Now if codices of papyrus had followed what seems to be the rule with codices of parchment, that "like" faces "like," one would have expected the sheets of a single-quire codex to alternate, ↓ and → alternately being laid downward, so that the pages of the folded codex would have come out ↓ →| → ↓ | ↓ →| → ↓ | etc. In fact, as we have already observed, this is not the way single-quire papyrus codices were normally put together, for they alternate ↓ → ↓ → to the central fold and then go into the reverse succession → ↓ → ↓. Here then, apparently, is an additional point in which the example of the parchment codex did not influence the practice of constructing papyrus codices.[16]

Speculatively two reasons may be advanced for this habit of placing ↓ on the outside right hand page of a gathering. One is that it was usual to gum the first sheet on a roll (the *protokollon,* which was normally left blank in a literary roll) with its fibers vertical, i.e., ↓, on the *inside* of a roll, in which all subsequent inside sheets were →. A second is that the *back* of a roll (except its first sheet) normally has its fibers ↓. If a codex is in fact made from "sheets" cut out of a roll, it would be expected that the maker laid each one above the other facing in the same direction as the roll from which they were cut. ↓ would then be face downward; and when the mass was folded centrally without being picked up and turned over, the first page would automatically also be ↓.

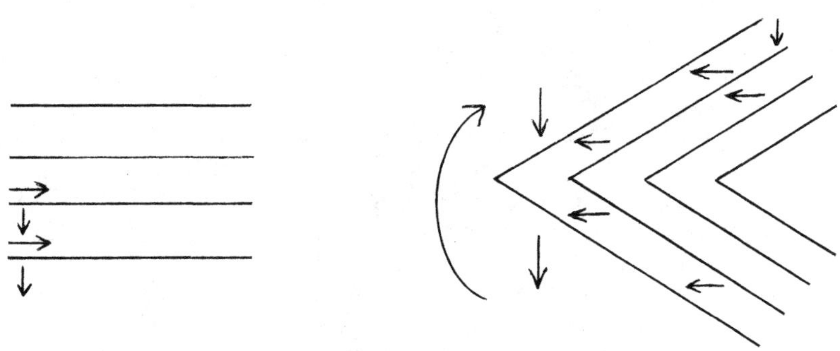

Fig. 11 Mode of folding a mass of papyrus sheets.

It is not, however, an invariable rule even in c. iii A.D. for the outside right-hand page of a papyrus codex to show ↓. A probable third century exception is offered by the Oxyrhynchus Philo codex (P. Oxy. 1173, 1356, 2158 + P. Haun. I 8 = **243**), if it is right to conclude that this manuscript is made up of sixes (seniones) (see p. 70). It seems probable that the Paris Philo (**244**) also may have → on the outside left-hand page, and then run in quaternions →↓→↓→↓||↓→ etc. The position as a whole can be checked in the following tabulation, set out analytically:

## TABLE 11

### Alternation of Fiber Direction in the Gatherings of Papyrus Codices

*A* *Single-quire codices*

With two exceptions (p. 65) the rule is ↓→↓→ to center, then →↓→↓.

*B* *Codices of multiple quires*

*I* Codices which certainly have ↓ on outside

(a) Uniones (must go ↓→→↓)

(1) Gospels and Acts, Ch. B. I (**P 45**), iii.

(2) Documents from Aphrodito commonly (H. I. Bell, quoted p. 61 above), ↓→→↓, vii.

(b) Multiple quires which alternate ↓→↓→ etc. to center (quaterniones, quiniones, seniones and larger)

(1) Hamburg *Praxeis Paulou* (**NT Apocryphi 9**), quaterniones, iii/iv, ↓→↓→ etc.

(2) Apology of Phileas, P. Bodmer XX, in P. Bodmer Composite (p. 79), quaternio E.G.T., iv.

(3) St. Hilary (**Lat. 5**), Vindob., v or vi.

(4) Heidelberg Minor Prophets (Septuagint 1) (**OT 191**), mixed quaterniones and quiniones, vii.

(5) Homer, *PSI* 1298 (**148**), v or vi.

(6) Demosthenes, P. Ryl. i 58 (**45**), quaternio, v.

*II* Codices which certainly have ↓ on outside but have like facing like ( ↓↓ or →→) inside

(1) P. Bodmer II St. John (**P 66**), c. A. D. 200–250.

(2) Documentary land tax register of the Arsinoite Nome (**Misc. 2**).

*III* Codices which certainly have → on outside, thereafter alternate

(1) Philo Paris BN suppl. gr. 1120 (**244**), quaternio, iii? Certainly an early example.

(2) Nativity of Mary, P. Bodmer I in P. Bodmer Composite (p. 79ff.), terniones, iv ?

(3) BM Or 7594 (**C 1**), Coptic Deuteronomy etc., quiniones and seniones, iv.

(4) 3 further Coptic examples, vi or later? W. E. Crum, *JTS* XI, 300–302; F. G. Kenyon, *Books and Readers*[2], p. 108, n. 1.

(5) *MPER* iv no. 24 (**OT 85**), Psalms as school-book, ? quaternio, iv-v.

(6) P. Amh. i 1 (**OT 223**), Ascension of Isaiah, v.

*IV* Codices which certainly have → on outside, but have like facing like ( ↓↓ or →→) inside

(1) Philo, P. Oxy. 1173, 1356 etc. (**243**), seniones, iii.

(2) Virgil glossary, P. Ryl. iii 478 + (**459**), quaterniones, iv.

(3) Cairo Menander (**227**), quaterniones, iv/v.

(4) Tourah codex I (**550**) (includes *Entretien d'Origène*), quaterniones, vi.

(5) Tourah codex II (**551**) (includes *Contra Celse*), quaterniones and quiniones, vi.

(6) Tourah codex III (**512**) Didymus *ad Ecclesiastem*, quaterniones, vi.
(7) Tourah codex IV (**513**) Didymus *ad Genesim*, quaterniones, vi.
(8) Tourah codex V (**514**) Didymus *ad Psalmos*, quaterniones, vi.
(9) Tourah codex VI (**515**) Didymus *ad Zachariam*, quaterniones, vi.
(10) Tourah codex VII (**516**) Didymus *ad Hiob*, quaterniones, vi.
(11) Tourah codex VIII (**517**) Commentary, single ternio, vii.
(12) Josephus, Milan Ambrosiana Ms Cimelio 1 (**Lat. 6**), quiniones, vi.
(13) St. Cyril, *de Adoratione* (**507**), quaterniones, vi/vii.
(14) Coptic Manichaean Homilies (**C 32**) ed. H. J. Polotsky, quaterniones, iv or v.

*V* Codices which certainly have like facing like ( ↓↓ and →→) inside, but in which the nature of the outside right-hand page is not known to me

(1) Ch. B. VI (**OT 36**), Numbers and Deuteronomy, ii/iii E. G. T.
(2) Ch. B. IV, 961, (**OT 5**), Genesis, iv.
(3) P. Rain. i 14 (**406**), Panegyric, iv or v (the two central sheets of the gathering survive).
(4) P. Oxy. 1374 (**25**), Aristophanes, v/vi.
(5) P. Oxy. 1370 (**72**), Euripides, v/vi.
(6) P. Oxy. 1818 (**170**), Homer, v or vi.
(7) Berlin Nonnus, *BKT* v 1, 94–106 (**236**), vi (editors describe as a *binio*, but I do not know what they mean).
(8) P. Oxy. 2258 (**28**), Callimachus (2 conjugate and consecutive leaves are →↓↓→), vi/vii.
(9) Isidore, Synonyma (**Lat. 7**), *CLA* vii 929.
(10) P. Ant. iii 182 (**9a**), Aelius Aristides (fr. 2 consists of conjugate and consecutive leaves ↓ →→ ↓, could be central sheet of a quaternio), vii.

The tabulation shows that gatherings with → outside do not begin to occur frequently till c. iv; and that in codices of multiple gatherings, when like is opposite to like, the first right-hand page is normally →; and that this formation also does not normally occur till c. iv. But the cases of the Philo codex (**244**) (B III 1, → outside, c. iii) and of the Bodmer II (**P 66**) St. John (↓ outside, multiple quires in which like faces like, not later than A.D. 250) prevent these generalizations being erected into laws. They also show that it is otiose to postulate a generalized development in two stages: (1) from ↓→↓→ to →↓→↓; (2) from →↓→↓ to internal like to like (→↓↓→). And their occurrence is a useful warning that the discovery of new evidence may at any time alter the general picture.

Nevertheless, it is worthwhile to make two observations. The first is that matching like with like will be almost forced on users of codices of single sheet gatherings. If the outside right-hand page is ↓, then the two inner pages of the sheet must necessarily be →→. This succession is, in fact, found in Ch. B. I, Gospels and Acts (**P 45**), c. iii. Following the "rule" of ↓ on the outside right-hand page, the last leaf of a gathering will also match the first of the subsequent gathering in the succession ↓→→↓ | ↓→→↓ . In this way the placing of like opposite to like would be achieved at the stage of planning the codex.[17] It would be no big further step to make a codex of multiple quires by laying sheets with ↓ and → alternately face down, so that when folded like would continue to face like. However, in the second sentence of this paragraph I wrote "almost forced," for a careless scribe could get the order wrong. There are wrongly placed sheets (a quaternion?) in P. Oxy. 1374 (**25**); in seniones alternating →↓→↓ in BM Ms Or. 7594; and a number of other false successions are enumerated by W. E. Crum, *JTS* xi (1910): 302, cf. F. G. Kenyon, *Books and*

*Readers*[2], p. 108, n. 1. The possibility that a scribe has confused the proper order of succession should be borne in mind when one is attempting to work out the original make-up from fragments.

Secondly, the pattern found in category B IV does from some time in the fourth century become the favoured make-up for codices consisting of quaternions, without however entirely supplanting category B Ib or B III.

Indeed it is put beyond doubt by the Philo codex P. Oxy. 1173 + 1356 etc. (**243**) that this pattern of make-up was used in the third century, though in a senio, not in a quaternio. But it would be absurd to suppose that what was used in a senio might not also be used in a quaternio. Certainly this make-up is found in the Virgil glossary (no. 2 in the list in B iv) which is probably not later than the middle of the fourth century. This is a conservative view about its date, which some scholars would bring down to the late third century (notably R. Marichal, *Pauli Sententiae, Fr. Leidense,* pp. 29, 34-36). A. Körte was the first scholar to establish the pattern of succession found in category B IV, and his reordering of the disjointed leaves of the Cairo Menander codex on this basis has found general acceptance. The pattern is as follows:

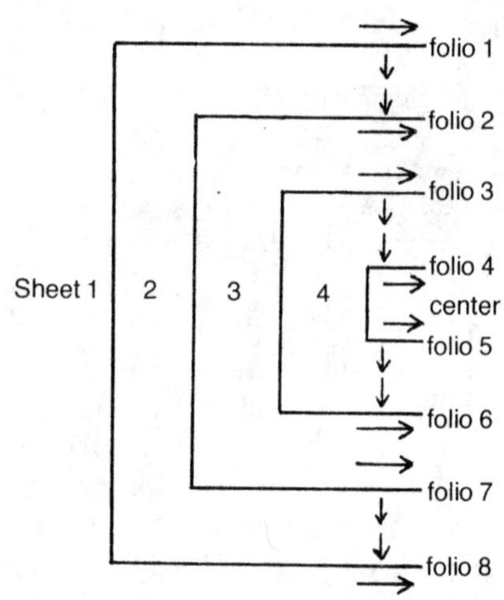


Fig. 12

## NOTES

[1]For example, by Sir Frederic Kenyon, *Books and Readers*[2], p. 106.

[2]C. R. Gregory, *Comptes Rendus Ac. Inscr.* (1885), 13: 261ff.; *Canon and Text of the New Testament* (Edinburgh, 1907), p. 324.

[3]The order may of course occasionally be disturbed through the carelessness of the scribe. Cf. A. S. Hunt's comments on P. Ryl. i 53 Odyssey (**184**), P. Ryl. i, p. 91.

[4]I have used these symbols with this meaning in *Greek Papyri* and *Greek Manuscripts of the Ancient World.* But I should warn the reader that it is not the meaning attached to them in *The Oxyrhynchus Papyri,* at any rate from Part XLI onward, where they stand for the direction of the writing in relation to the fibers. There → means "the writing is in the same direction as the fibers," ↓ "the writing runs across the fibers." In the case of a papyrus codex in which the writing is normally in a horizontal direction across the page, the upshot will of course be the same. But these two usages are likely to cause confusion when a detached piece of papyrus or a roll is concerned. On my system I can use the signs →↓ for pages of a papyrus codex which bear no writing.

[5]Figures of V. Martin. R. Kasser, P. Bodmer XXV, pp. 13 and 17 gives 13/13.3B x 28H.

[6]But see also the caution in Chapter Four, p. 46 and n. 12

[7]Cf. *BICS* vi (1959): 64; *Gnomon* (1969), p. 505 quoting as parallel Vindob. G. 2079b of A.D. 321 or 322.

[8]See the remarks of C. Bonner on the Michigan *Shepherd of Hermas* (**529**), pp. 11-12. He calls attention to the softness of the papyrus compared with paper. Even though bunched up at the fold papyrus will lie flat, which paper will not. Bonner's observation cannot be generalized to cover all such codices. The papyrus of the Menander is far from soft. Bonner does not suppose that "the tedious task of grading down the width" of the papyrus sheets would have often been carried out, and considers that the "irregularity of the front edge, as much as anything else, led to the abandonment of the large gathering in favour of smaller quires of regular size." He also expresses a doubt as to whether these early single-quire codices were given a binding cover.

[9]Chapter Two, p. 23

[10]In February 1973 I thought I had detected such a single-quire parchment codex in P. Cairo 274A and B (formerly Berlin 13274A and B; inadequately described in Pack$^2$ 270, 271) = **42**. This manuscript was found by Rubensohn at Hermopolis in 1906 and taken to Berlin; it was returned to Cairo in 1907. A photo of part of 274A is in W. Schubart, *Das Buch*$^2$, Abb. 26, p. 125 (whence Pack $^2$ 270), and the manuscript is listed in W. Schubart, *Einführung,* p. 475 (whence Pack$^2$ 271), but no reference is made to Dem. XVI *Pro Megalopolitanis* which 274A also contains. The first proper description was given, with full collation, by B. Haussmann, "Demosthenis Fragmenta in papyris et membranis servata," (Ph.D. dissertation, Leipzig, 1921), pp. 41-54. This dissertation is handwritten, not printed, which no doubt accounts for its rarity. I have not traced it in any library in England, and I have been able to consult the relevant pages only through the kindness of Wolfgang Müller of Berlin, who made a photocopy for me.

I inspected the original in Cairo in 1973, and photos were made of it by Professor L. Koenen and Dr. R. A. Coles. It then seemed to me that the two fragments demanded to be arranged as part of a single-quire codex according to the following system:

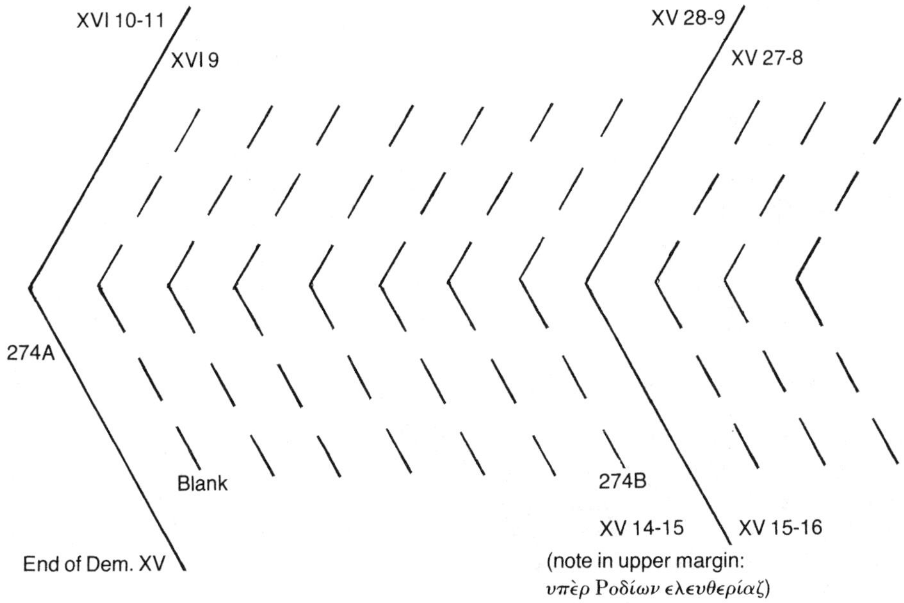


Fig. 13 The make-up of P. Cairo 274 as a codex: placing of the surviving sheets.

Haussmann shows that if the order of the speeches XIV, XVI, XV is adopted, the two fragments can be arranged in quaternions. This order is that of codices S and A (not F, as Haussmann) in the medieval tradition, cf. S. H. Butcher, preface to O. C. T. Demosthenes, pp. xvii-xviii. 274A will be the second sheet of quaternion 1; two complete quaternions were then lost; 274B will be the first sheet of quaternio 4. Such a system is more likely to have been in use in the fifth and sixth centuries. This arrangement will also explain the heading in Greek in the top right hand corner of 274B: the heading is at the start of a new gathering, for which it acts as gathering signature.

[11] K. Wessely, *Stud. Pal.* i (1901): iii-x claimed that a Hesiod manuscript (P. Rainer Inv. 19815) (**91**) had this form, but his reconstruction is fanciful. No doubt it began from a false interpretation of the figure λβ occurring at the foot of one page. This figure is stichometric, not a page number. I have examined the whole manuscript in photographs, and Dr. John Rea has checked it on the original. The authorities of the National Library in Vienna had already mounted it correctly, but I know of no published rectification.

[12] P. Bodmer II (1956), pp. 10-11. V. Martin supposed that this codex was made up as follows:

| | |
|---|---|
| Quire 1 quinio, with original first leaf lost | Pp. 1–18 |
| 2 quaternio | 19–34 |
| 3 unio, now lost | 35–38 |
| 4 quinio | 39–58 |
| 5 quinio | 59–78 |
| 6 octonio | 79–11[2] |

The plates, however, show there was an original gathering signature at the top right corner of each gathering: it is now cut away and I am not sure whether it was cut during the original binding, or on the occasion of rebinding. The figure is certainly identifiable at p. 17 where it can be restored as $>\overline{B}<$ (for the form, compare the gathering signatures in Tourah Codex II, J. Scherer, *Origene contre Celse,* plate I), and again on p. 77 (page οζ), where the figure is uncertain. I formerly read it as δ, C. H. Roberts as θ. but a re-examination of the codex made by Professor R. Kasser (letter of 29/3/71) suggests that it should be ϵ. Kasser reconstructs the make-up as follows:

| | Central parchment guard between pages |
|---|---|
| Quire 1 quaternio pp. 1–16 | 8–9 |
| 2 quinio [β] pp. 17–[36] (last leaf missing) | 26–27 |
| 3 senio pp. [37] – 60 (first leaf missing) | 48–49 |
| 4 quaternio pp. 61–76 | 68–69 |
| 5 nonio ?[ϵ] pp. 77–112 | 94–95 |
| 6 quaternio pp. 113–128 | Missing |
| 7 quaternio pp. [129]–[144] | Missing |
| 8 quaternio pp. [145–58 + 1 leaf blank] | Missing |

Professor Kasser supposes this was the original make-up. He writes: "A un certain moment le codex s'est usé, certains folios s'en sont détachés, et il a fallu effectuer une réparation au moyen des bandes de papyrus (inside, at pp. 2–15, 4–13; 62–75, 64–73; 114–27; outside at pp. 17–[36], 61–76). Au cours de cette opération, cependant, le folio p. 59–60 du cahier 3 a été relié au folio p. 77–78 du cahier 5. Je ne puis savoir à quoi on a relié alors les folios p. [37–38, perdu] et p. 111–112 (endommagé)."

[13] But this composition has been argued for Aristophanes, *BKT* v 2, p. 99 (**10**), on the basis of the numeration ϑ (top left) and ξϵ (top right), see p. 88, n. 6.

[14]The form of the Philo codex was determined as a sixer by Grenfell and Hunt, but they were not able to establish the fiber alternations. These are given by P. Oxy. 1356 fol. 4 and P. Haun. 8, which are consecutive conjugate leaves, as → ↓ ↓ → → ↓ etc. Confirmation of the format is offered by the fact that if p. 192 (the first page of P. Oxy. fol. 4) is the first page of a new gathering, there were precisely eight gatherings of sixes to precede it. In the case of *PSI* xi 1207, which is a consecutive conjugate leaf to P. Oxy. 1173 fol. 7, something has gone wrong with the total size of the gathering, which cannot have been a six. But the fiber alternations follow a similar pattern. For help in establishing the nature of P. Haun. 8 and for good photographs, I am indebted to Mr. Bülow-Jacobsen.

[15]J. Schwartz, *BIFAO* lxi (1962): 151 ff., if I have understood him correctly, suggests sevens for Homer, *Iliad* vi–xiii (**128**). But the regular alternation of → ↓ in leaves 3 to 36 suggests the second half of a single-quire codex. Cf. p. 57 and 66).

[16]The qualification "apparently" is needed. We do not have a succession of leaves from a parchment codex adequate to allow definite statements of their make up till iv A.D. That date is certainly later than a number of known papyrus codices made up in a single-quire or single-sheet quires. Just possibly earlier parchment codices were also capricious in their successions of hair sides and skin sides.

[17]It might therefore be argued that Ch. B. VI Numbers and Deuteronomy (**OT 36**), in which → is observed to face → and ↓ to face ↓ and the date assigned is early, is likelier to be a codex formed of uniones than arranged in one single quire.

CHAPTER

# 6

# The Codex and the Scribe

An interesting question now arises: did the scribe make up his codex and fasten it together before he copied his text into it? Could he buy a codex ready-made?

Only direct literary or documentary evidence can answer the second of these questions. We may proceed some way toward an answer to the first by considering what is implied in the procedure of copying a codex. Palaeographers have assumed in the past[1] that the great vellum codices were written sheet by sheet; that is, in order to be written the sheets were separated from the gathering into which they had been assembled (and through the whole body of which gatherings they were pricked). Each sheet was laid by itself in its turn on the scribe's knee or writing desk. Only when writing was completed were they reassembled and then stitched. That this was the procedure is mainly a matter of inference, but it is in itself eminently sensible. It makes two demands on the scribe: firstly, he needs to calculate fairly accurately the size of book he will eventually write so that he can have enough material to contain it; secondly, he must have some means of keeping the written sheets in the correct order.

Neither requirement would arise for a scribe used to writing on rolls. Should the latter find that his roll would not be long enough for the work he was copying, he could easily paste on to the end some extra sheets, or even a second roll; and the columns of the copy were necessarily in the right order. With a codex the case was different. A fairly accurate estimate was needed before starting. If the codex was formed of independent gatherings a miscalculation would not be serious, for an additional gathering or even a single leaf (cf. p. 64 above) could be added if required. In a single-quire papyrus codex the consequences would be more serious. Once the scribe had passed the central fold of his book it was too late to add another sheet except at the cost of having an empty leaf at the beginning, or of botching-in one or two loose single leaves in the middle or at the end. The former of these two devices is thought by H. A. Sanders to have been used in P. Oxy. 208 (**P 5**)[2] and by M. Krause and P. Labib in some of the Nag Hammadi codices; the latter was tried out in the middle in a shorthand manual BM Inv. 2561 (**420**), iii/iv, and at the end with the Coptic codex of I Clement (p. 13, **C 8**). There are not wanting examples also to show that a scribe, as he made progress with his copying, began to think that he would not succeed in getting his last pages in. In P. Bodmer xiv/xv Luke and John (**P 75**) the scribe makes his writing progressively smaller—and does succeed in getting home. The eye observes the change; quantitatively the change consists in getting more letters into the line. Page 3 (modern pagination) contains 39 lines to a page, averaging 24/25 letters to the line; p. 26 has 44 lines, but still averaging 24/25 letters; p. 98 has 43 lines, with an average of well over 30 letters to the line. The reverse process may be observed in P. Bodmer ii St. John (**P 66**), which is not a single-quire codex; the scribe begins to realize he has too much room and writes larger. Some statistics are given on p. 86.

In P. Bodmer xiv/xv it is not obvious how the second requirement (that of keeping the sheets in the correct order) was met. The manuscript is in excellent preservation, and after the first few leaves the original edges are intact. They show neither pagination nor gathering numbers. Was the book then put together and stitched before the scribe began copying? This is of course a possibility, but one is reluctant to accept it. It is hard to think of any form of book into which it would be harder to write regularly and evenly than a single-quire codex of thirty-six sheets (seventy-two leaves, 144 pages) which had already been stitched together. And this reluctance to believe can also be backed by measurement. T. C. Skeat has acutely observed (apropos of P. Ryl. Gk. 457[**P 52**], quoted by C. H. Roberts, in the *editio princeps*) that the reason why in that manuscript the lines on the left-hand page seem to be shorter than those on the right-hand page is that on the left-hand page the scribe is writing toward the central fold or gutter. If the sheets formed part of an already made-up book or quire (above all of a made-up single-quire codex) the scribe's difficulty would be far greater. I have indeed looked for other examples of the tendency noted by T. C. Skeat in P. Ryl. Gk. 457 on the part of the scribe, but I have found nothing convincing. In the papyrus codex of which we have just been speaking, P. Bodmer xiv/xv (**P 75**), the opposite seems to be the case. There are some left-hand pages which certainly have longer lines than those on the right-hand pages. For instance, in the pair pp. 35–36 (the pagination being modern, namely that of the *ed. pr.*) left-hand p. 36 has lines 8 cm. long; on the preceding right-hand page the lines are only 7.5 cm. long.

I conclude, therefore, that normally the scribe did write these pages when the sheets were still detached (before the volume was stitched), but that not every scribe copying a single-quire codex did so. To keep his sheets in the correct order without help of pagination would have required strict observance of a working routine: for example, only one sheet might have been removed from the bulk at any one time, and after one leaf, front and back, had been copied, it might have been replaced before the next sheet was taken. It would be possible to verify that the sheets were in the correct order for the binder at the moment that the scribe or the corrector collated the copy against its exemplar.

The Bodmer Luke/John codex is not unique in having no pagination, as will appear from the following short list of some other unpaged codices:

| | |
|---|---|
| Parchment, *Greek* literature: | Euripides, Cretans (**80**), ii? |
| | Odyssey, P. Ryl. i 53 (**184**), iv |
| | Dioscurides, Vindob. Med. 1, vi |
| *Greek* biblical: | Codex Sarravianus Colbertinus, iv |
| | Vaticanus, iv |
| | Alexandrinus, v |

| | | |
|---|---|---|
| Papyrus, | *Greek* magical: | *PGM* I iv (**M1**) iv |
| | | I v (**M2**) iv |
| | | *PGM* II xiii (**M3**) iv |
| | Chemical work | P. Lugd. Bat. "X" (**M4**) iv |
| | *Coptic* | (1) Elias Apocalypse (**C 10**) *TU* 17 (1899), iv |
| | | (2) Sahidic Apocalypse (**C 11**) ibid., iv? |
| | | (3) Coptic Exodus (**C 72**), *BIFAO* viii, 43ff., v or vi |
| | | (4) Achmimic Sirach (**C 73**), *ibid.* 64ff., vi |

A second general consideration will reinforce the argumentation adopted above. It is that pagination, when it occurs, is often written in a hand different from that of the original scribe (this point is not always reported by editors). It would seem, therefore, that it was not running pagination utilized by the scribe to keep his sheets in order, but was added subsequently (e.g., by a librarian). A few certain examples:

Pierpont Morgan *Iliad* (**140**), iv
Coptic I Letter of Clement (**C 8**)
P. Oxy. 697, Xenophon (**280**), ii
P. Oxy. 656, Genesis, (**OT 9**) ii/iii
Ch. B. XII (**OT 222**), Enoch and Melito.

Another observation points the same way. Campbell Bonner has remarked (*The Shepherd of Hermas*, pp. 8-9) that in the Michigan codex of that work page numeration was not added till after the codex was damaged, and had lost its beginning, since it starts at a point some distance from what is known from other sources to be the beginning of the text. Similarly, as will be seen later, pagination may restart inside a codex.

Running pagination may have been invented as early as the codex form itself. There are certainly examples of it continuously applied as early as the early third century.[3] But it would not seem to have been integral with the invention of the codex; otherwise one would have expected to find it as a part of every codex. It may have been developed in one center, from which it spread slowly; or right from the start an individual scribe may have refused to use it on esthetic grounds, and exercised his own judgment or been so instructed by his patron. The absence of pagination from the great vellum codices of the fourth century is probably to be explained as an act of deliberate choice.

It might indeed be argued that pagination was invented for other purposes (e. g., to facilitate reference) and that only gradually did scribes come to avail themselves of it for ordering the sheets of a codex. Such an argument might be based on those rolls of Greek literature in which a running figure is placed over a column of writing, and serves the same purpose as our own pagination (we should remember that *pagina* was the technical Latin term for a column of writing in a roll). These rolls are: *PSI* 1284, a history of the Diadochi, ii; an unpublished commentary on Theocritus from Oxyrhynchus, ii; Iulius Africanus, *Kestoi,* P. Oxy. iii 412, c. A. D. 250; and a roll of the *Epistle to the Hebrews* may be added, P. Oxy. iv 657, iii/iv. The idea that this numeration is there for reference purposes is supported by the filing practice of government officials in Egypt. Petitions, declarations, minutes of court action were filed by pasting the single sheets together to form rolls, which could then be cited by roll number and sheet number (e.g., τόμου β κολλήματος ρμ). A whole series of census returns so treated is to be seen in P. Brux. inv. E 7616 (P. Lugd. Bat. V). In favor of this theory is the probable date of the first two examples given above, viz. second century after Christ, a time before the codex is believed to have established itself as an acceptable format for Greek literature. Yet a residual doubt remains, and he would be an audacious man who asserted that the practice of giving a number could not have been transferred to the columns of the rolls in question by someone familiar with the habit of giving page numbers to equally early codices.

Even when employed pagination may be placed at different points on the page. The favorite place for it is undoubtedly the center of the upper margin. Some examples:

P. Oxy. 697 (**280**), Xenophon, ii
P. Oxy. 548 (**134**), Homer, iii
Pierpont Morgan *Iliad* (**140**), iv
*PSI* 977 (**127**), *Iliad*, iv-v
P. Reinach ii 69 (**142**), Homer v
*PSI* i 10 (**132**), *Iliad*, v-vi

But the page numeration may also be placed at the top outside edge. Some examples:

Callimachus hypomnema, P. Amh. ii 20 (**30**), iv
Coptic St. John "Q," iv
*PSI* 1298 (**148**), Homer, vi
*PSI* 1381 (**182**), Homer, vi

Some scribes did not number the odd pages, but only the even-numbered pages. Some examples:

P. Oxy. 1011 (**34**), Callimachus, iv/v
BM Add Ms 34473(1) (**47**), Demosthenes, ii
P. Oxy. 1780, St. John (**P 39**)
Leyden Anastasy 9 (**C 29**), Coptic letters of Abgar, etc.

Occasionally leaves, not pages, are numbered. The only instances I have met are: (1) *MPER* iv 51 (**548**), Origen commentary (but see p. 63) numbers $\overline{o}$, $\overline{\pi\epsilon}$ on first page of leaf; (2) P. Lond. Inv. 2562 (**419**), shorthand commentary, (H. J. M. Milne, *Shorthand Manuals*, pp. 2–8), on the first page of the leaf. Pagination at the foot does not occur. Where editors have thought they found it (as, for instance, in *MPER* i 4, (**324**), it is in fact a stichometric total of the number of lines on page.

It is also to be noted that in a number of codices a left-hand page is given an odd-page number. This can only mean that pagination started on an inside left-hand page, which in turn implies that the text of the work began on a left-hand page. In such cases it is possible that another work now lost (and separately paged) preceded that which survived; or that the previous right-hand page was deliberately left empty. Scholars have speculated whether in that case it was meant to serve as wrapper (Campbell Bonner, who considered that single-quire codices were frequently not given a binding (cf. Chapter Five, p. 69 n. 8); to carry the title (Grenfell and Hunt, on P. Oxy. 1229, Epistle of St. James); or to be glued to the binding cover (so H. Ibscher, *Der Kodex*, p. 13). Some examples:

Ch. B. II, Pauline Epistles (**P 46**), iii
Ch. B. V, Genesis (**OT 77**), iv
Philo, P. Oxy. 1173 etc. (**243**), iii

Epistle of St. James, P. Oxy. 1229 (**P 23**), iv
Mississippi Coptic Codex II + P. Bodmer XXII (**C 4**), iv
Achmimic Proverbs, Ms Berol. Oriental. 987 (**C 6**), iv
Psalms, P. Mich. 133 (**OT 65A**)
Demosthenes, pap., P. Ryl. i 58 (**45**), quaternio, v

Up to now the discussion has been about page numeration. In a single-quire codex it is the only numeration needed to keep the sheets in order. But in a codex of multiple quires the same function will be performed by a running number given to each quire: what is commonly termed a "gathering number" or "quire signature." The earliest examples of such that I know are to be found in the Bodmer papyrus II, the interpretation of which has already been discussed in Chapter Five, p. 70 n. 12. A little more may be said here about their nature. In this manuscript, at the top right hand, at its very edge, of p. 17 and p. 77, the ends of two parallel horizontal lines can be seen; lying between them to the left is a *diple* (>) followed by traces of ink. These traces are all that remains of the ancient figure, which was no doubt followed by a second *diple* facing in the reverse direction (<). This type of signature is preserved complete in Tourah Codex I (see plate I of J. Scherer, *Entretien d'Origène avec Héraclide*), in the form $>\overline{A}<$ . In the Bodmer manuscript these traces, which were not noticed by the first editor, are presumably all that was left by the binder's shears when he trimmed the pages for binding or for rebinding. They survive only at these two places in this manuscript. The ink and ductus seem compatible with an allocation to the original scribe, who in this case also added the page numbers. If this last guess is correct, they must be dated not later than A.D. 200-250 (cf. *Greek Manuscripts of the Ancient World,* no. 63), and are the earliest known examples of quire signatures. They are earlier than the signatures quoted by H. Ibscher from Mani codices (*Der Kodex,* p. 14), or the signatures in BM Ms Or. 7594 (**C 1**), which is unlikely to be later than A.D. 350.

These quire signatures are placed at the upper outside edge of the gathering concerned, a position which J. Irigoin has characterized as the normal one down to the ninth century after Christ (*Scriptorium* 12 [1958]: 222). It is not, however, canonical in the ancient world. The upper inside of this same page (i.e., top left of a right-hand page) is also of not infrequent occurrence, especially when both gathering numbers and pagination are inserted (sometimes by the same scribe). In these cases the gathering number is usually at the left, the page number at the right of the upper margin (in P. Bodmer II [**P 66**] both page and gathering numbers are at the upper right). If the gathering number is repeated, as it often is, on the last page of the gathering it is usually placed at the top inside edge, i.e., at the top right of its page. The center of the upper margin may also be the chosen position.

Different positions for quire signatures, sometimes coupled with pagination, may be shown in tabular form as follows:

A *Quire signatures and pagination*
Both at outside top edge of p. 1 of gatherings:
P. Bodmer II (**P 66**), iii.
Quire signature at top inside edge, page number at top outside of p. 1 of gathering:
Greek–Cairo Menander (**227**) (the only extant quire signature ς′, and page numbers κθ, λ obey this rule)[4]
P. Oxy. 1812 (**210**), Isocrates, last page of quire, $\overline{\iota\eta}$ top outside, $\overline{\delta}$ top inside,[5] vi
Aristophanes, *BKT* v 2 p. 103 (**10**), top inside θ = quire signature, top outside ξε,[6] v or vi

Coptic–BM Ms Or. 7594 (**C 1**), Deuteronomy, Jonah, Acts. iv
[gathering number is repeated at top inside on the last page of the gathering]
(vellum) BM Add. 5114 (**C 5**), Pistis Sophia, iv

B *Quire signature only*

Top outside (first page of gathering)

St. Cyril, De Adoratione (**507**), vi or vii (above line ending, repeated at top inside on last page of gathering)
P. Colt 1 (**458**)
P. Tourah I (**550**) (Entretien d'Origène), vi
(vellum) Freer Deuteronomy-Joshua (**OT 37**), vi

Top inside (first page of gathering)

(vellum) Homer Odyssey, P. Ryl. i 53 (**184**), iv
(papyrus) P. Tourah V Ad Psalmos (**514**)
P. Tourah VI Ad Zachariam (**515**)
P. Tourah III Ad Ecclesiastem (**512**) (*PTA* xvi p. xvii)

Top inside (last page of gathering)

(papyrus) Latin, Josephus, Milan Ambros. Cimelio Ms 1 (**Lat. 6**),[7] vi

Center of top margin

Codex Alexandrinus, v

Center of lower margin

Codex Vaticanus (Vat. gr. 1209), iv
Dioscurides, P. Vindob. Med. 1, vi
Augustine, Epistolae etc., Paris Bibl. Nat. 11641 (**Lat. 1**), vii/viii?

The basic system for Latin codices was to sign the quires with a Roman numeral preceded by a q or Q in the lower right-hand corner of the last page (cf. the remarks of E. A. Lowe at *CLA* vi:[vii]). I have counted 109 examples of this system in codices assigned in *CLA* to iv–vi. In three manuscripts the position is the middle of the lower margin, in one the left-hand corner. In two manuscripts, Greek numerals are found in the lower right-hand corner of the last page; in three others, though Roman numerals are used, the position is the left-hand corner of the first page.

To end this section it may be noted that another habit developed with the growth of the codex—that of giving a total at the foot of every page of the number of lines copied on that page. This is found, for instance, in:

| | | | |
|---|---|---|---|
| (1) Pastoral Poetry, *MPER* i no. 4 (**324**) | ii/iii | 48, 49 | Mistaken by editor for pagination. |
| (2) Callimachus, P. Berlin 13417A etc. (**32**) | iii | 37 | No pagination. |
| (3) Harris Homer, P. Lond. 126 (**106**) | iii | c. 50 | No pagination. |
| (4) Homer *PSI* i 13 (**137**) | iii | 37 | — |
| (5) Pierpont Morgan Homer (**140**) | iv | c. 40+ | Pagination also. |
| (6) Aratus P. Lond. ii 273+ (**8**) | iv | 61 | — |
| (7) Theocritus from Antinoe (**266**) | v–vi | 39–47 | No pagination. |
| (8) Hesiod, P. Rainer (**91**) | v | 32 | Mistaken by editor for pagination. Cf. p. 70, n. 17 above. |

This method of entering page-by-page stichometry is, to the best of my knowledge, an innovation of the codex. Stichometry in rolls is normally running and progressive by hundreds, not noted column by column. Such progressive stichometry in the roll is usually marked by a series of stichometric letters placed at the appropriate point in the side margin of the column, and totals are given only at the end of a roll. In the codex, progressive marginal stichometry is dropped. At least I know no example of its use.

In a number of codices pagination restarts in the middle. For instance, in BM Ms Or. 7594 (**C 1**), a well-written Coptic papyrus codex composed of quinions, and to be dated before A.D. 350, pages (ancient pagination) 1–145 contain Deuteronomy, followed by Jonah, beginning in mid-page, and paginated 1–8, and then Acts, paginated 1–112. The pagination seems to be added by a second hand. Since the separate sections begin in the middle of their respective quinions it does not seem that they were added as afterthoughts. But was this peculiar mixture Deuteronomy, Jonah, Acts planned from the outset?

Another probable example of a composite codex, the growth of which can be observed, is that of a number of biblical, patristic, and apocryphal texts in the Fondation Bodmer, details of which are set out in the enclosed table:

**TABLE 12**

**Contents of Bodmer Composite Codex (Codices)**

<table>
<tr><td>Nativity of Mary V Hand 1</td><td>quire 1 (threes) ancient pp. 1-12</td></tr>
<tr><td>14.2B x 15.5H</td><td>→↓|→↓|→↓‖↓→| etc.</td></tr>
<tr><td></td><td>quire 2 (fours) pp. 13-28 No details</td></tr>
<tr><td></td><td>quire 3 (fours) pp. 29-44 No details</td></tr>
<tr><td>ends p. 49</td><td>quire 4 (threes) pp. 45-56</td></tr>
<tr><td>Paul and Corinthians X Hand 2</td><td>↓→|→↓|↓→‖→↓|↓→|→↓|</td></tr>
<tr><td colspan="2">14.2 x 15.5 starts p. 50 ends p [57] ("like faces like")</td></tr>
<tr><td>11th Ode of Solomon XI Hand 2</td><td>quire 5 (fours?) (pp. 57-72?)</td></tr>
<tr><td>14.2 x 15.5 starts p. [57] ends p. 62</td><td>→↓|??|→↓|??‖??|↓→| | |<br>62/3<br>(false numeration, should be 61)</td></tr>
<tr><td>Epistle of Jude VII Hand 2?</td><td></td></tr>
<tr><td>14.2 x 15.5 starts p. 62 ends p. 68</td><td></td></tr>
<tr><td>Melito, Peri Pascha XIII Hand 3</td><td></td></tr>
<tr><td>Front title page [size?] p. [69?]</td><td></td></tr>
<tr><td colspan="2">[Pp. 1-2 lost = last leaf of quire 5 or not? A leaf in that case must be lost.]</td></tr>
<tr><td>Pp. 3 - begin</td><td>quire 6 (fours) 3-18</td></tr>
<tr><td>Size 14.2 x 16</td><td>↓→↓→↓→↓→‖→↓| etc.</td></tr>
<tr><td></td><td>quire 7 (fours) 19-34</td></tr>
<tr><td></td><td>As quire 6</td></tr>
<tr><td></td><td>quire 8 (fours) 35-50</td></tr>
<tr><td></td><td>As quire 6</td></tr>
<tr><td>ends p. 63</td><td>quire 9 (fours) 51-64 certain (66 ?)</td></tr>
<tr><td>Hymn Fragment XII p. 64</td><td>As quire 6</td></tr>
<tr><td>14.2 x 16</td><td></td></tr>
<tr><td>Apology of Phileas XX Hand 4</td><td></td></tr>
<tr><td>[? Title = last leaf of quire 9]</td><td>quire 10 (fours) [129–145]</td></tr>
<tr><td>14 x 15.5 text begins p.[129]</td><td>↓→↓→↓→↓→‖→↓| etc.</td></tr>
<tr><td>ends p.[146]</td><td>quire 11 (threes?)</td></tr>
</table>

[In V. Martin's reconstruction quire 10 is a 5 (quinio); but the fact that p. (145) is ↓ disproves Martin's reconstruction. There is no other quinio in the series here discussed, and p. (146) is likely to be first page of quire 11.]

| | |
|---|---|
| Psalms 33 and 34 IX Hand 5 | quire 11 (threes?) |
| (?14.2 x 15.5) | ↓ → \| ↓ → \| ? ? ‖ → ↓ \| ? |
| [Begin second page of this gathering and run to sixth page.] | |
| Epistle of Peter VIII Hand 6* | |
| (?14.2 x 15.5) begins p. 1 (= ? fourth leaf of quire 11) | |
| | quire 12 (fours) No details of make-up |
| Ends p. 36, followed | quire 13 (fours) No details (? begins ↓ →) |
| by a blank leaf | "Last quire of Ms" |

*M. Testuz identifies this hand with Hand 2. The published plate of p. 1 shows a hand whose letters have been remade, and neither confirms nor rebuts M. Testuz's identification. If the identification were certain, it would present conclusive evidence that the parts of this composite codex were intentionally copied in this order. Page 22 reproduced in a sale brochure for X-XII shows that Hand 2 has reappeared there.

This table repeats, corrects and adds to that given by M. Testuz in P. Bodmer VII-IX, pp. 8-9. But it is still not finally satisfactory. Doubtful questions could be resolved by inspection of the originals, about which M. Testuz gives inadequate information, often keeping silence about dimensions and the fiber-alternations of gatherings. I have visited the Bodmer Library more than once in the hope of settling these questions, but have not found the relevant portions available for study (and the Epistles of Peter are now separated from the remainder and at present in Rome).

It will be observed that there are four series of ancient paginations in this complex of manuscripts: (1) P. Bodmer V, X, XI, VII, pp. 1–68; (2) P. Bodmer XIII, pp. 3–63 + 64; (3) P. Bodmer XX, which seems to have begun at p. [129] (it does not seem to be possible to explain this starting-point on the assumption that it was thought by the scribe to the sum of the two preceding series); (4) P. Bodmer VIII, pp. 1–36, apparently at the end of the book.

Against the view that a single composite manuscript is before us is the larger size of P. Bodmer XIII (14.2 x 16) compared with what would have to be earlier and later gatherings (14.2 x 15.5). I have changed my mind more than once as to whether this consideration is finally decisive (see above Chap. one, p. 8). I incline now to think it is not, and to give more weight to the undoubted links at important places in the series. Such links are indisputable when a work begins in the later leaves of one quire and continues into the next: (V and X in quire 4; X, XI and VII in quire 5; XX and IX in quire 11). The evidence is compatible with such links in quire 9 (joining XIII and XX) and in quire 11 (joining IX and VIII). The only link that cannot satisfactorily be accounted for on evidence derived from Testuz is that of XIII and VII: quire 5 seems to be a leaf short if one supposes that the lost pages [1-2] of XIII are the last leaf of that quire. Two pages could have been left empty or held a short psalm.

For want, therefore, of positive evidence of linkage it cannot be taken as demonstrated that we have in this series a single composite codex that has, as it were, grown in size and content in front of our eyes. The absence of demonstration is a loss to the palaeographer in particular. If it were certain that the codex had grown in this way it would be surprising if any long interval of time separated its constituent parts. The hand of the Melito (XIII) or the Nativity (V) could not be dated much earlier than the Phileas (XX), which is undoubtedly of the fourth century.

A similar composite papyrus manuscript is the Greek *Acta Pauli* (**NT Apocryph. 9**) in Hamburg of about A.D. 300. This codex is in quaterniones. The first nineteen pages hold the Greek Πράξεις Παύλου (end-title, p.19). On p.20 the *Song of Songs* begins, written in old Fayumic, without front-title; it ends on p. 26 and is given an end-title. On p. 27 begin *The Lamentations of Jeremiah* in old Fayumic, and end on p. 36. Thereafter a section of the manuscript has been lost. It recommences at p. 49 with *Ecclesiastes* in Greek, followed at p. 63 by *Ecclesiastes* in Coptic. The end of the manuscript is lost. There are two figures ($\eta$ = 8 on p. 50, $\iota\alpha$ = 11 on p. 55, both written by first hand), the significance of which escapes me. In the *editio princeps* (p. 8), C. Schmidt argued from the absence of through pagination and of initial titles that the manuscript was a composite codex *(Sammelband).*

Lying behind the title "composite" given to these two codices is the suspicion that scribes did not care to waste writing material and would wish to fill any free pages left over at the end of a codex. Even if the matter chosen as filling was too long, in a quire of multiple gatherings additional gatherings could be added if required. This suspicion might be reinforced by a list of papyrus codices from these centuries containing heterogeneous material:

(1) The Harris Homer, BM Pap. 126 (**106**) = (*GMAW* 14), iii A.D. The Homer is written on one side only of the leaf; no other example of this manner of writing is known. (W. Schubart, *Das Buch*[2], p. 125, supposed that the scribe was unfamiliar with the proper procedure for copying a codex, and wrote on one side only as if it were a roll; a similar view is advanced by F. G. Kenyon, *Books and Readers*[2], p. 96. The interpretation rests on speculation only.) The codex contains other material than the Homer. On the back of the last three leaves are parts of Tryphon's *Ars Grammatica*, on the back of the fifth last leaf remains of accounts.

(2) P. Bon. 4 and 3 (**107**), ii/iii A.D., containing first a hexameter poem described as a *katabasis*, then a *Homeromanteion*.

(3) P. Bodmer Composite (described above pp. 79).

(4) An as yet unedited Bodmer papyrus of c. iv A.D. Parts of two or possibly three gatherings survive. Gathering 1 and the beginning of 2 contain *Susanna* in Greek. It is followed by some other apocryphal work, and then the beginning of Daniel, perhaps extending into gathering three. After a blank page, Thucydides VI, 1-3, was copied, breaking off where the gathering ends. It is impossible to say whether the whole of Thucydides VI would have been copied in a series of subsequent gatherings. [Addendum 1975. The Thucydides section and a note on the other contents have now been published by A. Carlini, *Museum Helveticum* xxxii (1975): 33ff. Carlini represents the gatherings as "terniones." On an earlier personal inspection I could not satisfy myself that this was the correct make-up, and I believe other reconstructions to be possible, but shall not argue them here.]

(5) P. Barcelona + P. Robinson inv. 201 (*Inno al Vierge* and *Seleccio de variants a les Catilinarias de Cicero*, ed. R. Roca-Puig: (**Lat. 4**), iv A.D. The manuscript begins with Cicero, *in Catilinam* I and II, and continues with a Latin metrical hymn to the Virgin.

Numbers 4 and 5 here are the earliest known examples of codices which combine Christian and pagan literature.

(6) P. Oxy. xxxiii 2656, Menander *Misoumenos* (**243a**), ed. princeps in *BICS* Suppl. xvii, iv A.D. On pages not occupied by the Menander, a later hand has copied a mathematical table of fractions for use as a ready reckoner. Since this copying is of a later date, this example is different in kind from the preceding.

(7) The Hamburg *Acta Pauli*, etc. (**NT Apocryph. 9**) just described.

(8) The Coptic Deuteronomy, Jonah, Acts, BM Ms Or. 7594 (**C 1**), just described.

(9) Mississippi Crosby Codex 1 (**C 3**), a single-quire papyrus codex of iii or iv A.D., contains a number of texts in Coptic. The first identifiable one is Melito, *Peri Pascha*, followed by a *Martyrdom under Antiochus* (= ii Macc. v 27-vii 50), ending on (ancient) p. 66. With the

following text, i Peter complete, page numeration begins afresh and runs from pp. 1–33. The next work is Jonah complete, page numeration again starts afresh, this time on a left-hand page. An additional damaged text came at the end.

(10) Ms d'Anastasy no. 9 (**C 29**). This papyrus book has already been mentioned because of its pagination on every second page (even-numbered left-hand pages) (see p. 76 above). It contains a mixture of prayers and apocryphal writings (Abgar to Christ, two letters of Christ to Abgar) etc. in Coptic.

A judgment of the value and purpose of these "composite codices" will be aided by a comparison with some rolls that are heterogeneous in content. Two examples will suffice:

(1) BM Pap. 131, the famous set of four rolls of *The Constitution of Athens* of c. A.D. 100. The principal roll (no. 1) was first used (on → side) for an agricultural account. Later on, a part of the back of this roll was utilized for a copy of a commentary on Demosthenes, *Meidias* P. Lit. Lond. 179). Only a column and a half were occupied by this text. When the scribe of the Aristotle took this used roll in order to make a copy of *The Constitution of Athens*, he turned it round and began on the back at the other end. On reaching the *Meidias*, he drew cancelling lines through it, and resumed his copying on a farther sheet placed after the *Meidias*. On this sheet, the writing of *The Constitution* is actually→, i.e., with the fibers; on the other side of it, across the fibers, are parts of three columns of a commentary on Callimachus *Aitia* (P. Lit. Lond. 181). I have not been able to determine whether this final sheet was the original *protocollon* of the agricultural roll (such a first sheet attached to a literary roll usually showed its fibers ↓ on the inside of the roll) or was deliberately added by the scribe of the Aristotle.

(2) BM Pap. 133 + 134, i B.C. The first part of this roll contains nine columns of a speech of Hyperides (P. Lit. Lond. 134). After a blank space of about 30 cm. a second scribe copied the Third Letter of Demosthenes (P. Lit. Lond. 130).

This list could be extended considerably, for instance, by adding all rolls which have one literary work on the recto, another on the verso. But this remark emphasises a difference between the two heterogeneous rolls just noted and the composite codices containing heterogeneous material. The latter are usually in the same writing (the Harris Homer or the Menander *Misoumenos* excepted), and were therefore probably written more or less at one time and place. Moreover, the texts they contain are usually longer than the farrago in rolls (1) and (2) above. It would perhaps, therefore, not be an error to see in them a growing recognition of the comprehensive character of a codex.

Comprehensiveness, as C. H. Roberts has already stressed, is one of the principal advantages of the codex form over the roll.[8] This factor is worth illustration from known or certainly calculable sizes of codices expressed in their number of pages. The highest page number from à papyrus codex that K. Ohly could quote in 1928 was from the third century Philo codex (**243**, P. Oxy. + P. Haun. 8 + *PSI* xi 1207), namely in the mid 200s. This number has now certainly been raised to 289 by the identification of *PSI* xi 1207 as part of this manuscript. This codex of c. iii, as we have seen (p. 70, n. 14 above), was in sixes. However, a papyrus codex of c. iv or v also in sixes is very much bigger—the Coptic Manichaean Psalm Book (**C 33**) has a gathering figure of 26, i.e., at least 638 pages, probably the largest number of pages known in any papyrus codex. Latin parchment codices can of course be much bigger still, e.g., *CLA* viii 1196 of A.D. 546 has fifty gatherings in quinions, that is, more than one thousand pages.

The Cairo Menander (**227**) of iv (or iv/v), a papyrus codex in quaternions, is much smaller: 10 quires = 160 pages, 5 plays, was the calculation of A. Körte, and his reconstruction is now firmly supported by its agreement with the evidence of the Bodmer Codex for *Samia* (**225**). Papyrus codices in quaternions in c. v and vi were bigger than this: of Tourah Codex VI (Didymus, *ad Zachariam,* vi, **515**) 406 actual pages survive, and Father Doutreleau argues that its minimum original compass was probably 26 quires of 16 pages each, i.e., at least 416 pages. In *Recherches de Science religieuse* xliii (1955): 161, n. 2, Father Doutreleau writes of 30 quires (=480 pages) as the size of the largest Tourah codices. This figure is well above the largest number of pages in any codex in single-quire form: 124 in the Pierpont Morgan *Iliad* (**140**) of c. iv, containing *Iliad* x-xvi, 62+ in the Bodmer Menander (three plays) also of c. iv, 280+ in the Milan Coptic codex of the Pauline Epistles of c. v.

For comparison, the number of pages in or contents of some other papyrus codices is set down:

| | | | |
|---|---|---|---|
| Callimachus[9] | P. Oxy. vii 1011 | **34** | 192 is the highest recorded pagination, iv or iv/v |
| Aristophanes | P. Oxy. xi 1374 | **25** | p. 196, v |
| Homer | P. Ant. iii 158 | **131a** | (number of pages unknown), iii, (*Il.* VIII-XVI) |
| | *PSI* i 10 | **132** | p. 189, vi (*Il.* VIII-XIII, and more?) |
| | *PSI* viii 977 | **127** | p. 103, iv–v (*Il.* I–VI, and more?) |
| | P. Rein ii 69 | **142** | p. 187 at *Il.* XI 152, v (*Il.* I–XII, and more?) |
| | *PSI* xiii 1298 | **148** | p. 92, v–vi (*Il.* XIII–XVI at least) |
| Xenophon | P. Varsov. 1 + P. Ryl. iii 549 | **281** | p. 235, iii (whole *Cyropaedia* in c. 300; pages ?). |

As a contrast to the papyrus codices, two parchment codices of Homer are:

| | | |
|---|---|---|
| P. Ryl. i 53 | **184** | iii/iv, quire signature "25" in *Odyss.* XXIII (i.e., 26 quires, each 16 pp. = 416 pp. for the whole *Odyssey*) |
| P. Amh. ii 23 | **188** | iv, p. 261 at *Odyss.* XV 161 (probably also whole *Odyssey*) |

The large size of the Didymus codices (26–30 quires, each of 16 pages, of dimensions which fall into group 2 "nearly square") has already been put by Father Doutreleau into relationship with a letter in which Saint Augustine discusses the make-up as a book of *De Civitate Dei:* "The number of quaterniones is 22, which is a serious undertaking to bind up into a single volume *(corpus).* If you wish it to be turned into two codices, the division should be arranged so that one codex holds ten books *(libri),* the other twelve . . . . If, however, you want more than two volumes *(corpora),* you must divide into five codices."[10] The importance of this division for the textual tradition of the *De Civ. Dei* was emphasized by the first editor and by others after him[11]; however, it is somewhat misleading to compare the 26–30 quires of the Didymus with the "22 quaterniones" of the letter of Augustine. In the latter the word "quaternio" is being used very loosely as equivalent to "liber," and it is out of the question that a quaternion in any contemporary codex could have contained a whole "book" *(liber)* of the *De Civ. Dei.* A fifth-century uncial manuscript of this work on parchment (Verona, Bibl. Capitolare XXVIII [26] = *CLA* iv 491) requires 30 quaternions for Books xi–xvi, i.e., an average of 5 quaternions per book; a sixth-century half-uncial manuscript contains Books i-ix in 40+ quaternions (Paris BN lat. 12214 = *CLA* v 635), i.e., 4½ quaternions per book. Supposing one took a papyrus codex written more closely, one still could not find a codex in which a single gathering of fours could hold a "book" of Augustine's work. The 1908 Teubner edition of B. Dombaert averages 31 lines (of 50 or so letters) to a page, and the early books occupy between 45 and 50 printed pages, the later about 42. A papyrus manuscript such as the Avitus of c. vi (BN lat. 8913 etc. = *CLA* v 573) contains about 27 lines (of no more than 26–34 letters) to a page; the Milan Josephus (Cimelio 1 = *CLA* iii 304) has 30–39 lines (of 50–55 letters) to a page. Something like 3 gatherings of fours would be needed in a manuscript written like the Josephus in order to hold a book of the *De Civitate Dei;* a larger number would be needed if the format were that of the Avitus.

The "Pandects," i.e., "the all-inclusive," is the Greek title of Justinian's great work of legal codification known as *Digesta* in Latin. One portion of Justinian's work is entitled *Codex Justinianus,* that is, comprehensiveness is the final aim of the codex. That a work should be all-inclusive is now its *raison d'être.* Such a work must needs be in large format, and the large format offers the opportunity to include alongside the sacred text the annotation the reader will need. Space for such annotation has been deliberately provided in the papyrus codex of Callimachus, P. Oxy. xx 2258 (**28**), page size 37B x 28H. This large page contained only twenty-three verses, occupying an area 20 B x 16H, and leaving side-margins each 8–10 cm. broad. "The margins," writes N. G. Wilson, "together are equivalent to half the width of the page."[12] If they were not designed for it, they certainly invite the generous commentary provided by the original scribe. We seem here to find a clear connection between format and the intention to include scholia.

But other aims than comprehensiveness no doubt animated the creators of such large books. They will have desired to create a book worthy of its contents (particularly when the contents are the sacred scriptures); they will have wished to create a book suitable as a splendid gift or to flatter the prestige of their patrons, grandees, churchmen, even local landowners. Illustration will have helped to satisfy this wish, and illustration also requires a generous provision of space and a large page. Such illustrations are to be seen in the book containing the Charioteers from Antinoe (Ch. one, p. 10), the Ambrosian *Iliad,* the Vienna Genesis; whole pages are devoted to the drawings of plants in the Vienna Dioscurides.

One further aspect of a large book has received little attention, and is worth examination. It is easier to read aloud to an assembly—a congregation—from a book in which the letters are written at a fair size than from one in which they are small. We are familiar with this practical point when we study lectionaries; the great codices in their "biblical majuscule" hands of the fourth, fifth, and subsequent centuries also come at once to mind. But the process may have begun at an earlier date. We know that there was a priestly office or order in the early church held by the *reader,* ἀναγνώστης. It was his duty to read the sacred scriptures aloud to the congregation. Such readers are mentioned in a list of the clergy of the church in Rome issued by Pope Cornelius about the middle of the third century after Christ and recorded by Eusebius "exorcists and readers together with sextons, 52."[13] H. Lietzmann writes of this priestly order: "they understood the difficult art of reading aloud at public worship with melodic and rhythmic correctness the prescribed Biblical lessons out of codices written without word-division or punctuation."[14] Persons belonging to this order proudly added the qualification ἀναγνώστης to their tombstones.[15] An individual *reader* whose church suffered in the persecution of A.D. 304 is mentioned in P. Oxy. xxxiii 2673, 8, and 34 where he is further described as "illiterate." What this means is that he was a "reader" of Coptic, not Greek texts.

Now, in some sense, all books produced in the ancient world were intended to be read out aloud.[16] But there would be a difference between the kind of book suitable for an individual reading to himself and that useful to a *reader* reading to instruct a congregation. It seems possible that the need to produce a book from which to read aloud to a congregation will account for some of the idiosyncratic features in the handwriting of early Christian codices. For instance, scholars have not been able to point to any precise palaeographic parallel for Chester Beatty Codex IX-X (**OT 183**). The handwriting has at one and the same time elements that are familiar and unfamiliar. As explanation I suggest that in it handwritings that are practised and clear but of no special merit have been produced to a greater size than normal to ease the task of reading aloud.

This suggestion can be tested statistically by comparing Christian and pagan papyrus codices assigned to roughly the same dates and belonging to the same format (i.e., "group" in the lists in Table 2). From the aberrants of Group 8 we may contrast:

| *"Christian"* | *Greek literature* |
|---|---|
| **OT 183**, **OT 207A**, Ch. Beatty IX-X<br>12. 8 x 34.4<br>49–54 lines<br>17–23 letters per line | (1) **150,** Homer, P. Merton 3<br>13.7 x [32.5]<br>52–54 lines<br>Hexameters, i.e., 32–38 letters<br>(2) **106**, Harris Homer<br>13.0 x 29.5<br>48–54 lines<br>Hexameters, i.e., 32–38 letters |

However, this comparison is not a fair one, since the "Christian" book is in prose and the Greek literature in verse; prose ought to be contrasted with prose. If one took from the same group two prose manuscripts (not, in my opinion of the same date as P. Chester Beatty) the discrepancy is, however, more striking still:

(3) **280**, Xenophon *Cyropaedia*,
P. Oxy. iv 697
12.5 x [33.1]
60 lines
40–45 letters per line

(4) **M1**, Magical *PGM* I iv
13.0 x 30.5?
50 lines
31–39 letters per line

From the main body of Group 8 the following two codices may be contrasted. Again it must be borne in mind that the codex of Greek literature is of verse, where the length of line is laid down; moreover, if we take the earlier date which has been suggested for the Christian manuscript, c. A.D. 175, there could be a century and a half between the two. I think that date improbable, but the time interval may still be nearly one hundred years.

| *"Christian"* | *Greek literature* |
|---|---|
| **P 75**, St. Luke, St. John, P. Bodmer XIV/XV | **225**, Bodmer Menander Codex |
| 13 x 26 | 13 x 27.5 |
| (See p. 74 above) | 47–54 lines (average 49–51) |
| p. 3: 39 lines, 24/25 letters | Trimeters 25–34 letters, |
| p. 24: 44 lines, 24/25 letters | average 28 |
| p. 98: 43 lines, 30+ letters | (longer lines in tetrameters) |

The following pair, both prose, may be contrasted from Group 9:

| *"Christian"* | *Greek literature* |
|---|---|
| **P 66**, St. John, P. Bodmer II | **243**, Philo, P. Oxy. + P. Haun + PSI |
| 14.2 x 16.2 | 15 x 17.5 |
| p. 1: 26 lines, average 31 letters | (several scribes) |
| p. 2: 23 lines, average 28 letters | e.g., fol. 7, 24/25 lines, 31+ letters |
| p. 26: 19 lines, average 21 letters | fol. 4 36 letters |
| p. 44: 20 lines, average 24/5 letters | |
| p. 68: 20 lines, average 23/4 letters | |
| p. 96: 15 lines, average 25 letters | |

Some other "Christian" manuscripts of which the same observation seems to hold (that they are the work of practiced scribes writing an ordinary type of hand, but writing it larger than usual) are:

Ch. B. VIII Jeremiah (**OT 202**)
XI Ecclesiasticus (**OT 181**)
XII Enoch & Melito (**OT 222**)
(perhaps) VI Numbers and Deuteronomy (**OT 36**) (Kenyon's plates are reduced)
Michigan Shepherd of Hermas (**529**)
P. Oxy, i 2 St. Matthew (**P 1**)
ii 208+ St. John (**P 5**)
Yale Genesis (**OT 7**)
P. Egerton "Unknown Gospel" (**NT Apocryph. 7**)

We should not expect to find this feature in all Christian books, but it seems to be present in a sufficient number for attention to be paid to it by palaeographers, and for the appropriate allowances to be made when datings are assigned.[17]

All the examples quoted so far have been of manuscripts with only a single column to the page, in which the lines are longish when compared with the length favored by classical practice of the second century or earlier, indeed they may be very long. Such a way of writing economizes in material, and this utilitarian motive may be one reason for its adoption (see Chapter Three, p. 35). But there is probably also an esthetic reason. Given that in a book of codex form each page is an easily apprehended unit of space when contrasted with the continuously extending space of the roll, the single column of writing inside that space—a solid block when contrasted with its margins—offers an esthetically satisfying appearance. In our modern books we are so familiar with the single block of print that an effort of imagination is needed to conceive of books in which it was not normal practice. On the basis of the Christian codices just instanced, it might be claimed that Christianity was the popularizer of the single broad column that fills the page. It is certainly true that early Christian papyrus codices favor the single-column format; and we have noted earlier (Chapter Three, p. 35) the interesting case of a manuscript, the Berlin Genesis (**OT 1**) which the scribe began to copy in two columns, but after eighteen pages changed to a single column with very long lines. However, even in the present state of knowledge such a claim on behalf of Christianity can be rejected as too sweeping. Not very many early codices of Greek prose literature survive compared with those of verse literature. Yet we may list the following examples written in single column:

| | | | |
|---|---|---|---|
| Xenophon | ii | **280** | 60 lines per page |
| Lollianus | ii | **223a** | 59+ lines per page |
| Plutarch | iii | **257** | 40+ lines per page |
| Astrology | iii | **341** | 40 lines per page, 43 letters per line |
| Philo | iii | **243** | 25 lines per page, over 30 letters per line |

[but note that Philo iii **244** is in two columns]

| | | | |
|---|---|---|---|
| Demosthenes commentary | ii/iii | **52** | total lines not known, 75+ letters per line |
| Thucydides commentary | iii | **279** | 45 lines per page, 60–70 letters per line. |

The last two examples are in a tradition well-established in the roll—for instance, the *Iliad* commentary in P. Oxy. viii 1086, or the parts of Aristotle's *Consitution of Athens* copied by the first scribe (*GMAW,* plates 58 and 60).

## NOTES

[1]The matter is currently the subject of controversy among mediaevalists. See for instance L. Gilissen, "La Composition des Cahiers, le Pliage du Parchemin et l'imposition," *Scriptorium* xxxvi (1972): 3ff.

[2]*HTR* (1938), p. 75. The same procedure is inferred by M. Krause and P. Labib (*MDAI* Kopt. Reihe I, p. 18) for Nag Hammadi Codices III and VI. Their argumentation is based apparently on the fact that pagination does not begin with what they regard as the resultant empty first leaf, the left-hand page of which carries a title (not apparently normal practice in these codices). Insofar as the argument rests on pagination prior to copying it seems to me insecure.

[3]A brief list, taken more or less at random:
NT: P. Bodmer II St. John (**P 66**), iii
P. Ch. B. III Revelation (**P 47**), iii
P. Oxy. i 2, St. Matthew (**P 1**), iii
Greek literature: Homer, P. Oxy. 548 (**134**)
Philo, P. Oxy. 1173 (**243**) etc.
K. Ohly, *Stichometrische Untersuchungen* (Leipzig, 1928), pp. 35ff., has collected a good deal of evidence.

[4]The discovery of parallels for this arrangement of the figures satisfactorily confirms Harmon's interpretation (apud Allinson Loeb ed., p. 12) of ϛ' as quire signature, which has been made the king-pin for reconstruction of the whole codex. Dr. R. A. Coles has confirmed for me from inspection of the original that the figure is to be read as ϛ', and that there is no corresponding figure Z (as Lefebvre thought) on the next page.

[5]Grenfell and Hunt interpreted $\delta$ as stichometric = line 400. Their interpretation and the interpretation as quire signature both run into difficulties. If $\delta$ is a quire signature, some other work preceded this speech. But normally *Ad Demonicum* is the first work in the Isocratean corpus.

[6]This Aristophanes has on the page which begins with →*Acharnians* 904 the figure $\theta$ in the top left corner, ξε in the top right corner. It has been pointed out that if the codex was composed of biniones, this is exactly the quire signature that would result on left and page numeration on right (8 x 8 pages reaches p. 64). The inference is attractive, since *Acharnians* will (by calculation) have begun about 27 pages earlier, i.e., at p. 38, and the manuscript's pagination cannot have begun afresh with each play.

[7]Roman numeral preceded by q.

[8]*The Codex*, pp. 202–04.

[9]The *Aitia* end on p. 185. Supposing 40 verses to a page, 7400 verses preceded. This may allow a guess at the minimum length of the *Aitia*, depending on its position in the Callimachean corpus.

[10]Ed. princeps by D. Lambert, *Rev. Benedictine* li (1935): 109ff.; thereafter. H. I. Marrou, *Vig. Christianae* iii (1949): 208ff.; R. Devreesse, *Introduction à l'étude des manuscrits grecs*, p. 79, n. 1, and p. 125, n. 2; B. V. E. Jones, *JTS*, n.s. xvi (1965): 142 ff.

[11]As observed already by Marrou, *loc. cit.*

[12]N. G. Wilson, *CQ*, n.s. xvii (1967): 249. Cf. *GMAW*, no. 47.

[13]*HE* vi 43.

[14]H. Lietzmann, *Geschichte d. alten Kirche* (1911-1961), p. 256. C. H. Roberts, *Cambridge History of the Bible*, 2: 64 notes the importance for the coherence of the early Church of "the rapid circulation of literature and its regular and public reading." He also calls attention (p. 62) to a copy of *The Shepherd of Hermas* marked for public reading. I presume him to be referring to P. Mich. inv. 44-H=P. Mich. 130 (C. Bonner, *HTR* xx [1927]: 108; *Idem., A Papyrus Codex of the Shepherd of Hermas*, p. 130). I do not know on what grounds the separating mark between vowels (col. i 7, 12) can be taken as evidence as marking for *public* reading.

[15]*ZPE* xi (1973): 4 and n. 28. Cf. P. Oxy. xli 2969, 4; M. Naldini, *Il cristianesimo in Egitto*, p. 38. Add K. A. Worp, 15 Wiener Papyri 14 v 21, (vi/vii).

[16]See Bernard W. Knox, *GRBS* ix (1968): 421.

[17]It is quite possible that P. Fuad inv. 266 Deuteronomy (*GMAW*, plate 56) should also be regarded as a text used for reading aloud in the synagogue.

CHAPTER

# 7

# The Form and Date of the Earliest Codices

The investigation begun in these lectures, incomplete though I know it to be, would prove seriously at fault if no attempt were made to formulate the characteristics of the earliest form of codex, and to discuss the date of the earliest examples. To attempt that task is the aim of this chapter.

It will be wise to begin with an inventory of early codices. I list them, therefore, complete down to iii/iv, paying special attention to those codices I assign to the second century after Christ, and the turning point between the second and third centuries (ii/iii). As far as this date I number each codex individually, using the notation "p" for papyrus, "d" (i.e., *derma*) for parchment. Numbers beginning with 2 (e.g., p. 201ff.) are used for texts assigned to the second century, p. 251ff. for ii/iii, p. 301ff. for the third century. I have grouped them separately, with prefix "C" for "Christian," "G" for "Greek" (G includes Latin).[1] Under a separate heading "Others" I also note those codices which other palaeographers whose judgment I respect have assigned to c.ii or ii/iii, but which I think belong to a later date.[2]

**TABLE 13**

**Inventory of Papyrus and Parchment Codices Dated Before c. iv**

Codices of c. ii

Papyrus

| | | | |
|---|---|---|---|
| p G | 201 | **2** | Achilles Tatius (date dubious) |
| | 202 | **207a** | Homeric lexicon |
| | 203 | **223a** | Lollianus |
| | 204 | **250** | Pindar |
| | 205 | **255a** | Plato *Republic* |
| | 206 | **280** | Xenophon |

| | | | |
|---|---|---|---|
| (Unverified) | 207 | **387** | Medical |
| (Unverified) | 208 | **389** | Medical |
| (Unverifiable) | | **27** | Berlin fragments of Ath. Pol. |

Other scholars add:

| | | |
|---|---|---|
| my p G | 309 | **52** |
| | 252 | **107** |
| | 315 | **100a** |
| | 329 | **139** |
| | 342 | **203a** |
| | 378 | **411** |

| | | |
|---|---|---|
| p C | 201 | **P 52**, P. Ryl. 457 |
| | 202 | **N T Apocryph. 7**, B.M. Egerton 2 |
| | 203 | **P 64/67**, St. Matthew |
| | 204 | **P 77**, St. Matthew |
| | 205 | **OT 24**, *VBP* iv 56 |

Other scholars add:

| | | |
|---|---|---|
| my p C | 252 | **OT 9** |
| | 253 | **OT 36** |
| | 312 | **P 32** |
| | 320 | **P 66** |
| | 328 | **OT 51** |
| | 336 | **OT 151** |
| | 251 | **OT 7** (P. Yale 1) |
| | 252 | **OT 9** |
| | 254 | **OT 97a** Psalms |
| | 255 | **OT 120** Psalms |
| | 325 | **OT 29** |
| | 339 | **OT 183** |
| | — | **OT 202** |

Codices assigned to ii/iii (i.e., ± A. D. 200)

| | | | |
|---|---|---|---|
| p G | 251 | **3a** | Aeschines Socraticus |
| | 252 | **107** | Homeromanteion (ii C. H. R.) |
| | 253 | **122** | Homer (i-ii ed.) |
| | 254 | **136a** | Homer |
| | 255 | **159a** | Homer |
| | 256 | **200c** | Homer |
| | 257 | **206a** | Hypotheses to Homer (if codex !) |
| | 258 | **224a** | Hypotheses to Lysias |
| | 259 | **251** | Pindar? |
| | 260 | **275** | Thuc. |
| | 261 | **324** | Pastoral Poetry |
| | 262 | **335** | Astronomical table |
| (Unverified) | 263 | **398** | Mythological fragment |
| | 264 | **407** | Declamation |
| | 265 | **408** | Oratorical |

| | | | |
|---|---|---|---|
| p C | 251 | | **OT 7** = P. Yale 1 |

| | | |
|---|---|---|
| | 252 | **OT 9**, Genesis |
| | 253 | **OT 36**, P. Ch. B. VI |
| | 254 | **OT 97a**, Psalms |
| | 255 | **OT 120**, Psalms |
| (Uncertain) | 256 | **OT 197**, Berlin Isaiah |
| (Uncertain) | 257 | **NT Apocryph. 1,** P. Oxy. i 1 |

| | | |
|---|---|---|
| Others add: | 203 | **P 64/P 67** |
| | 318 | Ch. B. II = **P 46** |

Codices assigned to the third century

| | | |
|---|---|---|
| p G | 301 | **1** |
| | 302 | **21** |
| | 303 | **32** |
| | 304 | **33** |
| | 305 | **35** |
| | 306 | **43** |
| | 307 | **46** |
| | 308 | **48**? |
| | 309 | **52** (ii C. H. R.) |
| | 310 | **53** |
| | 311 | **54** |
| | 312 | **90c** |
| | 313 | **93** |
| | 314 | **98**? |
| | 315 | **100a** (ii ed.) |
| | 316 | **102** |
| | 317 | **103** |
| | 318 | **106** |
| | 319 | **111** (iii/iv ed.) |
| | 320 | **113?** |
| | 321 | **116** |
| | 322 | **125**? |
| | 323 | **129** |
| | 324 | **131a** |
| | 325 | **132a** |
| | 326 | **133** (iii-iv ed.) |
| | 327 | **134** |
| | 328 | **137** |
| | 329 | **139** (ii ed.) |
| | 330 | **150** |
| | 331 | **151** |
| | 332 | **153** (iii/iv ed.) |
| | 333 | **158** |
| | 334 | **163** |
| | 335 | **165** |
| | 336 | **171** |
| | 337 | **171a** (ii/iii ed.) |
| | 338 | **192** |
| | 339 | **193** |
| | 340 | **195** |

341 **202**
342 **203a** (i-ii ed.)
343 **205**
344 **207**
345
346 **222**
347 **243**
348 **244**
349 **253**
350 **255**
351 **255B**
352 **257**
353 **258**
354 **272**
355 **279**
356 **279a**
357 **281**
358 **286**?
359 **293**
360 **303**
361 **305**
362 **307** (if codex!)
363 **308**
364 **328**
365 **329**
366 **341**
367 **342**
368
369 **356**
370 **359** (ii C.H.R.)
371 **374**
372 **386**
373 **391**
374 **392**
375 **396**
376 **397**
377 **410**
378 **411** (i/ii ed. pr.)
379 **423**
380 **428**
381 **441**
p C 301 **529** Hermas
302 **533** Hermas
303 **552**? Origen, Homilies
304 **553** Origen?
305 **NT Apocryph. 5**, Gospel of Mary
306 **NT Apocryph. 13**, Acts of Peter (E. G. T.)
307 **P 1**
308 **P 4**
309 **P 5**
310 **P 20**
311 **P 23**?

312 **P 27**
313 **P 28** (iv ed.)
314 **P 32**
315 **P 39**
316 **P 40**?
317 **P 45** Ch. B. I
318 **P 46** Ch. B. II
319 **P 47** Ch. B. III
320 **P 53**
321 **P 65**
322 **P 66** P. Bodmer II
323 **P 69**
324 **P 75** P. Bodmer xiv/xv
325
326 **OT 11a**
327 **OT 29**
328 **OT 31**
329 **OT 43** (v ed.)
330 **OT 51** (ii ed.)
331 **OT 51a**
332 **OT 60**
333 **OT 65**
334 **OT 65A**
335 **OT 110**
336 **OT 151** (ii C.H.R.)
337 **OT 164**
338 **OT 165**
339 **OT 183** Ch. B. IX-X (ii Wilckem, Galiano)
340 **OT 195**
341 **OT 198**
342 **OT 201A**
343 **OT 207A** (ii Wilckem)
344 **C3** (iii or iv?)

Codices assigned to iii/iv (± A.D. 300) (listed, not numbered):

p G **34a, 36, 115, 119, 120, 133a, 170a, 213?, 224, 285, 294, 297, 304, 331, 337, 340, 341, 356, 361, 388, 401, 402, 404, 412, 419, 420**
(total 25 + 1 dubious)

p C **536, 548, 552, 553, NT Apocr. 9, NT Apocr. 10, P29, P30, P35, P38, P48, P49, P78, OT 1, OT 11, OT 22, OT 75A, OT 121** (iv ed.), **OT 162** (iii ed.), **OT 172** (iii ed.), **OT 177** (iv ed.), **OT 180A, OT 187, OT 194A?, OT 200, OT 207**
(total 22)

Parchment codices (cf. p. 39)

Assigned to c. ii

| | | | |
|---|---|---|---|
| d G | 201 | **47** | Demosthenes |
| | 202 | **80** | Cretans |
| | 203 | **497** | Latin |

[I put Duke Univ. Plato **254** into iii/iv]

Assigned to ii/iii

| | | | |
|---|---|---|---|
| d G | 251 | **94a** | Hesiod |

Assigned to c. iii

| | | | |
|---|---|---|---|
| d G | 301 | **18** | Aristophanes |
| | 302 | **44** | Demosthenes |
| | 303 | **58** | Demosthenes |
| | 304 | **98** | Hippocrates |
| | 305 | **113?** | Homer |
| | 306 | **226** | Menander |
| | 307 | **229?** | Menander |
| | 308 | **248** | Pindar |
| | 309 | **277** | Thucydides |
| | 310 | **342** | Astrological |
| d C | 301 | **NT parch. 82** | |
| | 302 | **NT Parch. 107** | |
| | 303 | **NT Apocryph. 13** | |
| | 304 | **OT 2** | |
| | 305 | **OT 186** | |

Assigned to iii/iv

d G **119, 184, 188, 190, 216, 241, 254**
d C **NT Parch. 51, OT 29B, OT 121** (ed iv)

Regarding parchment codices these data add nothing to the tabulations whose significance has already been discussed in Chapter Three, p. 37 ff. (except one point to be mentioned shortly). Of papyrus codices, however, it will have been remarked that the number which I allow to be of second century date is fewer than that admitted by general consensus (e.g., in the lists of Roberts, and the allocations of Skeat and Bell). Particular manuscripts over which I differ include Ch. B. VI Numbers and Deuteronomy (**OT 36**) (c. A.D. 150 Kenyon and Wilcken, but not earlier than ii/iii in my view); Ch. B. IX–X (**OT 183, 207A**) (second century Wilcken, but third century, and relatively late third century, in my view); P. Yale 1 Genesis (**OT 7**) (A.D. 90) according to its first editors; I was myself once inclined to assign it to the middle of the second century, but I now think it should be assigned to c. ii/iii). These codices will shortly be subjected to a closer analysis of format and make-up. So also will be Ch. B. I (**P 45**) which displays some unique features.

Certain descriptive statements can be formulated from the groups set out in Table 1 in Chapter Two:

Group 5 has 2 examples dated iii/iv; the remaining 30 examples are iv, iv/v or later. Nothing in Group 5 is earlier than iii/iv or iv.

Group 8 has 2 examples dated ii/iii; the remaining 29 examples are iii, iii/iv or later. Nothing in Group 8 is earlier than ii/iii.

Group 9 "square," 9 examples, has nothing earlier than iii (a format such as 12/13 x 17/18 in **P 64/P 67** is not "square"); iii, iii/iv and iv predominate.

These statements about "negatives" ("nothing earlier than iii/iv") are descriptive statements, not enunciations of a law. The statistical sample is too small for prescription. Only a single example is needed in each group to push back the time span to an earlier date. Nevertheless the descriptive statements have a value as indications, and they put the onus of making a reasoned case on those who wish to extend the limits backward in time. I regard the descriptive statement about Group 9 as supporting my dating, already argued elsewhere on other grounds[3], that P. Bodmer II = **P 66** should be assigned to c. A.D. 200–250, not to c. ii. Likewise I regard the preponderance of c. iii or iii/iv instances in Group 8 as supporting my own dating, reached on the basis of morphological analysis, of P. Bodmer XIV/XV= **P 75** to c. A.D. 225–275 rather than to a period fifty years earlier.

An analogous argumentation may be applied to some of the cases labelled as "aberrant" in the lists. The Yale Genesis (**OT 7**) is not unique in aberrancy of format (14 x 20). An astrological treatise, *PSI* iii 158 (**341**), is 14 x 21; a St. John (**P 28**) is [13/12 x 20.5]. Both of these codices are assigned to c. iii. I think that the Yale Genesis should be assigned to a later date than that of its editors, at least to ii/iii, perhaps to iii.

Similarly Ch. B. VI Numbers and Deuteronomy = **OT 36** ([19 x 33]) can be paralleled in format by the Vienna pastoral poetry book, *MPER* i no. 4 = **324** ([20 x 33.5]) ii/iii, by the unpublished P. Oxy. Thucydides i 99–205 = **279a** ([19/18 x 34]), iii, and possibly by the Commentary on Demosthenes, *YCS* (1957), 81 (= **52**, in which the potential hazards of reconstruction are greater than usual). These supposed parallels in format are assigned to ii/iii or iii. On this basis Ch. B. VI can be assigned to not earlier than ii/iii, and if the handwriting also is assessed on the basis of parallels,[4] it should not in my opinion be assigned to a date earlier than ii/iii or iii.

Group 8 aberrants I are numerous enough to form a sub-group of their own. They are big codices, characteristically narrow (13.7 to 10.5B), and their height is between 2 and 3 times their breadth. One of the 9 examples is assigned to ii, 4 to iii, 2 to iv, 1 to a later date, and one (Ch. B. IX–X) is disputed. There is a case for supposing this format to be an early one. The way in which its large size fits the pattern can be seen from the following table, which records codices in which the number of lines per page exceeds 50.

Table 14 lists twenty-four papyrus codices, of which all but three are of Greek literature, which range in time from ii to iii/iv and have at least fifty lines to a page; there are only ten such codices from iv or later. It would seem as though large holding capacity was a prime recommendation for a papyrus codex in its developmental period (cf. Chapter Two, p. 23). The groups to which codices of not later than iii can be assigned are: Group 8, aberrants Class 1 of Group 8, and aberrants of Group 5. Four examples are placed in Group 1 (the largest sizes) and four in Group 3 or aberrants of Group 3, but their dimensions can be only approximately recovered, and no great weight should be placed on their precise grouping.

The small number of parchment codices in this table is noteworthy. Taken in conjunction with the evidence already presented in Chapter Three, p.39, it allows an important "negative" inference. Since parchment codices of large format are not recorded before c. iv, the Ambrosian *Iliad* (c. 29 x 32) is not to be dated earlier than the fourth century. We must, in consequence, refuse to accept the results of morphological analysis of its script, which has been held to point to a date in the third century[5]. Some features in its handwriting must therefore be due to deliberately archaic stylization by the scribe; if so, its date could be much later than the fourth century.

**TABLE 14**

**Codices Having Fifty or More Lines to a Page**

| *Date century* | *Reference* | *Content* | *Reference Number* | *Number of lines to page* | *Dimensions* |
|---|---|---|---|---|---|
| ii A.D. | P. Oxy. ined. | Plato, *Republic* | **255a** | [51] | — |
| | P. Oxy. iv 697 | Xenophon, *Cyropaedia* | **280** | [60] | 12.5 x [33.1] |
| | P. Köln | Lollianus, *Phoenikika* | **223a** | [59+] | [25/20 x 40/35] |
| ii/iii | B. Berol. 13236 (Pack[2] 1516) | Thucydides (Two columns per page) | **275** | [60] | [17 x 32] |
| | P. Ant. iii 162 | *Iliad* | **136a** | [51] | — |
| iii | *PSI* vi 720 | Aristophanes | **21** | [56] | [11 x 29] |
| | P. Lit. Lond. 126 | Demosthenes | **46** | [60] | [14 x 30?] |
| | P. Oxy. vi 873 | Hesiod, *Theogony* | **93** | [63] | [ x 36/37+] |
| | P. Oxy. xxxii 2647 | Hesiod, *Theogony* | **90c** | [58–61] | — |
| | P. Lond. 126 (Harris Homer) | *Iliad* ii-iv | **106** | 48–54 | 13 x 29.5 |
| | P. Merton i 3 | *Iliad* | **150** | [54] | 13.7 x [32.5] |
| | *PSI* x 1169 | *Iliad* | **151** | [59] | 15 x [29] |
| | P. Flor. ii 110 | *Iliad* | **158** | [63–65] | [ x 39] |
| | *PSI* ii 140 | *Iliad* | **171** | [63] | [15 x 28] |
| | *MPER* i no. 4 | Pastoral Poetry | **324** | [48–49] | [20 x 33.5] |
| | P. Oxy. ined. | Thucydides i 99-102 (two columns per page) | **279a*** | 55 | [18/19 x 34] |
| | P. Gen. 2 + P. Ryl. iii 548 | Thucydides ii (two columns per page) | **272** | [48–50] | — |

*See footnote to Table 3, p. 36. If Mr. Bulow-Jacobsen's identification of **279a** and **272** as parts of the same manuscript is sustained, the figures on pp. 35 and 95 must be reduced by one.

| | | | | | |
|---|---|---|---|---|---|
| | P. Ryl. iii 529 | Surgical Treatise (two columns per page) | **391** | 50 | [15.6 x 28] |
| *Biblical papyrus codices* | | | | | |
| ii/iii ? | (E. G. T.) Ch. B. VI | Numbers, Deuteronomy (Two columns per page) | **OT 36** | 31–38 | [19/18 x 33] |
| iii | (E. G. T.) Ch. B. IX–X | Daniel, Esther, etc. | **OT 207a** | 45–57 | 12.8 x 34.4 |
| iii/iv | P. Berol. inv. 13203 | Homer | **115** | 54–55 | — |
| | P. Oxy. iv 756 | Homer | **120** | 56 | — |
| | P. Flor. ii 110 | Homer | **158** | 65 | [ x 39] |
| iv | P. Lit. Lond. 34 etc. | Aratus | **8** | 63 | [16 x 32?] |
| | P. Lit. Lond. 40 | Dionysius | **60** | 58+ | [14/13 x 27.5/26.5] |
| | *PSI* ii 138 | Homer | **144** | 51 | [ x 24] |
| | P. Bodmer IV, XXV, XXVI | Menander | **225** | 47–54 | 13 x 27.5 |
| | P. Oxy. xiii 1615 | Sophocles | **261** | 60 | ? |
| | Paris BN suppl. gr. 574 | Magic PGM I iv | **M1** | 50 | 13 x 30.5 |
| iv or v | P. Oxy i 22 | Sophocles | **263** | 54 | [12.5 x 31] |
| v | P. Oslo inv. 1478 | Himerius | **97** | 59 | [21.5 x 35.5] |
| | P. Oxy viii 1097 | Cicero | **444** | 65–69 | [23 x 30] |
| v or vi | P. Oxy xiii 1614 | Pindar | **247** | 52? | [21 x 37] |
| Parchment iv | P. Ibscher 4 | Isocrates | **209** | [57] | — |
| | Membr. Petropolitana 388(P) | Menander | **227a** | 50? | [18/17 x 22/21?] |
| v | Codex Alexandrinus | Bible | **A** | 48–52 | 26.4 x 31.6 |

Two further supposed criteria of very great age can now be shown not to be essential features of an early codex. The first criterion is that a codex of early type is likely to have a square page or leaf. It may have; but squareness is not a *sine qua non* of an early codex. The tables for both papyrus and parchment codices discussed in Chapter Two make this clear. We may admit that some small sized papyrus codices (those of Group 9) and some parchment codices do have a format that approaches the square. But there is no representative as yet known of papyrus Group 9 earlier than the third century; Group 8 aberrant Class 1 can show an example in the second, and Group 8 itself has two examples assigned ii/iii; and we have also noted a number of papyrus codices of very large size which are of late ii or else ii/iii. Among parchment codices, the two examples accepted as of second century date (**47, 80**; Chapter Three, p. 38) do not have a square format. Equally the presence of a square written area (square $\beta$ =format) is not often attested in early Greek codices, though it seems to apply fairly well to Latin codices of the fourth century, as we have seen in the Appendix to Chapter Two.

**TABLE 15**

**Codices Having A Square Written Area ($\beta$ measurement)**

| | | | |
|---|---|---|---|
| iii | Papyrus | Philo **243** | 11.5 x 11.5 |
| | Papyrus | Philo **244** | 13.5 x 14.5 |
| | Papyrus | St. John **P66** | 11 x 11 |
| | Parchment | Aristophanes **18** | 10 x 11.5 |
| iii/iv | Parchment | Homer **188** | [11.5 x 11.2] |
| iv | Papyrus | Cicero **Lat. 4** | 10 x 10 |
| | Parchment | Demosthenes **56** | [11 x 12] |
| | Parchment | Isocrates **217** | 6.8 x 7 |
| | Parchment | Sallust **452** | 15 x 15 |
| | Parchment | St. John **NT Parch. 56** | 11 x 11 |
| | Parchment | I Kings **OT47** | 9 x 10 |
| iv/v | Papyrus | Virgil glossary **466** | 20.5 x 21.5 |
| | Papyrus | I John **P9** | [9 x 9] |
| v | Parchment | Cicero **449** | 8 x 8 |
| v-vi | Parchment | Ulpian **472A** | [16.5 x 16] |
| vi | Papyrus | Avitus **Lat. 2** | 26 x 28 |
| | Parchment | Homer **129a** | [15 x 15] |
| | Parchment | Sallust **453** | [14 x 14] |
| | Parchment | St. John **NT Parch. 66** | 12 x 12 |

It will be observed that seven, that is one-third, of the nineteen recorded cases are Latin manuscripts. When one adds to them the further thirty-five examples of this square $\beta$ measurement found in Latin parchment codices recorded in *CLA* (see p. 33) it begins to look as if there is a real difference between Greek and Latin codices with regard to this feature.

The second red herring to be discarded concerns make-up. H. Ibscher has laid it down[6] that the earliest make-up of papyrus codices was the single-quire form, and that the multiple-quire codex (including that in which the quires consist of single sheets, uniones) is derivative from it. He took it as self-evident that the inventor of the first codex laid a large number of sheets on top of each other and folded them in the center to make his book. It may be readily admitted that many undoubtedly early codices do follow this make-up. But the evidence will not sustain the erection of Ibscher's assertion into a law. Four points should be noted:

(1) It is true that there are not many codices in which the quires are single sheets (uniones). But in Ch.B.I (**P 45**) a certain example belonging to c. iii is to be recognized, and there are perhaps other examples among the Chester Beatty codices.

(2) There are certainly papyrus codices of early date which are not arranged in single quires. One of them is **P 64/P 67,** St. Matthew, which, I believe, is of the second century (a manuscript in two columns to the page).

(3) In so far as the term "codex" is derived from a set of wooden tablets (*plurium tabularum contextus*, see C. H. Roberts, *The Codex*, p. 172) one may suppose that it would have occurred as readily to a scribe to experiment with a "codex" of papyrus formed of a series of quires (whether each had only one or several sheets) as with a single-quire system. Wooden tablets may be singletons, but both terminology and actual finds show that they occurred frequently in sets in which up to 10 or 12 tablets were hinged together[7].

(4) Our uncertainty on this matter is the greater in the absence of evidence about how either early parchment codices or *membranae* were gathered. Though it has been demonstrated (above Chapter Five, p. 46 n.10) that the Cairo Demosthenes (**42**), a parchment codex of c. v, is not an example of this format, it is possible that examples may be found, so little is known of the make-up of early parchment codices.

For these reasons Ibscher's sweeping claim must be regarded as not substantiated.

The argumentation in this chapter has proceeded from relatively firm ground to less firm, and the next section is frankly speculative. An attempt has been made to find patterns and laws of development. But when the search is for the earliest examples of a phenomenon, the searcher is likely to encounter a number of cases which will fit into no system, and which may display unique features or may combine features that later on are sharply distinguished (features indeed which act as discriminants of separate groupings). From time to time I have written of "the developmental period in the history of the codex": is one to place these "unique" cases early in such a developmental period because no parallels have been found for them? Putting the question in this form at least makes one aware of the dangers in this concept of "a developmental period": that the particular cases inserted into it are in fact either failures of classification or fortuitously isolated in their nature. To point out such cases is, however, at least to warn investigators of eccentric features in them. It is time to consider four such cases. Three are provided by the Chester Beatty codices:

(1) Ch. B. I = **P 45**. What is apparently unique is the make-up in single-sheet quires (uniones). As a format the manuscript goes, however, tidily into Group 4, iii A.D. or later, and iii A.D. seems to me a satisfactory dating. Note that the written line is very long.

(2) Ch. B. VI = **OT 36**. On the basis of format (p. 95 above) I have acquiesced in a dating to ii/iii, i.e., ± A.D. 200. This is not the consensus date for the handwriting. U. Wilcken, H. I. Bell, C. H. Roberts and T. C. Skeat, have accepted Kenyon's dating to ii (c. A.D. 150). A. S. Hunt, however, pointed out[8] that the type of hand continues until well into the third century. I have myself elsewhere[9] reinforced Hunt's remark by quoting third century parallels for the handwriting. They are not of course finally decisive. The manuscript is written in two columns to the page (**P 64/P 67** of c. ii is in two columns); the make-up cannot be determined. It could be of uniones.

(3) Ch. B. IX-X = **OT 207A**, Ezekiel, Daniel, Esther, Susanna and Bel. In Chapter

One, p. 4, I proposed a date in the late third century on the basis of the handwriting, and after repeated reconsideration I adhere to this judgment. I know it is not the consensus dating (Wilcken even proposed the second century[10] for the Ezekiel hand and especially for the Esther). To me the nearest parallels for the Ezekiel (as for Ch. B. VIII Jeremiah) are P. Leiden "X" (**M 4**) and P. Holm. (**M 5**), both long ago assigned (and correctly, as I believe) to c. iv; and both the Ezekiel and Esther hands have more in common with handwritings dated to late c. iii or iii/iv (such as P. Cair. Isid. 2 of A.D. 298 and P. Herm. Rees 6 of c. A.D. 325) than with hands of ii/iii. But if this handwriting date is correct, it is fair to note that the format classification (aberrant Class 1 of Group 8) and the large number of lines per page would allow the manuscript to be placed earlier.

(4) P. Ryl. iii 457 = **P 52**, the early St. John fragment. For its format there are no parallels among early papyrus codices, but there are among later parchment codices. Further evidence is needed to show whether this fact has any significance. I have no evidence to invalidate the first editor's dating to the first half of the second century. But I should echo his warning about the need for caution. P. Amh. II 78, for instance, a petition of A.D. 184, shows a hand with similarities in its overall uprightness (or even slight lean to the left), roundness and scale, and in the forms of particular letters (the two forms of $\alpha$, the $\epsilon$, $\pi$, $\iota$ in particular). But the letters are crushed more closely together and not so even in size, as would in any case be expected in a document.

The Rylands papyrus may therefore be accepted as of the first half of the second century. It is the only codex in my list that I would place so early, for I would not be willing to admit any of the others to a date earlier than the second half of the century. While this appreciation removes to a slightly later period in time the particular manuscripts on which C. H. Roberts has built his account of the codex, I do not think it does any serious damage to his general theory. Indeed I should like to think that this independent critical assessment of the evidence has reinforced its acceptability.

## NOTES

[1]It might have been better to use "Biblical" instead of "Christian." Cf. Introduction, p. xxii.

[2]Especially the recent survey by C. H. Roberts, explicitly in *The Codex* and *Cambridge History of the Bible*, 2: 62; T. C. Skeat, *Cambridge History of the Bible*, 2: 69ff. (without explicit numeration); H. Hunger on **P 66** (cf. *GMAW*, no. 63).

[3]*GMAW*, no. 63.

[4]See my discussion in *Akten XIII Internat. Papyrologenkongress* (Marburg, 1974), p. 438.

[5]See R. Bianchi-Bandinelli, *Hellenistic-Byzantine Miniatures of the Iliad* (Olten, 1955), p. 45; W. H. Willis, *GRBS* xii (1971): 550, n. 22.

[6]H. Ibscher, *Jahrb. d. Einbandkunst* iv (1937): 11-12. The statement that all papyrus codices down to the end of the third century are in single-quire form was not true even in 1937.

[7]It might be a fascinating speculation to link particular sizes of wooden tablets to matching groups of codices. Somewhat too readily I tossed out some references in *Akten XIII Internat. Papyrologenkongress*, p. 437, n. 7, leaving the reader to draw the inference that the tablets published by P. J. Parsons in *JEA* xvii (1971): 165ff. of c. A.D. 250 measuring 13.7B x 30.5H could be set alongside papyrus codices of Group 8. But the preliminary collection of evidence for such a comparison has not yet begun. Among other things to which attention must be paid is the direction in which the writing is placed on the tablet—in the direction of the long or the short dimension? The Vienna tablet (Mittheil.MPER vi 1, (1897) = Callimachus fr. 260 Pf.) containing lines from the *Hecala* of Callimachus measures c. 52 cm.B, 8-10 cm.H. The Callimachus is written in the direction of the long dimension in three columns, just as if the tablet

were a roll. It is proper also for us to remind ourselves that we do not know what were the common dimensions of *membranae*, or what precise size was conveyed by the term *pugillares*.

[8]Introduction to *Chester Beatty Papyrus* VI. It should also be mentioned that the published facsimiles of this manuscript are reduced in scale, which creates a false impression.

[9]*Akten XIII Internat. Papyrologenkongress*, p. 438.

[10]*Archiv*, xi, p. 113, repeated with approval by the editors of *Papyrologische Texte und Abhandlungen*, Band V (1967):18.

## TABLE 16

### Consolidated List of Codices Consulted

This list offers in tabular form in columns certain basic information about the codices listed. Column 1 gives a serial number assigned by me; Col. 2 a short title or description; Col. 3 a condensed bibliographical reference; Col. 4 states whether the codex is of papyrus or parchment; Col. 5 gives its overall page dimensions ($\alpha$ measurement), B x H; Col. 6 the dimensions of the written area ( $\beta$ measurement), B x H; Col. 7 the dating (mine, not that of the original editor); Col. 8 the number of columns per page; Col. 9 the number of lines per column (page). If the information is given inside square brackets, it has been won by reconstruction and inference. In Col. 8 a figure in round brackets followed by a + sign means that that number of lines survive on the fragment. An obelos (†) prefixed to the serial number means that the codex has not been used in Tables 1 and 2; an asterisk similarly prefixed means I have seen either the original or a good photograph. When a query-mark is used in the tabulation, it signifies that from the publication or photograph or even original of the relevant text no answer can be elicited; when a dash (-) is used or a blank is left it means that I have not had the opportunity to study the text concerned.

The order of entries is as follows:-

1. Serial Numbers **1-556**, based on the order established in Pack[2]: i.e. Greek and Roman literary texts found in Egypt, followed by patristic texts. A considerable number of codices not included in Pack's list have been added at their proper place in the sequence.
2. **'BIBLE'**: the principal early codices of the Greek Bible not forming part of *recent* finds in Egypt.
3. **'CLASSICAL'**: seven important relatively early codices of Greek authors preserved mainly in libraries.
4. **C 1-53**: a selection of Coptic codices denoted by letter C and serial number (**C 41–53** are the Nag Hammadi codices).
5. **Lat. 1-8**: eight important Latin manuscripts on papyrus, all (except **Lat. 4**) preserved in western libraries, and not included in Pack[2]. A much longer list of about 300 Latin codices on parchment has not been printed (cf. p33).
6. **Lit. 1-10**: codices of the Greek liturgy.
7. **M 1-5**: magical or commonly-presumed magical books. (It will shortly be demonstrated by Dr. Hunt that **M 4** does not belong in this selection.)
8. **Misc. 1-4**: codices not falling into any of the other established classes.
9. **NT Apocrypha 1-17**.
10. **P 1-81** plus 2 unnumbered: papyrus codices of the New Testament following the now generally accepted numeration.
11. **NT Parch. 1-111**: a list compiled by myself of parchment codices of the New Testament found mainly in Egypt, following the canonical order of these books.
12. **OT 1-223**: a list compiled by myself of codices of the Old Testament, not distinguishing parchment and papyrus manuscripts into separate groups. The Apocrypha is included and the order followed is that of Tischendorf's Septuagint.

| 1 | 2 | 3 | 4 | 5 | 6 | 7 | 8 | 9 |
|---|---|---|---|---|---|---|---|---|
| **†1** | Achilles Tatius | Pack² 1 | pap. | ? | ? | iii | ? | ? |
| **†*2** | Achilles Tatius | Pack² 3 | pap. | ? | ? | ii | 2 cols ? | ? |
| **3** | Aeschines | Pack² 17 | parch. | 16.5 x 23.5 | ? | v | 2 | 30/29 |
| **†*3a** | Aeschines Socraticus | P. Oxy. xxxix 2890 | pap. | ? | ? | ii/iii | ? | ? |
| **† 4** | Apollonius Rhodius | Pack² 102 | parch. | ? | ? | vi? | 1 | 27 |
| **† 5** | Apollonius Rhodius | Pack² 105 | parch. | ? | 15 x 20 (ed.) | vii? (E. G. T.; ed. viii-ix) | 1 | 29 |
| **† 6** | Apollonius Rhodius | Pack² 110 | pap. | ? | ? | v | 1 | 40/43? |
| **† 7** | Appian roll? | Pack² 113 | pap. | ? | ? | iii? | | |
| ***8** | Aratus | Pack² 115 + 116 | pap. | [16 x 32] or [17 x 34] | [10 x 26] | iv | 1 | 63 |
| **† 9** | Aratus scholia | Pack² 119 | pap. | ? | ? | 'late' | | |
| **† 9a** | Aelius Aristides | P. Ant. iii 182 | pap. | [ x 34] | [19 x 24] | vii | 1 | ? |
| ***10** | Aristophanes | Pack² 139 | pap. | 25 x 37/36 | [14 x 26] | v or vi | 1 | 37–43 |
| **† 10a** | Aristophanes | Pack² 1578 | pap. | ? | ? | v or vi | ? | ? |
| **† 11** | Aristophanes | Pack² 140 | parch. | ? | ? | vi | 1 | (41 or 44?) |
| **† 12** | Aristophanes | Pack² 141 | pap. | ? | ? | iv-v | 1 | 40 |
| **† 13** | Aristophanes scholia | Pack² 142 + *Hermes* xcvi, 287 | parch. | ? | ? | iv | 1 | 23? |
| **†*14** | Aristophanes | Pack² 143 + P. Ant. iii 180, 211 | pap. | ? | ? | v? | 1 | 34 |
| ***15** | Aristophanes | Pack² 144 | pap. | 16 x [29] | 11 x [24] | iv (E. G. T.), v (edd.) | 1 | 36 |
| ***16** | Aristophanes | Pack² 145 | pap. | [25 x 33]? | [10 x 20]? | v | 1 | 37–38 |
| **† 17** | Aristophanes | Pack² 146 | parch. | ? | ? | v | 1 | 30, 34, 24 |
| **18** | Aristophanes | Pack² 147 | parch. | [13] x 16.5 | 10 x 11.5 | iii | 1 | 30 |
| **† 19** | Aristophanes | Pack² 148 | parch. | ? | ? | v or vi | ? | ? |

| | | | | | | | | |
|---|---|---|---|---|---|---|---|---|
| **20** | Aristophanes | Pack[2] 149 | parch. | [20 x 26] | [15 x 18] | v to vii | 1 | 36 |
| ***21** | Aristophanes | Pack[2] 150 | pap. | [11 x 29] | [10 x 25] | iii | 1 | 56 |
| ***22** | Aristophanes | Pack[2] 151 | pap. | [15 x 29] | [11.5 x 24] | v? | 1 | 44? |
| **23** | Aristophanes | Pack[2] 152 | pap. | [17 x 30]? | ? | v? | 1 | 31? |
| **†*24** | Aristophanes | Pack[2] 153 | pap. | ? | ? | v or vi? (E. G. T.) | 1 | 39, 42 |
| ***25** | Aristophanes | Pack[2] 155 | pap. | [25 x 32.7] | ? | v or vi (E. G. T.) | 1 | 45, 47, 48 |
| **26** | Aristotle | Pack[2] 158 | pap. | 16.6 x [31] | [14.3 x 25.5] | vi-vii | 1 | 42? |
| **† 27** | Aristotle, *Ath. Pol.* | Pack[2] 164 | pap. | ?[1] | ? | ii (M. Chambers) iv (F. G. Kenyon) | 1 | 37 |
| ***28** | Callimachus | Pack[2] 186 | pap. | [37 x 28] | [21 x 24.5] | vi? | 1 | 22 or 23 |
| **29** | Callimachus scholia | Pack[2] 187 | pap. | ? | ? | iv-v | 1 | 30? |
| **†*29a** | Callimachus | P. Ant. iii 179 | pap. | ? | [14/15 x 26] | v | 1 | 26, 27 |
| **† 30** | Callimachus, hypomnema | Pack[2] 190 | pap. | ? | ? | iv | 1 | (20+) |
| **†*31** | Callimachus | Pack[2] 192 | pap. | [ x 26/27] | ? | v or vi | 1 | 27 |
| **†*32** | Callimachus | Pack[2] 201 | pap. | [ x 24.5] | ? | iii? | 1 | 37–38 |
| **†*33** | Callimachus | Pack[2] 210 | pap. | ? | ? | iii | 1 | (31+) |
| ***34** | Callimachus | Pack[2] 215 | pap. | 18/19 x 30 | [12/13 x 26] | iv/v | 1 | 40, 41 |
| **†*34a** | Callimachus | P. Ant. iii 113 | pap. | ? | ? | iii-iv | 1 | (15+) |
| **† 34b** | Callimachus | P. Ant. iii 114 | pap. | ? | ? | iv-v | 1 | (7+) |
| **†*35** | Callimachus | Pack[2] 226 | pap. | ? | ? | iii | 1 | (16+) |
| **†*36** | Callimachus | Pack[2] 230 | pap. | ? | ? | iii-iv | 1 | (20+) |
| **37** | Chariton | Pack[2] 244 | parch. | 15 x 20 | ? | vii? | 2 | ? |
| **† 38** | Demosthenes | Pack[2] 260 | parch. | ? | ? | iv (E. G. T.), late v (Cavallo) | ? | [27?] |
| **39** | Demosthenes | Pack[2] 261 | parch. | [23 x 29] | ? | iv | 3 | 35, 33 |
| ***40** | Demosthenes | Pack[2] 263 | parch. | [10.5 x 14.3] | [8 x 10.5] | iv | 2 | 26 |
| **41** | Demosthenes | Pack[2] 266 | parch. | 16.5 x 21 | ? | iv | 2 | 27 |
| ***42** | Demosthenes xiv, xvi, xv | Pack[2] 270, 271[2] | parch. | 8.5 x 17.5 | 4.5 x 10 | v(?) | 1 | 24 |

[1]M. Chambers, *TAPA* xcvii (1967): 49ff. estimates at 15.3 x 24.

[2]See Chapter Five, p. 69 n. 10.

| 1 | 2 | 3 | 4 | 5 | 6 | 7 | 8 | 9 |
|---|---|---|---|---|---|---|---|---|
| **†*43** | Demosthenes | Pack$^2$ 278 | pap. | ? | ? | iii | ? | 65? |
| ***44** | Demosthenes | Pack$^2$ 280 | parch. | 17.8 x 22 | 10.6 x 14.4 | iii? | 2 | 28 |
| ***45** | Demosthenes | Pack$^2$ 290 | pap. | 10.2 x 15.7 | 7 x 12.5/13 | v? | 1 | 17-22 |
| ***46** | Demosthenes | Pack$^2$ 291 | pap. | [14 x 30?] | [11 x 26.5?] | iii | 1? | 63 |
| ***47** | Demosthenes | Pack$^2$ 293 | parch. | 16.5 x 19 | 11 x 14 | ii | 2 | 36 |
| **† 48** | Demosthenes Commentary | Pack$^2$ 294 | pap. | ? | ? | iii or later | 1 | ? |
| **†*49** | Demosthenes | Pack$^2$ 297 | parch. | ? | ? | v | 2 or 3? | (24+) |
| ***50** | Demosthenes roll | Pack$^2$ 302 + 303 | pap. | — | — | iii/iv | | |
| **† 51** | Demosthenes lexicon | Pack$^2$ 308 | pap. | ? | ? | iv-v | ? | ? |
| ***52** | Demosthenes Commentary | Pack$^2$ 311 | pap. | [20 x 30+] (Welles) | ? | iii (E. G. T.; ii ed., C. H. R.) | 1 | ? |
| **† 53** | Demosthenes | Pack$^2$ 313 | pap. | [ x 33] | ? | iii | 1? | 45? |
| **† 54** | Demosthenes | Pack$^2$ 314 | pap. | ? | ? | iii | 1? | 32–34 |
| **† 55** | Demosthenes lexicon | Pack$^2$ 317 | pap. | ? | ? | iv or v | ? | (38+) |
| ***56** | Demosthenes | Pack$^2$ 321 | parch. | [14 x 21] | [11 x 12] | iv | 2 | 25 |
| **†*57** | Demosthenes | Pack$^2$ 325 | parch. | ? | ? | v? | 1? | (14+) |
| **†*58** | Demosthenes | Pack$^2$ 340 | parch. | ? | ? | iii | 1 or 2? | (13+) |
| ***59** | Dio Chrysostom | Pack$^2$ 341 | pap. | [16 x 28.7] | ? | iv | 1 | 43 |
| ***60** | Dionysius | Pack$^2$ 343 | pap. | [13–14 x 26.5/ 27.5] | [7 x 18]? | iv? | 1 | 58+ |
| **† 61** | Dionysius Thrax | Pack$^2$ 345 | pap. | ? | ? | iv | 1 | (11+) |
| **† 62** | Dioscorus | Pack$^2$ 349 | pap. | ? | ? | vi? | 1 | 34 |
| **†*63** | Euphorion | Pack$^2$ 370 | parch. | ? | [11.5 x ] | iv (v, ed.) | 1 | (15+) |
| **†*64** | Eupolis | Pack$^2$ 375 | pap. | [18? x ] | ? | iv/v | 1 | ? |
| **†*65** | Euripides *Not* a codex[3] | Pack$^2$ 379 | pap. | | | | | |
| **† 66** | Euripides | Pack$^2$ 382 | parch. | ? | ? | vii? | 1 | 32, 35 |
| **67** | Euripides | Pack$^2$ 383 | pap. | [20 x 32.5] (E. G. T.)[4] | ? | v? | 1 | 30 |

| | | | | | | | | |
|---|---|---|---|---|---|---|---|---|
| † **68** | Euripides | Pack² 385 | pap. | [ x 28.5/30] | ? | vi? | 1 | 40 |
| ***69** | Euripides | Pack² 387 | pap. | [? 15 x 24.5] | ? | v-vi | 1 | 30 |
| † **70** | Euripides | Pack² 389 | pap. | ? | ? | v | 1 | 36 |
| † **71** | Euripides | Pack² 394 | pap. | [ x 27] | 17 x 19.5 | vi | 1 | 28 |
| ***72** | Euripides | Pack² 402 | pap. | [18 x 29.5] | ? | v | 1 | 37 |
| † **73** | Euripides | Pack² 403 | pap. | ? | ? | v? | 1 | 43 |
| ***74** | Euripides | Pack² 406 | pap. | [18 x 30] | [?14 x 21] | v-vi | 1 | 39–40 |
| †***75** | Euripides | Pack² 407 | parch. | ? | [ x 12.5] | iv-v | 1 | 30 |
| †***76** | Euripides | Pack² 409 | parch. | ? | [ x 16.8] | v | 1 | 36 |
| **77** | Euripides | Pack² 418 | pap. | [ x 30] | ? | vi | 1 | 30 |
| ***78** | Euripides Scholia | Pack² 419 | pap. | [18.5] x 31 | [17 x 24; 17 x 29] | vi | 1 | 35, 51 |
| ***79** | Euripides | Pack² 427 | pap. | 12 x 23[5] | ? | iv-v | 1 | 23, 26 |
| ***80** | Euripides | Pack² 437 | parch. | 11.5 x 14.5 | 7.5 x 10(10.5) | ii? | 1 | 26 |
| †***81** | Euripides | Pack² 441 | parch. | 14 x ? | 12 x ? | iv | 1 | (25+) |
| **82** | Euripides, *Oedipus* | Pack² 443 | *not* a codex | | | | | |
| † **83** | Euripides hypothesis? | Pack² 446 | pap. | ? | ? | vi? | ? | (10+) |
| **84** | Galen | Pack² 456 | pap. | 21.5 x 40.4 | ? | vi | 1 | 38, 41 |
| † **84a** | Galen | P. Ant. iii 186 | pap. | ? | ? | vi | 1? | (22+) |
| † **85** | Ps.–Gregorius | Pack² 457 | pap. | ? | ? | v? | 1? | (28+) |
| †***86** | Herodotus | Pack² 475 | parch. | ? | [13 x 17] | iv | 2 | 33–34? |
| †***87** | Herodotus epitome | Pack² 484 | parch. | ? | ? | iv | 1? | (14+) |
| † **88** | Hesiod | Pack² 487 | pap. | ? | ? | v | 1? | [43?] |
| † **89** | Hesiod | Pack² 488 | pap. | ? | ? | v-vi | 1 | [42] |
| ***90** | Hesiod | Pack² 494 | pap. | 13.5 x [23+] (cut down ?) | ? | iv-v | 1 | 33, 38 |
| † **90a** | Hesiod | P. Ant. iii 178 | pap. | ? | ? | iv-v | 1 | [26, 30+] |

[3]Cf. p. 9. And see J. Bingen, *CdE* (1965), 484.
[4]See p. 6.
[5]Possibly cut down.

| 1 | 2 | 3 | 4 | 5 | 6 | 7 | 8 | 9 |
|---|---|---|---|---|---|---|---|---|
| **†*90b** | Hesiod, *Theogony* | P. Oxy. xxxii 2644 | pap. | [22 x ] | 12/13 x [17] | v/vi | 1 | [35] |
| **†*90c** | Hesiod, *Theogony* | P. Oxy. xxxii 2647 | pap. | ? | [ x 22.8) | iii | 1 | [58–61] |
| **†*90d** | Hesiod, *Theogony* | P. Oxy. xxxii 2650 | pap. | ? | [ x 25.2] | iv to v | 1 | [40] |
| ***91** | Hesiod[6] | Pack² 499 | pap. | 19 x 29.5 | 13.5 x 21 | v | 1 | 30–35 |
| **†*92** | Hesiod | Pack² 501 | pap. | [ x 33.8] | ? | v-vi (E. G. T) | 1 | [43] |
| **93** | Hesiod | Pack² 503 | pap. | [ x 36/37+] | ? | iii | 1 | [63] |
| **† 94** | Hesiod | Pack² 517 | pap. | ? | ? | iv | 1 | [47+] |
| ***94a** | Hesiod | Pack² 514 | parch. | [14 x 17] | [11 x 13] | ii/iii (E. G. T.) | 1 | [25] |
| **†*95** | Hesiod | Pack² 533 | parch. | ? | ? | iv-v | 1? | (7+) |
| **† 96** | Hesiod? | Pack² 535 | pap. | ? | ? | v | 1? | ? |
| **97** | Himerius | Pack² 537 | pap. | [21.5 x 35.5] | ? | v | 1 | [59] |
| ***98** | Hippocrates | Pack² 543 | parch. | 11.4 x [16.2] | ? | iii? | 1 | [30, 32] |
| ***99** | Hippocrates | Pack² 544 | pap. | [28 x 33] | [? 20 x 25] | vi/vii | 1 | 44 |
| **† 99a** | Hippocrates | P. Ant. iii 183 | pap. | ? | ? | vi | 1? | ? |
| **† 99b** | Hippocrates | P. Ant. iii 184 | pap. | ? | ? | vi | 1? | (24+) |
| **† 99c** | Hippocrates | P. Ant. iii 185 | pap. | ? | ? | vi | 1? | (11+) |
| **† 100** | Hippolytus Romanus | Pack² 546 | pap. | ? | ? | vi or vii | 1? | (18+) |
| ***100a** | Homer, *Il.* I | *Cd'Ē* (1971), 313 | pap. | [13 x 26] (ed.) | ? | iii[7] (E. G. T.; ii, ed.) | 1 | 47 |
| **†*101** | Homer, *Il.* I[8] | Pack² 592 | pap. | ? | ? | v | 1 | (22+) |
| **† 102** | Homer, *Il.* I | Pack² 595 | pap. | ? | ? | iii | 1 | [45] |
| **†*103** | Homer, *Il.* I | Pack² 604 | pap. | ? | ? | iii | 1 | 48-49? |
| **† 104** | Homer, *Il.* I | Pack² 607 | pap. | ? | ? | iv | 1? | ? |
| ***104a** | Homer, *Il.* II | P. Oxy. xxxvi 2747 | pap. | 18.8 x 28.3 | 15 x 22.8 | v or vi | 1 | 38 |
| **† 105** | Homer, *Il.* II | Pack² 629 | pap. | ? | ? | v-vi | 1 | [45] |
| ***106** | Homer, *Il.* II–IV | Pack² 634 | pap. | 13 x 29.5 | 11.5 x 26 | iii | 1 | 48–54 |

| | | | | | | | | |
|---|---|---|---|---|---|---|---|---|
| † **107** | Homer, *Il.* II[9] | Pack$^2$ 645 | pap. | ? | ? | ii-iii (ii, C. H. R.) | 1? | ? |
| † **108** | Homer, *Il.* II | Pack$^2$ 654 | pap. | ? | ? | v | 1 | ? |
| **109** | vacant | | | | | | | |
| † **110** | Homer, *Il.* II | Pack$^2$ 658 | pap. | ? | ? | vi | 1 | [36] |
| ***111** | Homer, *Il.* II | Pack$^2$ 662 | pap. | [15] x 21+ | ? | iii (E. G. T.) | 1 | 29, 32 |
| †***112** | Homer, *Il.* II | Pack$^2$ 667 | pap. | [ x 22] | ? | v | 1 | [32] |
| † **113** | Homer, *Il.* III (Codex?) | Pack$^2$ 689 | parch. | ? | ? | iii? | ? | ? |
| † **114** | Homer, *Il.* III | Pack$^2$ 695 | pap. | ? | ? | iv-v | 1? | [35, 42] |
| † **115** | Homer, *Il.* III | Pack$^2$ 696 | pap. | ? | ? | iii-iv | 1? | [54, 55] |
| † **116** | Homer, *Il.* III | Pack$^2$ 701 | pap. | ? | ? | iii | 1 | [22, 23] |
| † **117** | Homer, *Il.* IV, VII | Pack$^2$ 719 | parch. | ? | ? | iv | 1? | [27–32] |
| **118** | Homer, *Il.* IV | Pack$^2$ 728 | parch. | [16 x 20] | ? | vi | 1? | 30 |
| | Homer, *Il.* IV | Pack$^2$ 729 | *not* a codex | | | | | |
| † **119** | Homer, *Il.* IV | Pack$^2$ 730 | parch. | ? | ? | iii-iv | 1 | 30 |
| † **120** | Homer, *Il.* V | Pack$^2$ 744 | pap. | ? | [ x 21.5] | iii-iv | 1 | [56] |
| **121** | see **M1** | Pack$^2$ 746 | | | | | | |
| †***122** | Homer, *Il.* V | Pack$^2$ 747 | pap. | ? | ? | ii/iii (E. G. T.) | 1 | [34] |
| † **123** | Homer, *Il.* V | Pack$^2$ 763 | parch. | ? | ? | iv | 1 | [20] |
| † **124** | Homer, *Il.* V | Pack$^2$ 764 | parch. | ? | ? | iv | 1 | [44, 46] |
| † **125** | Homer, *Il.* VI | Pack$^2$ 770 | pap. | ? | ? | iii? | 1 | [24] |
| † **126** | Homer, *Il.* VI | Pack$^2$ 777 | parch | ? | ? | iv? | 1 | [20] |
| **127** | Homer, *Il.* VI | Pack$^2$ 788 | pap. | [27 x 33]? | ? | iv-v | 1 | [35] |
| **128** | Homer, *Il.* VI–XIII | Pack$^2$ 789 | pap. | [15 x 25] | [11 x 19/21] | iv | 1 | [41–44] |
| ***129** | Homer, *Il.* VII | Pack$^2$ 802 | pap. | [17] x 24.5 | [14] x 22 | iii | 1 | 33 |
| ***129a** | Homer, *Il.* VII | P. Ant. iii 157 | parch. | [19? x 22] | [15 x 15] | vi-vii? | 1 | [27] |

[6]Reexamined by J. Rea from original and by me from photographs. Cf. p. 70 n. 11.
[7]Cf. P. Oxy. xliii 3093 introd.
[8]See p. 9
[9]Homeromanteion. Part of same codex as Pack$^2$ 1801.

| 1 | 2 | 3 | 4 | 5 | 6 | 7 | 8 | 9 |
|---|---|---|---|---|---|---|---|---|
| **†*130** | Homer, *Il.* VII | Pack$^2$ 805 | parch. | ? | [ x 18] | iv | 1 | [37] |
| **† 131** | Homer, *Il.* VII | Pack$^2$ 812 | parch. | ? | ? | iv-v | 1 | [25] |
| **131a** | Homer, *Il.* VIII–XVI | P. Ant. iii 158 | pap. | 16.5 x 25 | ? | iii | 1 | [35–44] |
| ***132** | Homer, *Il.* VIII–XIII | Pack$^2$ 833 | pap. | [27 x 33/34][10] | ? | v-vi (M. Manfredi, G. Cavallo[10]; iv ed. pr.) | 1 | 30–35 |
| **† 132a** | Homer, *Il.* IX | P. Ant. iii 159 | pap. | ? | ? | iii | 1 | [45] |
| **†*133** | Homer, *Il.* IX | Pack$^2$ 836 | pap. | ? | [ x 19] | iii (E. G. T.) | 1 | [56] |
| **133a** | Homer, *Il.* IX | P. Ant. iii 160 | pap. | 18 x 29 | ? | late iii to iv | 1 | 38–41 |
| ***134** | Homer, *Il.* IX | Pack$^2$ 841 | pap. | [12.8] x 16.7 | [10.8 x 13.7] | iii | 1 | 34 |
| **† 135** | Homer, *Il.* IX | Pack$^2$ 843 | pap. | ? | ? | v | 1 | [38] |
| **†*135a** | Homer, *Il.* IX–X | P. Ant. iii 161 | pap. | [ x 32] | [ x 27] | v (ed.; iv E. G. T.) | 1 | [35–40] |
| **†*136** | Homer, *Il.* IX | Pack$^2$ 850 | pap. | ? | ? | iv | 1 | [34] |
| **† 136a** | Homer, *Il.* X | P. Ant. iii 162 | pap. | ? | ? | ii to iii | 1 | [51] |
| **† 137** | Homer, *Il.* X | Pack$^2$ 858 | pap. | ? | ? | iii | 1 | [37] |
| **† 138** | Homer, *Il.* X | Pack$^2$ 864 | pap. | ? | ? | v | ? | ? |
| **†*139** | Homer, *Il.* XI | Pack$^2$ 868 | pap. | ? | ? | ii ed., iii E. G. T. | 1 | [35] |
| ***140** | Homer, *Il.* XI–XVI | Pack$^2$ 870 | pap. | 14(12.5) x 27 | 10 x 23 | iv | 1 | 29–42 |
| **† 141** | Homer, *Il.* XI | Pack$^2$ 872 | pap. | ? | ? | v-vi | 1 | [27–30] |
| **† 142** | Homer, *Il.* XI | Pack$^2$ 873 | pap. | [ x 28/29] | [ x 22] | v | 1 | [32, 34] |
| **† 143** | Homer, *Il.* XI | Pack$^2$ 877 | parch. | ? | ? | (?iv-v) | 1 | [30] |
| **† 144** | Homer, *Il.* XI | Pack$^2$ 878 | pap. | [ x 24] | [ x 18] | iv | 1 | [51] |
| **† 145** | Homer, *Il.* XI | Pack$^2$ 884 | pap. | ? | ? | v | 1 | [38, 40] |
| **146** | Homer, *Il.* XI | Pack$^2$ 885 | pap. | [18 x 28](ed.) | [14 x 20] | iv | 1 | [32, 33] |
| **† 147** | Homer, *Il.* XI | Pack$^2$ 888 | pap. | ? | [ x 23.5] | vi | 1 | [39, 38] |
| **148** | Homer, *Il.* XIII–XXIII | Pack$^2$ 904 | pap. | 23.5 x 29 | 14.5 x 19.5 | v-vi | 1 | 26–29 |
| ***149** | Homer, *Il.* XIII 512ff. | Pack$^2$ 911; *BASP* x (1973): 47ff | pap. | 21 x [32] | 15.4 x [21/22] | v (E. G. T.) | 1 | 33 |

| | | | | | | | | |
|---|---|---|---|---|---|---|---|---|
| ***150** | Homer, *Il.* XIV | Pack² 915 | pap. | 13.7 x [32.5] | 11 x [29] | iii | 1 | [54] |
| ***151** | Homer, *Il.* XIV | Pack² 917 | pap. | 15 x [29] | 13 x [25.8] | iii | 1 | [59] |
| † **152** | Homer, *Il.* XV | Pack² 923 | pap. | ? | ? | vi | 1? | [30?] |
| ***153** | Homer, *Il.* XV | Pack² 924 | pap. | [15.5 x 27] | [13 x 20] | iii (E. G. T.) | 1 | [39, 41] |
| † **154** | Homer, *Il.* XV–XXIII | Pack² 925 | pap. | ? | ? | v | 1? | 28 |
| † **155** | Homer, *Il.* XV | Pack² 926 | pap. | [ x 38] | ? | v-vi | 1 | [36] |
| † **156** | Homer, *Il.* XVI | Pack² 932 | parch. | ? | ? | v | 1? | [33, 34] |
| **157** | Homer, *Il.* XVI | Pack² 933 | pap. | [20 x 25] | ? | v | 1 | [40] |
| ***158** | Homer, *Il.* XVI | Pack² 937 | pap. | [ x 39]? | ? | iii (E. G. T.) | 1 | [65] |
| † **159.** | Homer, *Il.* XVI | Pack² 939 | pap. | ? | ? | iv/v | 1? | [32, 33] |
| † **159a** | Homer, *Il.* XVI | P. Ant. iii 163 | pap. | ? | ? | ii to iii | 1? | [39] |
| † **159b** | Homer, *Il.* XVII | P. Ant. iii 164 | pap. | ? | ? | iv | 1 | [48] |
| † **160** | Homer, *Il.* XVII | Pack² 946 | parch. | ? | ? | iv-v | 1? | [34] |
| ***161** | Homer, *Il.* XVII–XVIII | Pack² 948 | pap. | [18.5 x 31.5][11] | [14+ x 25] | v or vi | 1 | [33–40] |
| † **162** | Homer, *Il.* XVIII | Pack² 954 | parch. | ? | ? | iv-v | 1? | [36] |
| † **162a** | Homer, *Il.* XVIII, XXIII | P. Ant. iii 165 | pap. | ? | ? | iv | 1 | [43, 46] |
| † **163** | Homer, *Il.* XVIII | Pack² 957 | pap. | ? | ? | iii | 1 | [33] |
| †***164** | Homer, *Il.* XVIII | Pack² 961 | pap. | [ x 26]? | ? | iv (iv-v ed.) | 1 | [40, 41] |
| †***165** | Homer, *Il.* XIX | Pack² 964 | pap. | [ x 26] | [ x 21] | iii | 1 | [34, 36] |
| † **166** | Homer, *Il.* XX | Pack² 971 | pap. | ? | ? | iv | 1 | [29] |
| †***167** | Homer, *Il.* XX | Pack² 974 | pap. | [ x 33]? | [ x 28]? | iv | 1 | [45] |
| † **167a** | Homer, *Il.* XXI | P. Ant. iii 166 | parch. | ? | ? | iv | 1 | [43] |
| †***168** | Homer, *Il.* XXI | Pack² 984 | parch. | 26.3 x [ ] | 18/19 x [22/23?] | vi | 1 | 33–34 |
| † **169** | Homer, *Il.* XXI–XXII | Pack² 985 | parch. | ? | ? | iv | 1? | [33+] |
| ***170** | Homer, *Il.* XXII–XXIII | Pack² 988 | pap. | [23.5 x 32][12] | [14.5 x 26] | v-vi | 1 | 44, 36 |

[10] *Acta* XIV Pap. Congress p. 49.
[11] Lameere gives [20 x 33] and [ x 27].
[12] Lameere gives [25 x 34], [14.5 x 28].

| 1 | 2 | 3 | 4 | 5 | 6 | 7 | 8 | 9 |
|---|---|---|---|---|---|---|---|---|
| † **170a** | Homer, *Il.* XXII | P. Ant. iii 167 | pap. | ? | ? | iii to iv | 1 | [49] |
| **171** | Homer, *Il.* XXIII | Pack² 1000 | pap. | [15 x 28] | [12.5 x 19] | iii | 1 | [63] |
| †***171a** | Homer, *Il.* XXIII | Pack² 1003 | pap. | ? | [ x 30+] | iii (E. G. T. ii/iii ed.) | 1 | [45] |
| **172** | Homer, *Il.* XXIV | Pack² 1018 | parch. | 7.7 x 9.7(?+)[13] | ? | iv | 1 | 26 |
| † **173** | Homer, *Od.* I | Pack² 1026 | pap. | ? | ? | v | 1 | [31, 32] |
| † **174** | Homer, *Od.* I | Pack² 1027 | parch. | ? | ? | v | 1 | [26] |
| † **175** | Homer, *Od.* III | Pack² 1040 | parch. | ? | ? | iv | ? | ? |
| **175a** | Homer, *Od.* IV, XIV | P. Ant. iii 168 | pap. | ? | ? | iv to v | ? | [52, 48] |
| ***176** | Homer, *Od.* V | Pack² 1058 | pap. | [19/20 x 26/27] | [16 x 18.6] | iv | 1 | [27] |
| † **177** | Homer, *Od.* VI | Pack² 1066 | parch. | ? | ? | iv | 1 | [31] |
| **178** | Homer, *Od.* VII | Pack² 1067 | parch. | 15 x 17 | ? | iv | 1 | 30 |
| † **179** | Homer, *Od.* IX | Pack² 1074 | pap. | ? | ? | iv | 1 | [44] |
| † **180** | Homer, *Od.* IX | Pack² 1082 | pap. | ? | ? | v | 1 | [49] |
| † **181** | Homer, *Od.* X | Pack² 1086 | pap. | ? | ? | vi | ? | ? |
| † **181a** | Homer, *Od.* XI | P. Ant. iii 169 | parch. | ? | ? | iv | 1 | [33] |
| † **182** | Homer, *Od.* XI | Pack² 1097 | pap. | ? | ? | vi | 1 | [33] |
| † **183** | Homer, *Od.* XII | Pack² 1105 | parch. | ? | ? | v | 1 | [33] |
| ***184** | Homer, *Od.* XII–XXIV | Pack² 1106 | parch. | 13 x 16.8 | 11.3 x 13.5 | iii/iv | 1 | 28–34 |
| † **185** | Homer, *Od.* XIII | Pack² 1109 | pap. | ? | ? | v-vi | 1 | [27–28] |
| †***185a** | Homer, *Od.* XIII–XVI | P. Ant. iii 171 | pap. | ? | ? | v (ed.; ? earlier) | 1 | [49, 52] |
| †***185b** | Homer, *Od.* XIII | P. Ant. iii 172 | parch. | ? | ? | v | 1 | [31] |
| † **186** | Homer, *Od.* XIV | Pack² 1111 | pap. | ? | ? | vi-vii | ? | ? |
| † **187** | Homer, *Od.* XIV | Pack² 1113 | parch. | ? | [ x 15] | iv-v | 1 | [29/30] |
| ***188** | Homer, *Od.* XV | Pack² 1114 | parch | [14.7 x 16] | ? | iii/iv | 1 | [29] |
| ***189** | Homer, *Od.* XV, XVII | Pack² 1115 | pap. | 24 x 35 | [ x 25] | vi/vii (ed.) (?vi E. G. T.) | 1 | [33, 34] |
| †***189a** | Homer, *Od.* XV | P. Ant. iii 173 | pap. | ? | [ x 26.5] | v | 1 | [38] |
| † **190** | Homer, *Od.* XV | Pack² 1117 | parch. | ? | ? | iii-iv | 1 | [33-34] |

| | | | | | | | | |
|---|---|---|---|---|---|---|---|---|
| † **191** | Homer, *Od.* XV | Pack$^2$ 1118 | parch. | ? | ? | iv-v | ? | [34?] |
| † **192** | Homer, *Od.* XVI | Pack$^2$ 1123 | pap. | ? | ? | iii | 1 | [45] |
| † **193** | Homer, *Od.* XVII | Pack$^2$ 1125 | pap. | ? | ? | iii | 1 | [46] |
| † **194** | Homer, *Od.* XVII | Pack$^2$ 1126 | parch. | ? | ? | iv | 1? | [23–25?] |
| † **195** | Homer, *Od.* XVII | Pack$^2$ 1131 | pap. | ? | ? | iii | 1 | ? |
| †***196** | Homer, *Od.* XVIII | Pack$^2$ 1133 | pap. | ?[14] | ? | vi-vii | 1 | [41] |
| **197** | Homer, *Od.* XVIII | Pack$^2$ 1134 | parch. | [19 x 19][15] | ? | iv | 1 | [25] |
| † **198** | Homer, *Od.* XIX | Pack$^2$ 1140 | parch. | ? | ? | iv-v | 1? | ? |
| † **199** | Homer, *Od.* XXI | Pack$^2$ 1144 | parch. | ? | ? | iv? | ? | [30?] |
| ***199a** | Homer, *Od.* XXII | P. Ant. iii 174 | pap. | 14.5 x [28.5/29] | 12/12.5 x 25 | vi (ed.), iv E. G. T. | 1 | [41, 46] |
| † **200** | Homer, *Od.* XXIII | Pack$^2$ 1150 | parch. | ? | ? | iv | ? | [19?] |
| †***200a** | Homer, *Od.* XXIII | P. Ant. iii 175 | pap. | ? | ? | iv to v | 1 | [50] |
| †***200b** | Homer, *Od.* XXIV | P. Ant. iii 176 | parch. | ? | [12/14 x ] | v | 1 | [32] |
| † **200c** | Homer, *Od.* XXIV | P. Ant. iii 177 | pap. | ? | ? | ii to iii | 1 | [32?] |
| †***201** | Commentary to *Il.* I Codex?[16] | Pack$^2$ 1159 | pap. | 12/13 x 23 | ? | iii/iv | ? | 35 |
| †***202** | Glossary to *Il.* I | Pack$^2$ 1167 | pap. | ? | ? | iii | ? | (12+) |
| † **203** | Comm. on *Il.* II etc. | Pack$^2$ 1171 | pap. | ? | ? | vi | 2 | (25+) |
| †***203a** | Comm. on *Il.* VI | Pack$^2$ 1183 | pap. | ? | ? | iii (E. G. T.)[17] | ? | (12+?) |
| † **204** | Lexicon to *Il.* XI | Pack$^2$ 1192 | parch. | 18 x [ ] | ? | vii | 1 | (34+) |
| † **205** | Lexicon to *Il.* XIII | Pack$^2$ 1195 | pap. | ? | [10 x 30]? | iii | 2 | (19+) |
| † **206** | Scholia on *Il.* etc. | Pack$^2$ 1203 | parch. | ? | ? | v | ? | ? |
| †***206a** | Hypotheses to Homer[18] | Pack$^2$ 1206 | pap. | ? | [ x 16.5]? | ii-early iii | ? | [24?] |
| † **207** | Scholia to *Od.* | Pack$^2$ 1209 | pap. | ? | ? | iii | ? | (15+) |
| †***207a** | Lexicon to Homer | P. Oxy. xxx 2517 | pap. | ? | ? | ii | ? | (20+) |

[13]Information from Wolfgang Müller.

[14]Grenfell and Hunt estimate the size as 19 x 34. I cannot reconcile this with my photograph.

[15]Zereteli calculates [20 x 20].

[16]Back ( → ) carries no writing. Wilcken did not offer any discussion.

[17]Editor dates i-ii, and does not note that a codex is involved.

[18]Not clear that this is a codex. Note that same hand wrote both sides.

| 1 | 2 | 3 | 4 | 5 | 6 | 7 | 8 | 9 |
|---|---|---|---|---|---|---|---|---|
| **208** | Isocrates | Pack$^2$ 1241 | pap. | [14 x 16] | [10 x 12] | iv | 1 | [21?] |
| † **209** | Isocrates | Pack$^2$ 1247 | parch. | ? | ? | iv | 2 | [57] |
| ***210** | Isocrates | Pack$^2$ 1249 | pap. | 13.7 x 19.7 | 10.5 x 12.7 | v or vi | 1 | 23, 25 |
| ***211** | Isocrates | Pack$^2$ 1250 | pap. | [17/18.5] x 25.6 | [14/15] x 19.6 | iv | 1 | 34 |
| ***212** | Isocrates | Pack$^2$ 1254 | *not* a codex | | | | | |
| † **213** | Isocrates | Pack$^2$ 1258[19] | pap. | ? | ? | iii/iv | 1 | 26 |
| ***214** | Isocrates | Pack$^2$ 1259 | pap. | [14 x 16.6][20]? | [12 x 14]? | v? | 1 | [16?] |
| † **215** | Isocrates | Pack$^2$ 1265 | parch. | ? | ? | iv | ? | ? |
| ***216** | Isocrates | Pack$^2$ 1266 | parch. | [8.8 x 10] | [5.2 x 6.9] | iii/iv (iii ed.) | 1 | 18 |
| ***217** | Isocrates | Pack$^2$ 1268 | parch. | [9] x 10 | 6.8 x 7 | iv | 1 | 16, 17 |
| **218** | Isocrates | Pack$^2$ 1269 | parch. | [20 x 16] (ed.) | ? | v | 2 | 29 |
| † **219** | Isocrates | Pack$^2$ 1275 | pap. | ?[21] | ? | iv-v | 1 | 30? |
| †***220** | Isocrates | Pack$^2$ 1276 | parch. | ? | ? | iv | ? | (7+) |
| ***221** | Isocrates | Pack$^2$ 1277 | parch. | [13 x 18] | [10 x 14] | iv | 2 | [30] |
| **222** | Josephus | Pack$^2$ 1283 | pap. | [20 x 25] (ed.) | ? | iii | 1 | [30] |
| †***223** | Libanius | Pack$^2$ 1284 | pap. | ? | ? | vii (?, ed. viii/ix) | 1 | [30] |
| ***223a** | Lollianus | A. Henrichs, *Die Phoinikika des Lollianos* | pap. | [25/20 x 40/35] | ? | late ii | 1 | 59+ |
| ***224** | Lysias | Pack$^2$ 1290 | pap. | [18/19 x 31/32] | ? | iii/iv | 2 | 45 |
| ***224a** | Hypotheses of Lysias' speeches | P. Oxy. xxxi 2537 | pap. | [13/13.5] x 24.5 | [12] x 22/23 | ii/iii | 1? | 45, 48 |
| ***225** | Menander | Pack$^2$ 1298 | pap. | 13 x 27.5 | 11 x 23.5 | iv (iii ed.) | 1 | 47–54 |
| † **226** | Menander | Pack$^2$ 1299 | parch. | ? | ? | iii | 1 | [29] |
| ***227** | Menander | Pack$^2$ 1301 | pap. | 18 x 30 (18.5 x 31.5) | 13 x 22 | iv/v | 1 | 33–38 |
| † **227a** | Menander | Schedae Petropolitanae | parch. | ? | ? | iv | 1 | (27+)[22] |
| †***228** | Menander | Pack$^2$ 1302[23] | parch. | ? | ? | iv | 1 | (22+) |

| | | | | | | | | |
|---|---|---|---|---|---|---|---|---|
| **229** | Menander | Pack$^{2}$ 1303 | parch. | 15 x 16 | ? | iii? | 1 | 30, 31 |
| ***230** | Menander | Pack$^{2}$ 1306 | pap. | [18 x 30] | ? | v? | 1 | 43, 44 |
| † **231** | Menander | Pack$^{2}$ 1307 | pap. | ? | ? | iv | 1 | (31+) |
| † **232** | Menander | Pack$^{2}$ 1308 | pap. | ? | ? | iv | ? | (3+) |
| ***233** | Menander | Pack$^{2}$ 1314 | pap. | [17 x 31/32] | ? | v/vi | 1 | [35] |
| † **234** | Menander | Pack$^{2}$ 1315 | parch. | ? | ? | iv or v (E. G. T.) | 1 | [34?] |
| ***234a** | Menander | P. Oxy. xxxiii 2656 | pap. | 14 x 30+ | ? | iv | 1 | 35–40 |
| ***235** | Menander | Pack$^{2}$ 1318 | parch. | 14 x 22 | 10 x 17.7 | iv or v | 1 | 24–28 |
| **236** | Nonnus | Pack$^{2}$ 1329 | pap. | [28 x 40] | ? | vi[24] | 1 | 44–48 |
| † **237** | Oppian | Pack$^{2}$ 1331 | pap. | ? | ? | iv | 1 | [39] |
| † **238** | Oracula Sybillina | Pack$^{2}$ 1332 | parch. | ? | ? | iv | 1 | [20] |
| † **239** | Palaephatus | Pack$^{2}$ 1333 | | | | | | |
| ***240** | Pamprepius | Pack$^{2}$ 1334 | pap. | [16 x 25] | 11 x 21.4 | v/vi | 1 | [44–46] |
| † **241** | Parthenius | Pack$^{2}$ 1337 | parch. | ? | ? | iii-iv | 1 | (16+) |
| † **242** | Parthenius | Pack$^{2}$ 1338 | parch. | ? | ? | iv-v | 1? | ? |
| ***243** | Philo | Pack$^{2}$ 1344 | pap. | 15 x 17.5 | 11.5 x 11.5 | iii | 1 | 22–24 |
| ***244** | Philo | Pack$^{2}$ 1345 | pap. | 16.5 x 17.8 | 12 x 15 | iii (A. S. Hunt, E. G. T.) | 2 | 35–41 |
| † **245** | Philo | Pack$^{2}$ 1346 | pap. | ? | 10 x [ ] | iv-v | 1? | — |
| † **246** | Philostratus | Pack$^{2}$ 1347 | pap. | 18.5 x [ ] | 14 x [ ] | iv | 1? | (34?) |
| ***247** | Pindar | Pack$^{2}$ 1352 | pap. | [21 x 37] | ? | v or vi | 1 | [52?] |
| † **248** | Pindar | Pack$^{2}$ 1354 | parch. | ? | ? | iii | 1 | ? |
| † **249** | Pindar, scholia on | Pack$^{2}$ 1356 | pap. | ? | ? | vi? | ? | ? |
| †***250** | Pindar, Paeans | Pack$^{2}$ 1362 | pap. | [22 x 32] | [15/11 x 22] | ii (ed., E. G. T.) | ? | [43–44] |
| † **251** | Pindar? | Pack$^{2}$ 1379 | pap. | ? | ? | ii-iii (ed.) | ? | (14+) |
| †***252** | Plato, Theaetetus | Pack$^{2}$ 1394 | parch. | ? | [ x 16] | vi (ed., v? E. G. T.) | 2[25] | 24 |

[19]+ Pack$^{2}$ 2534, see *Cd'É* (1966), 341.
[20]Ed. supposed page had 2 columns; I have treated it as a double leaf, 1 column to a page.
[21]In *MPER* iv, p. 137 the size is estimated at [22 x 45]. Such a size is without parallel.
[22]Cf. *GRBS* x (1969): esp. p. 311. The type could have been 17/18B x 21+H, containing 50 verses per page.
[23]Cf. *GRBS* x (1969): 312. A codex of type 17/18B x 22/23H would be conceivable.
[24]Schubart, *Pal.*, p. 142.
[25]Ed. supposes one column. But the horizontal ruling continues outside the vertical bounds, and suggests a double column format.

| 1 | 2 | 3 | 4 | 5 | 6 | 7 | 8 | 9 |
|---|---|---|---|---|---|---|---|---|
| † **253** | Plato, Gorgias | Pack$^2$ 1415 | pap. | ? | [ x 16.8] | iii | 1 | 28 |
| ***254** | Plato, Parmenides | *GRBS* xii (1971): 539 | parch. | [19 x 24] (ed.) | ? | iii/iv (E. G. T.; ii ed.) | 2 | [29] |
| † **255** | Plato, Republic | Pack$^2$ 1420 | pap. | ? | ? | iii | ? | (6+) |
| **255a** | Plato, Republic | P. Oxy. xliv 3157 | pap. | ? | [ x 22?] | ii | 1? | (c. 51) |
| † **255b** | Ps.–Plato | P. Ant. iii 181 | pap. | ? | ? | early iii | ? | (11+) |
| **256** | Ps.–Plato | Pack$^2$ 1429 | parch. | [11/12 x 18] | ? | iv | 2 | [33] |
| ***257** | Plutarch | Pack$^2$ 1432 | pap. | [21 x 35/36] | ? | iii | 1 | [40+] |
| †***258** | Ptolemy[26] | Pack$^2$ 1437 | pap. | ? | ? | iii | 2 | (32+) |
| † **259** | Sappho | Pack$^2$ 1440 | parch. | ? | ? | vii | 1? | (5+) |
| † **260** | Sappho—*not a* codex![27] | Pack$^2$ 1451 | parch. | ? | ? | vii? | ? | ? |
| †***261** | Sophocles | Pack$^2$ 1462 | pap. | | [12 x 21]? | iv | 1 | [60] |
| †***262** | Sophocles[28] | Pack$^2$ 1464 | parch. | ? | ? | vi-vii | ? | (9+) |
| ***263** | Sophocles | Pack$^2$ 1468 | pap. | [12.5 x 31] | [10 x 24.5] | iv or v | 1 | 54 |
| † **264** | Sophocles | Pack$^2$ 1469 | pap. | ? | ? | v-vi | 1? | [43] |
| † **265** | Soranus | Pack$^2$ 1483 | pap. | ? | [13 x ] | iv | 1 | (19+) |
| ***266** | Theocritus | Pack$^2$ 1487 | pap. | 21 x 28.4 | 18 x 24 | v/vi | 1 | 39–48 |
| † **267** | Theocritus | Pack$^2$ 1488 | parch. | ? | ? | v-vi | ? | [32] |
| † **268** | Theocritus | Pack$^2$ 1490 | pap. | 24 x [ ] | ? | v | 1 | [25, 32] |
| † **269** | Theocritus | Pack$^2$ 1491 | parch. | ? | ? | vi-vii | ? | (5+) |
| † **270** | Theocritus | Pack$^2$ 1493 | pap. | ? | ? | iv? | ? | ? |
| † **271** | Theocritus | Pack$^2$ 1494 | pap. | is *not* a codex | | ii | | |
| † **272** | Thucydides | Pack$^2$ 1511 | pap. | ? | [15 x 26] | iii | 2 | 48–50 |
| ***273** | Thucydides | Pack$^2$ 1513 | parch. | [11.8] x 14.3 | 9 x 9.7 | iv | 1 | 21 |
| † **274** | Thucydides | Pack$^2$ 1515 | parch. | ? | ? | iv-v | ? | ? |
| ***275** | Thucydides | Pack$^2$ 1516 | pap. | [17 x 32] (ed.) | ? | ii/iii | 2 | 60 |
| ***276** | Thucydides | Pack$^2$ 1521 | parch. | ? | ? | v-vi | ?[29] | (22+) |
| ***277** | Thucydides | Pack$^2$ 1533 | parch. | [11/12 x 14/15] | [9 x 11] | iii | 2 | [32] |
| **278** | Thucydides | Pack$^2$ 1534 | parch. | [14 x 17.8] (ed.) | ? | v-vi | 1 | (28+) |

| | | | | | | | | |
|---|---|---|---|---|---|---|---|---|
| † **279** | Thucydides Commentary | Pack² 1535 | pap. | [25 x 31] (ed.) | ? | iii | 1 | [45?] |
| ***279a** | Thucydides I 99– | P. Oxy. ined. | pap. | [19/18 x 34] | ? | iii | 2 | 55 |
| | Tryphon[30] | Pack² 1539 = *BICS* xxii (1975):65 | pap. | | | | | |
| ***280** | Xenophon | Pack² 1546 | pap. | 12.5 x [33.1] | 11 x [29] | ii | 1 | 60 |
| ***281** | Xenophon, *Cyropaedia* | Pack² 1547 | pap. | [13.5 x 23]? (E. G. T.) | ? | iii | 1 | [32–35] |
| † **282** | Xenophon[31] *Hellenica* | Pack² 1553 | parch. | ? | [ x 16/17] | iv | 2? | [32] |
| † **283** | Xenophon, *Mem.* | Pack² 1560 | parch. | 8.3 x [ ] | 3 | iv | 2 | [20] |
| † **284** | Verse anthology | Pack² 1578 | pap. | ? | ? | v | ? | ? |
| † **285** | Anthology? | Pack² 1581 | pap. | ? | ? | iii-iv | 1? | ? |
| | Anthol. Pal.[32] | Pack² 1599 | | | | | | |
| † **286** | Verses | Pack² 1609 | pap. | ? | ? | iii (Oellacher), iii-iv (Pack) | 1? | (13+) |
| †***287** | Epigrams | Pack² 1611 | pap. | ?[33] | ? | v-vi | 1 | 45 |
| † **288** | Old Comedy? | Pack² 1627 | pap. | ? | ? | v | ? | ? |
| † **289** | Scholia on comedy | Pack² 1630 | pap. | ? | ? | v | ? | ? |
| † **290** | Old Comedy | Pack² 1631 | pap. | 'At least [20 x 30] (ed.) | ? | iv-v | ? | ? |
| †***291** | Menander? | Pack² 1642 | parch. | ? | [12.5/13 x 16][34] | iv | ? | ? |
| † **292** | Menander? | Pack² 1644 | pap. | ? | ? | iv? | ? | ? |
| † **293** | New Comedy | Pack² 1652 | pap. | ? | ? | iii | 1? | (6+) |
| † **294** | Menander? | Pack² 1659 | pap. | [12/13 x ] | [10/11 x ] | iii/iv | 1 | (23+) |

[26] Not certainly a codex. If the astronomical tables of P. Ryl. 523 (on the back) are part of Ptolemy's text, it could be a 'utility' codex c. 11/12 x 13/14.
[27] It should be examined to see whether it could be part of an orihon.
[28] Not certainly a codex.
[29] Uncertain whether to be restored as in 1 or 2 columns.
[30] Same codex as **106**.
[31] Presumably a codex.
[32] Part of same codex as **90**.
[33] See Seider, *Gr. Pal.* Abb. 63. At least [21 x 28].
[34] Editor reconstructs as 2 columns to a page. But this is the only known example of a verse Ms with 2 columns. My reconstruction assumes 1 column of 40/45 verses per page.

| 1 | 2 | 3 | 4 | 5 | 6 | 7 | 8 | 9 |
|---|---|---|---|---|---|---|---|---|
| † **295** | Comedy | Pack² 1664 | pap. | ? | ? | v | ? | ? |
| †***296** | New Comedy | Pack² 1669 | pap. | ? | ? | iv-v | 1 | (22+) |
| † **297** | Comedy | Pack² 1672 | pap. | ? | ? | iii-iv | 1? | (14+) |
| † **298** | Comedy | Pack² 1687 | pap. | ? | ? | v? | 1? | (10+) |
| † **299** | Commentary on tragedy | Pack² 1714 | pap. | ? | ? | iv-v | ? | (7+) |
| † **300** | Tragedy? | Pack² 1725 | pap. | ? | ? | v | ? | (17+) |
| † **301** | Epic | Pack² 1773 | pap. | ? | ? | iv | ? | (10+) |
| † **302** | Epic | Pack² 1775 | pap. | [ ] x 34 | ? | iv | 1 | 42 |
| † **303** | Epic? | Pack² 1777 | pap. | ? | ? | iii | 1? | (16+) |
| † **304** | Epic | Pack² 1784 | pap. | ? | ? | iii-iv | 1? | (12+) |
| † **305** | Epic | Pack² 1786 | pap. | ? | ? | iii | 1? | (25+) |
| † **306** | Epic? | Pack² 1789 | parch. | ? | ? | iv-v | 1? | (6+) |
| † **307** | Epic[35] | Pack² 1790 | pap. | ? | ? | iii | ? | ? |
| † **308** | Epic? | Pack² 1792 | pap. | ? | ? | iii | 1? | (21+, 22+) |
| † **309** | Epic? | Pack² 1798 | pap. | ? | ? | iv | 1 | (23+) |
| | Epic Katabasis[36] | Pack² 1801 | | | | | | |
| † **310** | Epic | Pack² 1803 | pap. | ? | ? | iv-v | 1? | (13+) |
| † **311** | Epic | Pack² 1825 | pap. | ? | ? | iv-v | 1? | (13+) |
| † **312** | Epic | Pack² 1826 | pap. | ? | ? | vi | 1? | (10+) |
| † **313** | Epic[37] | Pack² 1831 | pap. | ? | ? | iii-iv | 1? | (18, 19) |
| † **314** | Epic (Colluthus?) | Pack² 1835 | pap. | ? | ? | v-vi | 1? | (19+) |
| †***315** | Epic | Pack² 1844 | pap. | ? | ? | v/vi (E. G. T.; iv ed.) | 1 | (13+) |
| † **316** | Epic | Pack² 1848 | pap. | ? (very tall) | ? | iv | 1 | (20+) |
| † **317** | Epic? | Pack² 1849 | pap. | ? | ? | iv | 1? | (46+) |
| †***317a** | Epicedia | Pack² 1851 | pap. | 22 x [ ] | ? | iv | 1 | (30+) |
| †***318** | Panegyric | Pack² 1852 | pap. | ?[38] | ? | v | 1 | (22+) |
| † **319** | Encomium | Pack² 1853 | pap. | ? | a [12 x ] | iv | 1? | (31+) |
| † **320** | Epic | Pack² 1854 | pap. | 14 x [ ] | ? | v | 1 | (30+) |
| †***321** | Epic? | Pack² 1855 | pap. | ? | ? | iv (E. G. T.; v-vi ed.) | 1 | (19+) |

| | | | | | | | | |
|---|---|---|---|---|---|---|---|---|
| † **322** | Epic | Pack$^2$ 1856 | parch. | ? | ? | iv-v | 1 | (16+) |
| †***323** | Epic | Pack$^2$ 1857 | parch. | 3 | ? | vi? | 1? | (6+) |
| **324** | Pastoral | Pack$^2$ 1858 | pap. | [20 x 33.5][39] | [16 x 25] | ii/iii | 1 | 48, 49 |
| **325** | See **M1** | Pack$^2$ 1866 | | | | | | |
| **326** | *Not* a codex! | Pack$^2$ 1869 | | | | | | |
| | See **319** | Pack$^2$ 1888 | | | | | | |
| † **327** | Lyric fragments[40] | Pack$^2$ 1899 | pap. | ? | ? | iv | ? | ? |
| †***328** | Commentary | Pack$^2$ 1952 | pap. | ? | ? | iii (E. G. T.) | ? | (15+) |
| †***329** | Hexameters | Pack$^2$ 1957 | pap. | ? | ? | iii | 1? | (16+) |
| † **330** | Verse | Pack$^2$ 1974 | parch. | ? | ? | iv-v | ? | ? |
| † **331** | Prose Maxims | Pack$^2$ 1991 | pap. | ? | ? | iii-iv | ? | (19+) |
| **332** | Magic<br>See **M4** | Pack$^2$ 1997 | | | | | | |
| **333** | See **M5** | Pack$^2$ 1998 | | | | | | |
| ***334** | Planetary tables | Pack$^2$ 2010 | pap. | 14.8 x 22.5[41] | ? | iv | tables | — |
| †***335** | Astronomical Tables | Pack$^2$ 2014 | pap. | ? | ? | ii/iii | ? | (18+) |
| † **336** | Astronomical ephemeris | Pack$^2$ 2020 | pap. | ? | ? | v | ? | ? |
| †***337** | Royal Canon | P. Oxy. xxxi 2551[42] | pap. | ? | ? | iii/iv | 1? | 27+ |
| **338** | See **258** | Pack$^2$ 2028 | | | | | | |
| † **339** | Ephemeris | Pack$^2$ 2037 | pap. | ?[43] | ? | v | ? | ? |
| † **340** | Astrological Treatise | Pack$^2$ 2039 | pap. | ? | ? | iii/iv | 1 | (27/28?) |

[35] Uncertain whether roll or codex.
[36] Part of same codex as **107**.
[37] May be school exercise continued to back of sheet.
[38] Could be [18 x 30].
[39] Calculated from the stichometry. The date assigned by E. G. T. on basis of the editor's parallels.
[40] Presumably (a) at least is codex; (b) may not be.
[41] See corrections of O. Neugebauer, *Osiris* xiii (1958): 112; *Proc. Am. Philosoph. Soc.* cvi (1962): 385-86.
[42] Either conjugate leaf with one column per page (size [9B x 27H] unparalleled!), or single leaf with curious two-column page.
[43] Perhaps [17 x 35] ed.

| 1 | 2 | 3 | 4 | 5 | 6 | 7 | 8 | 9 |
|---|---|---|---|---|---|---|---|---|
| ***341** | Treatise on the Planets | Pack$^2$ 2053 | pap. | 14 x 21 | 12.5 x 17.5 | iii | 1 | 40, 41 |
| **342** | Astrol. frag. | Pack$^2$ 2062 | parch. | 11.5 x 19 | ? | iii (Youtie) | 1 | 28, 26 |
| **343** | See **M1** | Pack$^2$ 2067 | | | | | | |
| † **344** | Life of Aesop | Pack$^2$ 2072 | pap. | ? | ? | iv? | 1? | (13+) |
| † **345** | Life of Aesop | Pack$^2$ 2073 | pap. | [ x 17/18] (ed.) | ? | iv-v | 1 | 35 |
| † **346** | Life of Aesop | Pack$^2$ 2075 | pap. | [ ] x 32 | [ ] x 27 | vii? | 1 | 52 |
| ***347** | Life of Alcibiades | Pack$^2$ 2077 | parch. | 18 x 21.6 | 13 x 15 | v | 2 | 30 |
| † **348** | Herbal | Pack$^2$ 2095 | pap. | ? | ? | v | ? | ? |
| † **349** | Treatise on Divination *Not* a codex. | Pack$^2$ 2104 | pap. | | | iii-iv | | |
| ***350** | Palmomancy | Pack$^2$ 2112 | pap. | 6.6 x 7.5 | 5 x 6 | iv | 1 | 14–17 |
| † **351** | Palmomancy | Pack$^2$ 2113 | pap. | ? | ? | iv | 1 | (29+) |
| † **352** | Cyril Glossary[44] | Pack$^2$ 2119 | pap. | ? | ? | vii | ? | ? |
| † **353** | Lexicon | Pack$^2$ 2125 | pap. | ? | ? | iv? | 2 (more?) | (22+) |
| ***354** | Glossary | Pack$^2$ 2126 | pap. | 14.8 x [ ][45] | 8 x [ ] | vi | 1 | (17+) |
| † **355** | Greek Coptic Glossary | Pack$^2$ 2133 | paper | 9 x 12 | ? | x or xi? | 4? | ? |
| † **355a** | ?School book Codex? | Pack$^2$ 2140 | pap. | ? | ? | iv? | 2 | 15(?+) |
| † **355b** | "Study book" Lexicon, grammar | A. Wouters, *Ancient Society* iii (1972): 259[46] | pap. | 13 x 18 | ? | v (E. A. L.) iv (E. G. T.) | ? | 30 |
| †***356** | Grammatical treatise | Pack$^2$ 2145 | pap. | ? | [ ] x 11.6 | iii (E. G. T.) | 1 | 18 |
| † **357** | Grammatical treatise | Pack$^2$ 2147 | parch. | ? | ? | vi-vii | 1? | (12+) |
| † **358** | Grammatical treatise | Pack$^2$ 2153 | parch. | ? | ? | vii | ? | (22+) |
| †***359** | Grammatical treatise | Pack$^2$ 2155 | pap. | ? | ? | iii (E. G. T.)[47] | ? | (30+) |

| | | | | | | | | |
|---|---|---|---|---|---|---|---|---|
| † **360** | Grammatical | Pack$^2$ 2161 | pap. | ? | ? | v-vi | ? | (7+) |
| † **361** | Conjugation | Pack$^2$ 2164 | pap. | ? | 19 x 9.8 | iii-iv | 4? | 21 |
| † **362** | Grammatical fragment | Pack$^2$ 2168 | pap. | ? | ? | v | ? | (10+) |
| †***363** | Prosodical treatise | Pack$^2$ 2169 | parch. | 16.5 x [ ] | 11.5 x [ ] | iv | 1 | (22+) |
| **364** | is part of **365** | | | | | | | |
| † **365** | Metrical treatise | Pack$^2$ 2173+ 2174 | pap. | ? | ? | v | 1? | (13+) |
| † **366** | Treatise on metrics | Pack$^2$ 2175 | pap. | ? | ? | v-vi | ? | (9+) |
| † **367** | History | Pack$^2$ 2182 | pap. | [ x 32+] | ? | v | 1 | (33+) |
| †***368** | History of Rome | Pack$^2$ 2211 | parch. | ? | 10/11 x [ ] | v | 1 | (22+) |
| †***369** | Chronicle (illustrated) | Pack$^2$ 2243 | parch. | [16 x 28] (ed.)[48] | ? | iv-v | 2 | 55 |
| †***370** | World chronicle | Pack$^2$ 2244 | pap. | ?[49] | ? | vi-vii | Illustrated 31 | |
| †***370a** | (Antinoe charioteers) | Pack$^2$ 2916; *JEA* xvii (1931): 1 = *JHS* xciii (1973): 192 | pap. | [22? x ] | ? | vi | 1 | ? |
| †***371** | History? | Pack$^2$ 2245 | pap. | 15.2 x [ ] | 8.5 x [ ] | v-vi? | 1 | (14+) |
| † **372** | History? | Pack$^2$ 2253 | parch. | ? | ? | iv | 1? | (7+) |
| † **373** | History? | Pack$^2$ 2261 | pap. | ? | ? | v | ? | ? |
| † **374** | History | Pack$^2$ 2268 | pap. | ? | ? | iii | 1 | (22+) |
| † **375** | Commentary on Roman Law | Pack$^2$ 2277 | pap. | ?[50] | ? | v-vi | 1? | (34+) |
| †***376** | Juridical fragment | Pack$^2$ 2278 | parch. | ? | ? | vi? | 1? | (7+) |
| **377** | vacant | | | | | | | |

[44] **524** is part of same codex.
[45] Could well have been 14.8 x [30/32].
[46] It seems likely that *CLA* Suppl. 1683 refers to this text.
[47] ii ed., *CHR*.
[48] It is not clear how much estimate is involved in this figure.
[49] [24 x 30] ed. But [22 x 32] or [25 x 33] is to be preferred.
[50] Over 30 cm. H.

| 1 | 2 | 3 | 4 | 5 | 6 | 7 | 8 | 9 |
|---|---|---|---|---|---|---|---|---|
| **†*378** | Summary of Digest | Pack$^2$ 2279 | pap. | ?[51] | ? | vi | 1? | (11+) |
| **† 379** | Juridical fragment | Pack$^2$ 2280 | pap. | ? | ? | v | 1? | (7+) |
| **†*380** | Juridical fragment | Pack$^2$ 2281 = *CLA* Suppl. 1783 | pap. | ? | ? | v | 1 | (29) |
| **† 381** | Register of constitutions | Pack$^2$ 2282 | pap. | ? | ? | iv-v | ?[52] | (13+) |
| **† 382** | Juridical fragment | Pack$^2$ 2284 | pap. | ? | ? | vi-vii | 1 | (22+) |
| **383** | Rhetorical Catechism | Pack$^2$ 2288 | pap. | 25 x 30 (ed.) | ? | v-vi | 2 | 42–44 |
| **†*384** | Mathematical tables | Pack$^2$ 2306 | pap. | 27.5 x 31.5?[53] | ? | vi | 6, 5 on pp. 1-2, then 2 | 49, 35 |
| **† 385** | Mathematical treatise | Pack$^2$ 2325 | pap. | ? | ? | iv | 1 | (10+) |
| **† 386** | Medical aphorisms | Pack$^2$ 2338 | pap. | ? | ? | iii | 1 | (20+) |
| **† 387** | Medical catechism[54] | Pack$^2$ 2340 | pap. | ? | ? | ii? | 1? | (32+, 37+) |
| **† 388** | Anatomical catechism | Pack$^2$ 2341 | pap. | ?[55] | ? | iii-iv | 1 | 24 (?+) |
| **† 389** | Medical treatise | Pack$^2$ 2355 | pap. | ? | ? | i-ii (so ed.) | 1? | (10+) |
| **† 390** | Medical treatise | Pack$^2$ 2362 | pap. | ? | ? | iv | 1? | (11+) |
| ***391** | Surgical treatise | Pack$^2$ 2376 | pap. | [15.6 x 28] | 13 x 21 | iii | 2 | 50 |
| **† 392** | Treatise | Pack$^2$ 2389 | pap. | ? | ? | iii | 1? | (14, 15+) |
| **† 393** | Medical prescriptions | Pack$^2$ 2390 | pap. | ? | ? | vi | 1? | (10+) |
| **†*393a** | Prescriptions Magical? | P. Ant. ii 65 | parch. | ? | ? | v | ? | (10+) |
| **†*393b** | Prescriptions Magico-medical | Pack$^2$ 2391 | pap. | 21 x [ ][56] | 16 x [ ] | v (ed. ? earlier) | 2 | (15+) |
| **† 394** | Medical prescriptions | Pack$^2$ 2393 | parch. | ? | ? | v-vi | 1? | (15+) |

| | | | | | | | | |
|---|---|---|---|---|---|---|---|---|
| † **395** | Medical prescriptions | Pack$^2$ 2411 | pap.? | ? | ? | v? | 1? | (7+) |
| † **396** | Medical prescriptions[57] | Pack$^2$ 2415 | parch. | ? | ? | iii | 1? | (14+) |
| † **397** | Mythological fragment | Pack$^2$ 2461 | pap. | ? | ? | iii | 1? | (8+) |
| † **398** | Mythological fragment | Pack$^2$ 2462 | pap. | ? | ? | ii-iii (ed.) | 1? | (11+) |
| † **399** | Treatise on priests[58] | Pack$^2$ 2484 | pap. | | | | | |
| † **400** | Declamation | Pack$^2$ 2497 | pap. | ? | ? | v | 2 | 36 (?+) |
| † **401** | Declamation | Pack$^2$ 2503 | pap. | ? | ? | iii-iv | 1 | (13+) |
| † **402** | Isaeus? | Pack$^2$ 2505 | pap. | ? | ? | iii/iv | ? | (13+) |
| † **403** | Encomium | Pack$^2$ 2526 | pap. | ? | ? | v-vi | 1 | (16+) |
| † **404** | Rhetorical exercises | Pack$^2$ 2528 | pap. | 17 x [ ][59] | 15.5 x [ ] | iii-iv | 1 | (18+) |
| † **405** | Oration | Pack$^2$ 2530 | pap. | ? | ? | iv-v | 1 | (23+) |
| **406** | Panegyric | Pack$^2$ 2531 | pap. | 15 x 32 (ed.) | 8 x 21 (ed.) | iv-v | 1 | 37–40 |
| | Pack$^2$ 2534 is part of same codex as **213** | | | | | | | |
| † **407** | Declamation | Pack$^2$ 2550 | pap. | 10 x [ ] (?) | ? | ii-iii | 1 | (17+) |
| † **408** | Oratory | Pack$^2$ 2552 | pap. | ? | ? | ii-iii | 1 | (14+) |
| ***409** | Aristotelian physics | Pack$^2$ 2565 | pap. | 20 x 30 | 14 x 24 | vi/vii (ed. vii-viii) | 1 | 33 |
| **410** | Philosophical | Pack$^2$ 2573 | pap. | [15.5 x 23.5] (ed.) | [8 x 13] (ed.) | iii | 1? | ? |

[51] [20 x 30] ed.
[52] A supposed second column may be marginal notes.
[53] Or should it be 31.5 x 27.5?
[54] Presumably codex.
[55] Possibly [14] x 16?
[56] Editor does not say codex, but hand, lay-out, and subject matter are the same on the back.
[57] It is not clear that a codex is involved.
[58] Probably not a codex but an opisthograph roll. If a codex, it is 30 x [ ], an unparalleled shape.
[59] Ed. suggests 17 x [32]

| 1 | 2 | 3 | 4 | 5 | 6 | 7 | 8 | 9 |
|---|---|---|---|---|---|---|---|---|
| †***411** | Medical fragment | Pack$^2$ 2578[60] | pap. | — | [10/10.5 x ] | iii (E. G. T.; iii or iii/iv Manfredi) | 1 | (15+) |
| † **412** | Romance of Sesonchosis | Pack$^2$ 2619 | pap. | ? | ? | iii-iv | 1 | (13–15+) |
| **413** | [Lucian], Lucius (Asinus) | Pack$^2$ 2637 + J. Lenaerts, *Cd'É* (1974), 115 | parch. | [7.5 x 17] Lenaerts | [5 x 12] Lenaerts | iv | 1 | [27] |
| † **414** | Romance? | Pack$^2$ 2638 | parch. | ? | ? | vi | 1 | (10+) |
| ***415** | Schoolbook | Pack$^2$ 2643 | pap. | 8 x 9 | ? | iv | 1 | 12+ |
| **416** | Schoolbook | Pack$^2$ 2644 | parch. | [6 x 10] (ed.) | ? | "Byz." | 1 | 13 |
| ***416a** | Schoolbook | *Ancient Society* i (1970): 201ff. | pap. | 14.5 x [21+] | 11.5 x [ ] | iv | 1 or 2 | 28(+) |
| †***417** | Shorthand | Pack$^2$ 2754 | pap. | ? | ? | iv-v | ? | ? |
| †***418** | Shorthand | Pack$^2$ 2756 | pap. | ? | ? | iv | 2 | ? |
| ***419** | Shorthand | Pack$^2$ 2759 | pap. | 12.0 x 24.5 | — | iii-iv | 2 double cols. | ? |
| ***420** | Shorthand | Pack$^2$ 2760 | pap. | 15 x 23.5 | — | iii-iv | 2 double cols. | ? |
| ***421** | Shorthand | Pack$^2$ 2761 | pap. | 18.3/18.5 x 20.5[61] | ? | iv-v | 2 | 15 |
| †***422** | Shorthand | Pack$^2$ 2762 | pap. | ? | ? | ? | 2 | ? |
| †***423** | Shorthand | Pack$^2$ 2763 | pap. | ? | ? | iii | 2 | ? |
| †***424** | Shorthand | Pack$^2$ 2764 | pap. | ? | ? | v | 2 | ? |
| † **425** | Shorthand | Pack$^2$ 2777 | pap. | ? | ? | vi-vii | ? | ? |
| † **425a** | Shorthand | *Aegyptus* xx (1940): 5 | pap. | ? | ? | v | ? | (13+) |
| † **426** | Prose frag. | Pack$^2$ 2797 | parch. | ? | ? | vi | 1? | (5+) |
| † **427** | Prose frag. | Pack$^2$ 2809 | pap. | ? | ? | vii | 1? | (12+) |
| † **428** | Prose frag. | Pack$^2$ 2814 | pap. | ? | ? | iii | 1? | (15+) |
| † **429** | Prose frag. | Pack$^2$ 2846 | pap. | ? | ? | iv | 1? | (13+) |

| | | | | | | | | |
|---|---|---|---|---|---|---|---|---|
| † **430** | Marginal commentary? | Pack² 2864 | pap. | ? | ? | v | ? | (5) |
| † **431** | Marginal commentary | Pack² 2865 | pap. | ? | ? | v | ? | ? |
| † **432** | Marginal commentary? | Pack² 2866 | pap. | ? | ? | vi | ? | (12+) |
| † **433** | Scholia | Pack² 2867 | pap. | ? | ? | v | 1? | (4+) |
| † **434** | Prose frag. | Pack² 2868 | pap. | ? | ? | vi-vii | 1? | (21+) |
| † **435** | Prose frag.? | Pack² 2869 | pap. | ? | ? | v | 1? | (8+) |
| † **436** | Prose frag. | Pack² 2870 | pap. | ? | ? | iv/v | 2 | (11+) |
| † **437** | Prose? | Pack² 2873 | pap. | ? | ? | iv? | ? | (11+) |
| † **438** | Prose? | Pack² 2874 | pap. | 18.5 x [ ] | 3 | v-vi | ? | ? |
| † **438a** | Medical frag. | *MPER* iii 58 | pap. | ? | ? | v | 1? | (7+) |
| † **438b** | Indeterminate | *MPER* iv 55 | parch. | ? | ? | iv-v | ? | (6+) |
| † **439** | Prose? | Pack² 2877 | pap. | ? | ? | vi | 1? | (16+) |
| † **440** | Prose | Pack² 2878 | pap.? | ? | ? | v-vi | 1? | (9+) |
| † **441** | Prose | Pack² 2883 | pap. | ? | ? | iii | 1? | (3+) |
| † **442** | Prose? | Pack² 2887 | pap. | ? | ? | iv | ? | (6+) |
| † **443** | Prose | Pack² 2888 | pap. | ? | ? | 'late' | ? | (8+) |
| † **443a** | Prose | Pack² 2895 | pap. | ? | ? | v or later | ? | (2+) |
| ***444** | Cicero | Pack² 2918, *CLA* ii 210 | pap. | [23 x 30+] | 17 x [ ] | v | 1 | [65, 69] |
| ***445** | Cicero | Pack² 2919, *CLA* ii 226 | pap. | [20.5] x 29 | [ ] x 18 | v | 1 | 22 |
| ***446** | Cicero | Pack² 2921, *CLA* iii 286 | pap. | [17.5 x 25][62] | [13.5 x 19] | v-vi | 1 | [30] |
| ***446a** | Cicero, in Cat. I, II[63] | P. Barcin. | pap. | 11.4 x 12.6 | 8.5 x 10 | iv | 1 | 24 |

[60]See M. Manfredi, *SIFC* xvi.

[61]Milne's figures (p. 8) neglect the fact that fr. 1 is full width of double-leaf.

[62]Ramorini 20 x 28; E. A. Lowe 22 x 28.

[63]Same composite codex as Psalmus responsorius.

| 1 | 2 | 3 | 4 | 5 | 6 | 7 | 8 | 9 |
|---|---|---|---|---|---|---|---|---|
| ***447** | Cicero | Pack$^{2}$ 2922, *CLA* x 1519 | pap. | [30 x 40]? | ? | iv-v | 2 double | [50?] |
| †***448** | Cicero | Pack$^{2}$ 2923, *CLA* ii 224 | pap. | ? | ? | v (ed., iii-iv Mallon) | 1 double col.? | (17+) |
| ***449** | Cicero | Pack$^{2}$ 2924, *CLA* iii 1043 | parch. | [13+] x 14.5 | 8 x 8 | v | 1 | 17 |
| ***450** | Juvenal | Pack$^{2}$ 2925, *CLA* Supp. 1710 | parch. | 17 x 22.7 | 12 x 16.7 | v/vi | 1 | 25 |
| †***451** | Lucan | Pack$^{2}$ 2928, *CLA* ii 175 | parch. | ? | ? | v-vi | 1 | [18] |
| †***452** | Sallust | Pack$^{2}$ 2930, *CLA* viii 1054 | parch. | [ ] x 16.3+ | [15 x 15] | iv | 2 | 18 |
| †***452a** | Sallust | P. Ant. iii 154[64], *CLA* Supp. 1712 | parch. | ? | ? | iv | 1? | (6+) |
| ***453** | Sallust | Pack$^{2}$ 2931, *CLA* ii 246 | pap. | [17 x 23] | [14 x 14] | v | 1 | [17] |
| †***454** | Sallust | Pack$^{2}$ 2932, *CLA* iii 288 | pap. | ? | ? | iv | 1 | [32] |
| ***455** | Terence | Pack$^{2}$ 2934, *CLA* Supp. 1717 | pap. | [22] x 31 | 15/16 x 22 | iv | 1 | 34–35 |
| †***455a** | Terence, *Andria* | *CLA* x 1537 | pap. | ? | [18] x [ ] | iv | 1 | (25) |
| ***456** | Vergil, glossary | Pack$^{2}$ 2936, *CLA* xi 1651 | parch. | 19.4 x [24] | ? | v | double col. | [28?] |
| ***457** | Vergil | Pack$^{2}$ 2937, *CLA* Supp. 1708 | pap. | [27.5 x 41] (ed.) | ? | iv | 1 | 25 |
| ***458** | Vergil glossary | Pack$^{2}$ 2939, *CLA* xi 1652 | pap. | 20 x 27.5 | 13/14 x 19 | vi? | double col. | 26 |

| | | | | | | | | |
|---|---|---|---|---|---|---|---|---|
| ***459** | Vergil glossary | Pack$^2$ 2940[65] | pap. | [20 x 35] | ? | iv | double col. | 36–40 |
| †***460** | Vergil | Pack$^2$ 2941, *CLA* ii 134 | pap. | ? | ? | v | ? | 25 |
| **461** | Vergil Rewritten | Pack$^2$ 2942 | *not* a codex | | | | | |
| †***462** | Vergil Palimpsest | Pack$^2$ 2943[66], *CLA* iii 306 | parch. | ? | ? | v-vi | 2 | 30 |
| †***463** | Vergil | Pack$^2$ 2944, *CLA* x 1569 | parch. | ? | ? | iv? | ? | [23] |
| †***464** | Vergil | Pack$^2$ 2945, *CLA* xi 1653 | pap. | ?[67] | ? | vi (ed.), v (E. A. L.) | 1 | 34 |
| †***465** | Vergil glossary | Pack$^2$ 2946, *CLA* iii 290 | pap. | 30 x [ ] | ? | iv-v | 2 double cols. | (33+) |
| †***466** | Vergil glossary | Pack$^2$ 2948, *CLA* x 1570 | pap. | ?[68] | 20.5 x 21.5 | iv-v | 2 double cols. | [25–26] |
| ***467** | Vergil | Pack$^2$ 2949, *CLA* iii 287 | pap. | [19/20 x 29/30] (E. G. T.) | [14 x 19] | v | 1 | [34] |
| ***468** | Vergil and Greek Paraphrase | Pack$^2$ 2950, *CLA* ii 137 | parch. | [?14] x [ ] | 9.5 x [ ] | v-vi | double col. | [35+] |
| †***469** | Vergil | Pack$^2$ 2951,[69] *CLA* x 1522 | parch. | ? | ? | v | 2 | (10+) |
| ***470** | Vergil | Pack$^2$ 2952, *CLA* Supp. 1709 | parch. | [ x 27/28] | [ x 17] | iv | 1 | [24] |
| ***471** | Gaius | Pack$^2$ 2953, *CLA* iii 292 | parch. | 16/17 x [29?] (ed.)[70] | 9 x 18 (ed.) | iv-vi | 1 | 22 |

[64]Morel, *CR* (1968), p. 23.

[65]Cf. *ZPE* (1973), p. 219. Size [24 x 36], C. H. R. On the date cf. Cavallo p. 51, n.1.

[66]Add *Studi C. Castiglioni* (1957), 355.

[67][19/20 x 29/30] ed.

[68]Not certain if codex. Ed. suggests [27 x 29/30], which is an unparalleled dimension.

[69]And *Helikon* IV: 343.

[70]Ed. nowhere states the height of individual fragments. I suspect 29cm. is an over-estimate.

| 1 | 2 | 3 | 4 | 5 | 6 | 7 | 8 | 9 |
|---|---|---|---|---|---|---|---|---|
| **†*472** | Papinian | Pack$^2$ 2955, *CLA* viii 1037, Supp. p. 25 | parch. | ? | ? | iv-v | 2 | (28+) |
| **†*472a** | Ulpianus, Disputationes | Pack$^2$ 2962, *CLA* vi 834 | parch. | ?[71] | [16.5 x 16] | v-vi | 2 | [29] |
| **†*473** | Paulus | Pack$^2$ 2956, *CLA* x 1577 | parch. | x [18.5] | [11 x 13.5] | iii-iv | 1 | (23+) |
| **†*474** | Paulus | Pack$^2$ 2957, *CLA* viii 1042, x p. 27 | parch. | 20+ x [ ] | 16 x [ ] | iv | 1 | (16+) |
| **† 474a** | Commentary on Paulus etc.[73] | Pack$^2$ 2958 | pap. | ? | ? | v? | ? | ? |
| **†*474b** | Ulpian | Pack$^2$ 2959, *CLA* x 1471 | parch. | ? | 9.2 x [ ] | v | 1 | (9+) |
| **†*475** | Ulpian | Pack$^2$ 2960, *CLA* Supp. 1697 | parch. | ? | [ x 25?] | iv | 2 | [50?] |
| ***476** | Codex Theodosianus | Pack$^2$ 2963, *CLA* ii 211 | parch. | [22.5 x 30/31] | [ x 16.5] (E. G. T.) | v-vi (E. A. L.) | 1 | [31] |
| **†*477** | Latin uncertain[74] | Pack$^2$ 2964 | parch. | | | | | |
| **†*478** | Index of Stephanus | Pack$^2$ 2965[75] | pap. | 20.6 x 37.7+ | 17 x 30+ | vi | 1 | 35 |
| **†*479** | Digest? and scholia | Pack$^2$ 2966, *CLA* viii 1221 | pap. | ? | ? | vi (E. A. L.) | ? | (15+) |
| ***480** | Digest | Pack$^2$ 2967, *CLA* Supp. 1723 | pap. | [25/26 x 36]? | [20 x 26]? | vi | 1 | [32] |
| ***481** | Index to Codex Iust. | Pack$^2$ 2969 *CLA* Supp. 1713 | pap. | [22.4 x 34.3] | 14.3 x 22.5 | vi | 1 | 30 |

| | | | | | | | | |
|---|---|---|---|---|---|---|---|---|
| ***482** | Codex Iust. | Pack² 2970, *CLA* iii 293 | pap. | [23 x 33] (E. G. T.; [ x 28], ed.) | [18 x 24] | vi | 1 | [30?] |
| **†*483** | Codex Iust. | Pack² 2971, *CLA* v 700 | pap. | ? | ? | vi | ? | (6+) |
| **†*484** | Juridical frag. | Pack² 2972, *CLA* ii 248 | parch. | ? | ? | iv-v | ? | (7+) |
| **†*485** | Juridical frag. | Pack² 2974, *CLA* Supp. 1722 | pap. | ? | ? | iv | ? | (8+) |
| **†*486** | Juridical frag. | Pack² 2975, *CLA* Supp. 1715 | parch. | 11 x [ ][76] | 7/7.5 x [ ] | iv or v | 1? | (10+) |
| **†*487** | Juridical frag. | Pack² 2976, *CLA* viii 1218 | pap. | ? | ? | vi (E. A. L.) | ? | (14+) |
| **†*488** | Juridical frag. | Pack² 2978, *CLA* xi 1657 | pap. | ? | ? | iv-v | ? | (9+) |
| **†*489** | Juridical frag. | Pack² 2979, *CLA* Supp. 1707 | parch. | ? | 1 col. = 5.4 $\beta$ B | iv | 2 | (9+) |
| **†*490** | Legal definitions | Pack² 2982 | pap. | [ x 33][77] | ? | iv-v | 1 | [33] |
| **†*491** | Work on Criminal Law | Pack² 2984, *CLA* x 1538 | pap. | ? | ? | vi | 1 | (20+) |
| **†*492** | Juridical frag. | Pack² 2985, *CLA* viii 1033 | parch. | ? | [20] x [ ] (E. A. L.) | iv-v (E. A. L.) | 2 | (16+) |

[71]*CLA* vi 834, [23] x 30.
[72]*CLA* x 1577.
[73]Not clear from *BCH* iv (1880): 449 whether these are from a codex.
[74]Same manuscript as **OT 213.** That *Bel* in good Greek Capitals of iv/v should be written over the Codex Theodosianus (in small format) seems to me an impossibility.
[75]W. Wodke, *Christentum am Roten Meer* (1971), pp. 122ff.
[76]Assuming part of a conjugate leaf to be represented.
[77]Ed. gives no measurements for single fragments and estimates page at 30.5 x 36 (BH?).

| 1 | 2 | 3 | 4 | 5 | 6 | 7 | 8 | 9 |
|---|---|---|---|---|---|---|---|---|
| **†*493** | Juridical frag. | Pack² 2988, *CLA* Supp. 1696 | pap. | ? | ? | v (E. A. L.) | ? | (6+) |
| **†*494** | Juridical frag. | Pack² 2989, *CLA* viii 1039 | parch. | ? | ? | iv-v | ? | (33+) |
| **† 495** | Juridical frag. | Pack² 2990 | parch. | ? | ? | iv-v | ? | ? |
| **†*496** | Juridical frag. | Pack² 2991, *CLA* Supp. 1756 | pap. | ? | ? | iv-v (E. A. L.) | ? | (12+) |
| **†*496a** | Latin-Greek Grammar | Pack² 2997, *CLA* v 697 | parch. | 24 x [ ] | ? | v-vi | 2 | (23+) |
| **†*497** | Latin historical fragment | Pack² 3000, *CLA* ii 207, x 1539 | parch. | ? | ? | i A.D.[78] | 1? | (11+) |
| **† 498** | Latin-Greek Lexicon | Pack² 3007 | pap. | 17 x 18.5?[79] | ? | iv | 2 | ? |
| ***499** | Latin-Greek-Coptic Conversation Manual | Pack² 3009 | pap. | 19 x 26.5 | ? | vi | 2? | 35+ |
| **†*500** | Latin | Pack² 3018, *CLA* xi 1643 | parch. | ? | ? | vi? | 1? | (6+) |
| **†*501** | Latin unidentified | Pack² 3025, *CLA* viii 1041 | parch. | ? | ? | v-vi | ? | (6+) |
| **† 501a** | Andreas Cretensis | *Jahrb. Öst. Byz. Gesellsch.* iv (1955): 1 | paper | — | — | ix | | |
| **†*502** | Aristides Apologia | Pack² Patr. 2, P. Oxy. xv 1778 | pap. | ? | ? | iv | 1 | (19+) |
| **503** | Aristides Apologia[80] | Pack² Patr. 3, P. Lit. Lond. 223 | pap. | 13.1 x 19.5 | 10.5 x 15 | iv | 1 | 24, 27 |

| | | | | | | | | |
|---|---|---|---|---|---|---|---|---|
| † **503a** | Barnabas | *PSI* vii 757[81] | pap. | ? | ? | iv or v | 1 | (20+) |
| **504** | Basil of Caesarea | Pack² Patr. 5 = *BKT* vi 21 | pap. | [15.5 x 22] (ed.) | ? | v | 1 | [27] |
| † **505** | Basil of Caesarea | Pack² Patr. 6= P. Rein ii 62 | pap. | ? | ? | v | 1? | (17+) |
| † **505a** | Basil of Caesarea | *PSI* xiii 1296a, palimpsest[82] | parch. | | | vii/viii | | |
| † **506** | Clement of Alex.? | Pack² Patr. 10 = *JTS* xxx (1928/9): 179 | pap. | ? | ? | iv? | 1? | (14?+) |
| ***507** | St. Cyril | Pack² Patr. 13 = J. Irigoin, Type Copte p. 36 | pap. | 21.5 x 34.5/35.5[83] | 12.5/13 x 22.5 | vi or vi/vii | 1 | 29 or 30 |
| † **508** | St. Cyril | Pack² Patr. 15 = P. Rain. inv. 19913 | parch. | ? | ? | vi | ? | ? |
| **509** | St. Cyril | *CQ* xliii (1949): 5 | parch. | 28 x 38 | ? | viii | 2 | 38 |
| † **510** | John of Damascus | Pack² Patr. 17, *BKT* vi 119 | paper | ? | ? | x | ? | ? |
| ***511** | Didache | Pack² Patr. 18, P. Oxy. xv 1782 | parch. | 5 x 5.8 | — | iv or v | 1 | 7/8 |
| **512** | Didymus on Ecclesiastes | Tourah Codex III (see *Recherches de Science religieuse* lv (1967): 547ff.) | pap. | 23.5/24 x 27/27.5 | 15.5 x 18 | vi | 1 | ? |

[78] J. Mallon, *Emerita* XVII (1949): 1.
[79] May not be a codex.
[80] This leaf also contained Song of Solomon, = **OT 175.**
[81] R. A. Kraft, *Vig. Chr.* II (1967): 150.
[83] Part of same text as **N. T. Parch. 111.**
[83] E. G. T.

| 1 | 2 | 3 | 4 | 5 | 6 | 7 | 8 | 9 |
|---|---|---|---|---|---|---|---|---|
| **513** | Didymus on Genesis | Tourah Codex IV | pap. | 23 x 27 | | vi | 1 | |
| **514** | Didymus on Psalms | Pack² Patr. 19 = Tourah Codex V | pap. | 24.5 x 26.5/27 | 17/18 x 18.5/19 | vi | 1 | 30 |
| **515** | Didymus on Zachariah | Pack² Patr. 20, 21 = Tourah Codex VI | pap. | 22.5 x 27 | 15.5/18 x 19/22.5 | vi | 1 | 27 |
| **516** | Didymus on Job | Tourah Codex VII | pap. | 14.5/15.5 x 33 | 9.5/10.5 x 24 | vi | 1 | 34–36 |
| **517** | Didymus Homily | Tourah Codex VIII | pap. | 22 x 28.5 | ? | vi | ? | ? |
| † **518** | Didymus | Pack² Patr. 22, P. Iand. v 69 | pap. | | | iv | | |
| † **519** | St. Ephraem | Pack² Patr. 23 = *Wien. Stud.* xi (1889): 177 | pap. | | | vi | | |
| †***520** | St. Ephraem | Pack² Patr. 24 = *Biblica* i (1920): 371[84] | pap. | 31.5 x [ ] | ? | vii | 2 | 30 (?+) |
| † **521** | Eusebius | Pack² Patr. 25 = Monastery of Epiphanius ii 584 | pap. | | | vi-vii | | |
| † **522** | Gregory Nazianzus | Pack² Patr. 26 = *PSI* v 550 | parch. | | | ix-x | | |
| † **522a** | Gregory Nazianzus See **240** | Pack² Patr. 27 = *S. B. Wien. Akad.* 1928, Abh. 3, 87 | pap. | | | | | |

| | | | | | | | | |
|---|---|---|---|---|---|---|---|---|
| **523** | Gregory of Nyssa | Pack² Patr. 28 = *BKT* vi 38 | pap. | [16 x 22] (ed.) | ? | v | 1 | 25 |
| † **524** | Ps.=Gregory Thaumaturgus[85] | P. Colt. ii 9 | pap. | ? | ? | vii | 1 | [20–28?] |
| †***525** | Hermas | Pack² Patr. 29 = P. Amh. ii 190 | pap. | ? | [ x 18?] | vi | 1 | 30? |
| † **526** | Hermas | Pack² Patr. 30 = P. Harris 128 + *JTS* xlviii (1947): 204 | pap. | ? | ? | v | 1? | [8+] |
| ***527** | Hermas | Pack² Patr. 32 = P. Oxy. xv 1783 | parch. | 9.3 x [12/13] | 7 x 7.5/8 | iv | 1 | [14] |
| †***528** | Hermas | Pack² Patr. 33 = P. Oxy. i 5 | pap. | ? | 9.8 x [ ] | iv or v (E. G. T.) | 1 | (16+) |
| ***529** | Shepherd of Hermas | Pack² Patr. 34 = Mich. pap. 129 (inv. 917) | pap. | 11.3/11.5 x 25 | 8/9 x 19/20 | late iii | 1 | 30 |
| ***530** | Hermas | Pack² Patr. 35 = P. Oxy. ix 1172 | pap. | [13.5 x 20] | 11 x 17 | iv | 1 | 25 |
| † **531** | Hermas | Pack² Patr. 37 = P. Hamb. inv. 24 | parch. | | | iv-v | | |
| † **532** | Hermas | Pack² Patr. 38 = *Aegyptus* xvii (1937): 456 | parch. | | | iv | | |

[84]Now in Bibliothèque Nationale, Paris. See *Journal des Savants* (1970), p. 85 and Pl. I.
[85]Part of same manuscript as **352.**

| 1 | 2 | 3 | 4 | 5 | 6 | 7 | 8 | 9 |
|---|---|---|---|---|---|---|---|---|
| **†*533** | Hermas | Pack$^2$ Patr. 39 = P. Oxy. xv 1828 | parch. | ? | ? | iii | 1 | (6+) |
| **† 534** | Hermas | Pack$^2$ Patr. 40 = *BKT* vi 17 | pap. | ? | ? | vi | 1 | (15, 17) |
| ***535** | Hermas | Pack$^2$ Patr. 41 = P. Oxy. xiii 1599 | pap. | 19.8 x 24.5 | 13.5 x 18.5 | iv | 1 | 28 |
| **† 536** | Hermas | Pack$^2$ Patr. 42 = P. Oxy. iii 404 | pap. | ? | ? | iii-iv | 1? | (22+) |
| **537** | Ignatius of Antioch | Pack$^2$ Patr. 43 = *BKT* vi 1 | pap. | 19.5 x 31 | 15 x 23.5 | v | 1 | 28, 29 |
| **538** | John Chrysostom | *MPER* iv 54 | *not* a codex | | | | | |
| **† 539** | John Chrysostom? | P. Ant. iii 111 | pap. | 23.5 (?+) x [ ] | ? | vi/vii | 2 | (16+) |
| **540** | Irenaeus | F. Uebel, *Eirene* III (1964): 51 | *not* a codex | | | | | |
| **541** | Isaiah Abbas | *Annuaire de l'Inst. de Philol. et d'Hist. ar. et slaves* vii (1939): 127 | *not* a codex | | | | | |
| **† 542** | Isaiah Abbas | *Aegyptus* xxxii (1952): 464 | pap. | | | vi/vii | | |
| ***543** | Melito, On The Passion | Pack$^2$ Patr. 46 = P. Ch. B. XII + P. Mich. inv. 5333 | pap. | 14 x [27] | 11 x 23 | iv | 1 | 41–46 |

| | | | | | | | | |
|---|---|---|---|---|---|---|---|---|
| **†*544** | Melito | Pack$^2$ Patr. 47 = P. Oxy. xiii 1600 | pap. | [ x 25/26] | ? | v | 1? | (30)? |
| ***545** | Melito | Pack$^2$ Patr. 48 = P. Bodmer xiii[87] | | | | | | |
| **† 546** | Melito? | Pack$^2$ Patr. 49 = P. Oxy. xvii 2074 | pap. | ?[88] | ? | v | 1 | 21, 20 |
| **† 547** | Life of St. Nephon | Pack$^2$ Patr. 50 = *Aegyptus* xiii (1933): 11 | pap. | | | xi-xii | | |
| ***548** | Origen, Comm. on Genesis | Pack$^2$ Patr. 51 | pap. | [18/17 x 24] | 14.7 x 19.5 | iii/iv or iv | 1 | 40, 46 |
| **† 549** | Origen, Commentary Origen, Homily | Pack$^2$ Patr. 52 = *MPER* iv 51 same codex as **549** | pap. | ?[89] | ? | iv-v | 1 | (15+) |
| ***550** | Origen | Pack$^2$ Patr. 58, 53 = Tourah Codex I[90] | pap. | 14.5 x 32 | 10 x 22/23 | vi | 1 | 33–37 |
| ***551** | Origen | Pack$^2$ Patr. 54, 56, 57 = Tourah Codex II | pap. | 18 x 27.5 | 13.75 x 21.5 | vi | 1 | 34–37 |
| **† 552** | Origen | Pack$^2$ Patr. 55 = P. Bonon. 1, 1 | pap. | ? | ? | iii | 1 | (22–23+) |

[86]Same codex as Enoch **OT 222.**
[87]Part of the composite codex, see pp. 79–80.
[88]Ed. '11.8 x 14.5, not far from being complete.'
[89]Ed. suggests [19 x 25/30]. A second work of Origen in this same codex has full Breadth 18.5 and contains 28+ lines.
[90]See *Recherches de science religieuse* LV (1967): 547.

| 1 | 2 | 3 | 4 | 5 | 6 | 7 | 8 | 9 |
|---|---|---|---|---|---|---|---|---|
| **†*553** | Origen? | Pack$^2$ Patr. 60 = BM Egerton pap. 3 | pap. | [15.2] x [ ] | ? | iii | 2 | 32+ |
| **†*554** | Romanus | Pack$^2$ Patr. 62 = *MPER* iii 41 | pap. | ? | ? | v | 1 | (9+) |
| **† 555** | Diatessaron? | Pack$^2$ Patr. 64 = *ZNTW* xxxvii (1938): 223 | pap. | ? | ? | v-vi | | |
| **†*556** | Theophilus of Alexandria | P. Oxy. xxxi 2531 | pap. | ? | ? | vi? | 1? | (19?) |
| ***BIBLE Aleph** | | Codex Sinaiticus, BM Add. 43725 | parch. | 35 x 40[91] | 25 x 24 (4 cols.) | iv | 4 and 2 | 48 |
| ***Bible 'A'** | Alexandrinas | BM Royal Mss 1D. V–VIII | parch. | 26.4 x 31.6 | 20 x 22.4 | v | 2 | 46-52, usually |
| ***Bible 'B'** | Vaticanus | Vat gr. 1209 | parch. | 27 x 27[92] | | iv | 3 | 42 |
| ***Bible 'C'** | Codex Ephraemi rescriptus | Paris BN gr. 9 | parch. | 27 x 33[93] | | vi (Cavallo) | 1 | 40-46 |
| ***Bible 'D'** | Codex Bezae | Cambridge Nn 2-41 | parch. | 22 x 25.4[94] (Metzger) | | v | 1 | 33 |
| ***Bible 'D$^P$'** | Claromontanus, St. Paul | Paris BN gr. 107 | parch. | 19.7 x 24.8[95] (Pal. Soc.) | | v | 1 | 21 |
| ***Bible 'E'** | Laudianus Acts | Bodl. Laud. gr. 35 | parch. | 21.5/22.6 x 26.1/27.1 | | vi or vii | 2 | 22-26 |
| ***Bible 'G'** | Sarravianus-Colbertinus Heptateuch | Leyden Voss. gr. Quadratus 8 + BN gr. 17 + Leningrad | parch. | 23.8 x 25 | 17 x 16 | iv/v | 2 | 27/28 |

| | | | | | | | |
|---|---|---|---|---|---|---|---|
| ***Bible 'H'** | Coislinianus, St. Paul | Paris Coislin. 202 + BN supp. gr. 1074 (+ Athos, Kiev, Leningrad, Moscow, Turin) | parch. | 25 x 30[96] (Cavallo, Turin Leaf) | v/vi | 1 | 16 |
| ***Bible 'M'** | Octateuch-Kings Coislinianus 1 | Paris Coislin. 1 | parch. | 25 x 36 | vi | 2 | 49 |
| ***Bible 'N'** | Purpureus Petro-politanus—Gospels | Leningrad Publ. Lib. cod. gr. 537 + Athens, Lerma, BM, NY, Patmos, Rome, Vienna | parch. | 28.5/28.8 x 33/33.7 (Hatch) | vi | 2 | 16 |
| ***Bible 'O'** | Sinopensis purpureus—Matthew | Paris BN suppl. gr. 1286 | parch. | 25 x 30 | vi | 1 | 15, 16 |
| ***Bible 'Q'** | Marchalianus—Prophets | Vat. gr. 2125 | parch. | 17.9 x 29.5 | vii/viii | 1 | 29 |
| ***Bible 'K'** | Nitriensis, St. Luke = **N. T. Parch. 38** | BM Add. 17211 | parch. | 21.3/23.4 x 28.8/30.5 | v late | 2 | 25 |
| ***Bible 'T'** | Codex Borgianus, Gospels = **N. T. Parch. 44** | Borg. Copt. 109[65] | parch. | 18.8/21 x 22.3/24.9 (Hatch) | vi? | 2 | 27-31 |
| ***Bible Ξ** | Codex Zacynthius (Luke) | Brit. & Foreign Bible Soc.no. 24 | parch. | | | | |

[91] T. C. Skeat, *Cambr. Hist. Bible*, p. 77.
[92] *Pal. Soc.* I, 104, 25.4 x 26.7.
[93] 25.6/26.4 x 31.4/32.5 Hatch.
[94] 17/22.9 x 25.8/26.7 Hatch.
[95] 19/20.1 x 24.5/24.8 Hatch.
[96] 18.2/21.7 x 26.2/28.2 Hatch (Paris leaf).

| 1 | 2 | 3 | 4 | 5 | 6 | 7 | 8 | 9 |
|---|---|---|---|---|---|---|---|---|
| ***Bible Σ** | Rossanensis purpureus, Gospels | Rossano | parch. | 26 x 30.7 | | vi | 2 | 20 |
| **Bible Φ** | Beratinus purpureus (Gospels) | Berat | parch. | | | vi | | |
| ***Bible** | Genesis | Vienna Theol. gr. 31 | parch. | 27 x 33.3 (probably trimmed down)[97] | | vi | 1 | 15 + miniature across full width |
| **CLASSICAL 1** | Cassius Dio | Vat. gr. 1288 | parch. | 22.9 x 30.5 (cut: once 'square'?) | ? | v | 3? | 42 |
| ***CLASSICAL 2** | Dioscorides | Vienna Med. gr. 1 | parch. | 29 x 34.6 (measured E. G. T.), 30.5 x 36.5 (Pal. Soc.), 29.2 x 37 (Cavallo) | | c. A.D. 510 | 1 | 27+ |
| **†*CLASSICAL 3** | Euripides Phaethon Palimpsest | | parch. | | | | | |
| **†*CLASSICAL 4** | Euripides 'H' Jerusalem palimpsest | | parch. | 12/14 x 17/18 | | x? | 1 | |
| ***CLASSICAL 5** | Homer Ilias Ambrosiana | Ambros. 1019 olim F. 205 inf. | parch. | [28.8 x 32.6) (Bianchi Bandinelli) | | vi? | 1 | (illustrated) |
| ***CLASSICAL 6** | Homer, 'Cureton Iliad' | BM Add. 17210 | parch. | 23.8 x 30.2 (Pal. Soc.) | | v/vi | 1 | 33 |
| ***CLASSICAL 7** | Strabo Palimpsest | Vat. gr. 2306 | parch. | 26 x 28.1 (Cavallo) | | vi | | |

| | | | | | | | | |
|---|---|---|---|---|---|---|---|---|
| ***C 1** | Deut., Jonah, Acts | BM Or. 7594[98] | pap. | 16.5 x 29.2 ([31] Budge) | 12 x 23 | A.D. 330-350 (Cavallo v) | 1 | 29–38 |
| ***C 2** | St. John | 'Q', Brit. & Foreign Bible Soc.[99] | pap. | 12 x 25.3 ([12.5 x 25]) | 8.5 x 20.5 | iv | 1 | 34–37 |
| ***C 3** | ?, Melito, 1 Peter, Jonah, + | Mississippi Coptic i[100] | pap. | 15.2 x 14.6 | c. 13 x 10 | iii or iv | 2 | 11–18 |
| ***C 4** | Jeremiah, Lamentations, etc. | P. Bodmer xxii + Mississippi Coptic ii | parch. | 12 x 14 (14.8 Willis) | 9 x 9.8 | iv (Willis), iv/v (Kasser) | 1 | 18 |
| ***C 5** | Pistis Sophia | BM Or. Add. 5114 (Crum, Catal. 367) | parch. | 17 x 21.2 | 14 x 16.7 | iv or v? | 2 | 30–34 |
| ***C 6** | Proverbs | Berlin Or. oct. 987[101] | pap. | 14.3 x 12.2 | | iv? | 1 | 15–17 |
| ***C 7** | Pauline Epistles | P. Vogliano v | pap. | 16.5 x 27.5 | 11 x 19.5 | v? | 1 | 28–31 |
| ***C 8** | 1 Clement | Berlin Or. fol. 3065[102] | pap. | 12 x 25 | 8 x 12 | iv? | 1 | 28–32 |
| ***C 9** | Epistula Apostolorum | Inst. fr. arch. Or.[103] | pap. | 14 x 15 | 10.5 x 9.5 | iv (E.G.T.) | 1 | 14–15 |
| ***C 10** | Apocalypse of Elias | Paris BN copte 135 + Berlin P 1862[104] | pap. | 12.5/13 x 14.5/15.5 | 8.5/9 x 10/12.5 | iv or v | 1 | 21 |

[97] H. Gerstinger, *Wiener Genesis*, I. p. 31.
[98] Wallis Budge, *Coptic Biblical Texts in the Dialect of Upper Egypt* (1912); H. Thompson, *The New Biblical Papyrus* (1913).
[99] Ed. H. Thompson (1924).
[100] W. H. Willis, *Proc. IX Int. Congress Papyrology*, pp. 383ff.
[101] A. Böhlig, *Der Achm. Proverbientext* (Studien z. Erforschung d. christl. Ägyptens 3, xxi, 1958).
[102] *Texte und Untersuchungen* 32 (1908), Heft 1.
[103] *Texte und Untersuchungen* 43.
[104] *Texte und Untersuchungen* 17, 3a.

| 1 | 2 | 3 | 4 | 5 | 6 | 7 | 8 | 9 |
|---|---|---|---|---|---|---|---|---|
| ***C11** | Apocalypse of Elias and of Sophonaia | Paris BN copte 135[105] | pap. | 9.5/11 x 25 | 7/8 x 22/23 | v? | 1 | |
| ***C 12** | Exodus | Paris BN copte 135[106] | pap. | 18 x 25 | 14.5 x 21 | v or vi | 1 | 39–43 |
| **C 13** | Sirach | BN copte 135[107] | pap. | 19 x 33.5 | 15.5 x ? | vi? | 1 | |
| **†*C 14** | 2 Maccabees Roll | BN copte 135[108] | pap. | | | v? | | |
| **C 15** | Luke | BN copte 135[109] | pap. | [15] x 25 | | iv or v | 1 | 35–37 |
| ***C 16** | | Phillipps Codex A (W. E. Crum, Der *Papcodex . . . der Phillipps bibliothek* . . . [1915]) | pap. | 14 x 18.5 | 10.5/11 x 14.5 | vi/vii | 1 | 20 |
| **† C 17** | | Phillipps Codex B | parch. | | | A.D. 1003 | | |
| ***C 18** | Acts | Pierpont Morgan Glazier G 67 | parch. | 10 x 11.5 | | iv or v | 1 | 16 |
| **† C 19** | Extracts from Synaxary | Pierpont Morgan Coptic C 31 | paper | | | c. A.D. 860 | | |
| ***C 20** | Prayer of Mary | P. Iand. Inv. 9 A & B | pap. | 12.5 x 13 | | vi? | 1 | 17 |
| **†*C 21** | | Phillipps Coptic[110] | pap. | | | viii? | | |
| **† C 22** | Salomonic Bks[110a] | | pap. | 27 x 36 | | vii or viii | | |
| **† C 23** | | BM Or. 5000, Crum Coptic Cat. 940 | | | | | | |

| | | | | | | | | |
|---|---|---|---|---|---|---|---|---|
| † **C 24** | | BM Or. 5001, Crum Coptic Cat. 171 | | | | | | |
| **C 25** | Job | Mich. inv. 1290,[111] 1292, 1293, 1517 | pap. | 15 x 27.8 | | ? | | |
| † **C 26** | | Mich. inv. copt. 3992[112] | pap. | 9/10 x 14/15 | ? | iii?, not later than iv | | |
| ***C 27** | 1 Peter | BM Or. 4918(2)[113] | parch. | 6.5 x [7.5] | 4.2 x [6.9] | v | 1 | [12] |
| **C 28** | St. John | Mich. inv. 6896[114] | parch. | 5.3 x 6.5 (?+) | | ? | | |
| ***C 29** | Prayers, Abgar, Liturgy, etc. | Ms d'Anastasy 9[115] | pap. | 14 x 21.7 | 10 x 16.5 | vi or vii | 1 | 27 |
| ***C 30** | Isaiah | P. Bodmer xxiii | pap. | [13.5 x 20] | 9.5 x 14.5/16 | iv | 1 | 23–26 |
| **C 31** | Manichaean Kephalaia[116] | P. Berl. | pap. | 18 x 31.5 | 13 x 22 | iv or v | 1 | |
| **C 32** | Manichaean Homilies | P. Ch. B., ed. H. J. Polotsky | pap. | 18 x 31.5 | 13 x 20 | iv or v | 1 | 33 |
| ***C 33** | Manichaean Psalm Book | P. Ch. B., ed. C. R. C. Alberry | pap. | 17.5 x 27 | 10/11 x 16.5/17.5 | iv (or v?) | 1 | 30 |

[105] *Texte und Untersuchungen* 17, 4.
[106] *BIFAO* viii 43.
[107] *BIFAO* viii 64.
[108] *BIFAO* viii 68.
[109] *BIFAO* viii 76.
[110] Sotheby's Catalogue 30. xi. 71, lot 484.
[110a] H.Thompson, *The Coptic (Sahidic) Version of Certain Books Of the O.T.*, 1908; W. E. Crum, *JTS* xi (1910): 310 ff.
[111] Described in Worrell, *Coptic Texts in Univ. Mich.*, p. 5.
[112] Described only, *ibid.* p. 5.
[113] W. H. Willis, *Studies . . . B. L. Ullmann* I (1964): 265.
[114] Described in Worrell, *Coptic Texts* (cf. C **25**), p. 7.
[115] W. Pleyte and P. A. Boeser, *Manuscrits Coptes du Musée d'Antiquités des Pays-Bas*, (Leiden, 1897), pp. 441ff.
[116] Sizes as given in *SB Berlin* (1933), p. 82.

| 1 | 2 | 3 | 4 | 5 | 6 | 7 | 8 | 9 |
|---|---|---|---|---|---|---|---|---|
| ***C 34** | NT Apocrypha | Berlin P. 8502 (TU 60, 1955) | pap. | 13.5/10 x 15[117] | 10/7 x 11/ 13.8 | v | 1 | 17–24 |
| **C 35** | Pauline Letters (Sahidic) | Vienna K 7661-7, *SB Wein* (1914). no. 5 | pap. | 25.5 x [33] | ? | v-vi | 2 | 33/34 |
| ***C 41** | | Nag Hammadi I[118] | pap. | 14.4 x 30 | | iv | 1 | ? |
| ***C 42** | | Nag Hammadi II | pap. | 15.4/14.5-13.8/13.5 x 28.4 | | iv | 1 | |
| ***C 43** | | Nag Hammadi III | pap. | 15.6/7–14.1 x 25.7 | | iv | 1 | |
| ***C 44** | | Nag Hammadi IV | pap. | 10.7/12.3-13.2/12.4 x 23.6 | | iv | 1 | |
| ***C 45** | | Nag Hammadi V | pap. | 13.3/12.3/ 11.3 x 24 | | iv | 1 | |
| ***C 46** | | Nag Hammadi VI | pap. | 14.7/14.9-12.9 x 27.9 | | iv | 1 | |
| ***C 47** | | Nag Hammadi VII | pap. | 17.3/17.5-15.2 x 29.1 | | iv (after A.D. 342) | 1 | |
| ***C 48** | | Nag Hammadi VIII | pap. | 14.7/14.9-12.0 x 24.2 | | iv | 1 | |
| ***C 49** | | Nag Hammadi IX | pap. | 13.7/15.1 x 26.3 | | iv | 1 | |
| ***C 50** | | Nag Hammadi X | pap. | 12.1-11.4 x 25.6 [? 26.9] | | iv | 1 | |
| ***C 51** | | Nag Hammadi XI | pap. | 14.3/14.2/ 13.7 x 28.2 | | iv | 1 | |
| ***C 52** | | Nag Hammadi XII | pap. | [19 x 26][119] | | iv | 1 | |

| | | | | | | | | |
|---|---|---|---|---|---|---|---|---|
| ***C 53** | | Nag Hammadi XIII | pap. | 13.8 x 27.2 | | iv | 1 | |
| ***Lat. 1** | Augustine | Paris BN Lat. 11641 + Gen.. M. I 16 (97) P Leningrad F1 (*CLA* v 614) | pap. and parch. | 22 x 32/33 | 16 x 25 | vii-viii (E. A. L.) | 1 | 28–33 |
| ***Lat. 2** | Avitus | Paris BN Lat. 8913 + 8914 (*CLA* v 573) | pap. | 29/29.6 x 30/30.3 | 26 x 28 | vi | 1 | 18–23 |
| †***Lat. 3** | Breviarium Alarici | Paris BN Lat. 12475 (pp. 1-19) (p. 10) (*CLA* v 703a, b) | pap. | ? | ? | vi or vii | 1 | (19+) |
| ***Lat. 4** | Cicero Cat. i, ii, Psalmus Responsorius | see **446a** P. Barc. | pap. | 11.4 x 12.6[120] | c. 10 x 10 | iv | 1 | 23 |
| ***Lat. 5** | Hilarius, de Trinitate, etc. | Vindob. lat. 2160 + etc. (*CLA* x 1507) | pap. | 20.4 x 27.2 | 12/14 x 21.5/22 | vi (before 556) | 1 | c. 30 |
| ***Lat. 6** | Josephus, Antiquitates | Milan, Ambrosiana Cimelio Ms 1 (*CLA* iii 304) | pap. | 24 x 34 | 18 x 24.5/26 | vi | 1 | 30–39 |
| ***Lat. 7** | Isidorus, Synonyma | St. Gall. Stiftsbibl. 226 + etc. (*CLA* vii 929) | pap. | 15.5 x 22.5 (? cut down) | 11/11.5 x 16 | vii | 1 | 20–24 |

[117]Variations in size of a single quire codex.

[118]Numbering follows M. Krause, *MDAIK* xviii and xix (1962 and 1963); see further J. M. Robinson, *The Facsimile Edition of the Nag Hammadi Codices* (1972), 17-19. The sizes have been remeasured by J. M. Robinson: when three measurements are given for B(readth), the first is early in the codex, the second at the middle, the third at the end.

[119]Surviving pieces are 15.2 x 23.8.

[120]Largest recorded dimensions.

| 1 | 2 | 3 | 4 | 5 | 6 | 7 | 8 | 9 |
|---|---|---|---|---|---|---|---|---|
| † **Lat. 8** | Justinian, Digest | Pommersfelden, Lat. pap. 1, *CLA* ix 1351 | pap. | ?[121] | ? | vi | 1 | [30] |
| † **Lit. 1** | Marcus anaphora | P. Ryl. iii 465 + P. Lit. Lond. 232[122] | parch. | ? | ? | vi/vii | 1? | (11+) |
| **Lit. 2** | Euchologium | C. H. Roberts, E. B. Capelle, *An Early Euchologium* (1949) | pap. | [17.5 x 26.5] (minimum ed.) | ? | vi | 1 | 27–32 |
| † **Lit. 3** | Hymn Possibly *not* a codex | P. Erlangen 2 | pap. | ? | ? | vi/vii? | 1 | (15+) |
| ***Lit. 4** | Liturgical Book | BM Egerton pap. 5[123] | pap. | 16 x 19 | 13 x 15 | iv–v | 1 | 17/18 |
| † **Lit. 5** | 'Great prayer' | *Klio* xli, 234; *Klio* xlii, 337 | parch. | | | ? | | |
| **Lit. 6** | Legend of St. George | P. Colt ii 6 | pap. | 10 x 23.5 | ? | vii | 1 | 16 |
| †***Lit. 7** | Martyrology of St. Mamas | P. Oxy. vi 851 | pap. | [20] x [ ] | 16 x [ ] | v or vi | 1 | (3+) |
| ***Lit. 8** | Prayers | P. Berol. 13415[124] | pap. | 16 x 28 | 14 x 23 | v (E. G. T.; iv ed.) | 1 | 36 |
| **Lit. 9** | Liturgical Book | *VBP* iv 58 | pap. | 16.5 x 19.7 | ? | viii? | 1 | 26, [29] |
| **Lit. 10** | Acrostic Hymn | BKT vi 8 p. 125 | pap. | 4.5 x 6 | | iv | | 7–8 |
| ***M1** | Magic | *PGM* I iv (Paris BN suppl. gr. 574) | pap. | 9.5/13 x 27/30.5 | e.g. 10 x 26.5 | iv | 1 | 50 |
| ***M2** | Magic | Pack[2] 1866 = P. Lond. i 46 = *PGM* I v | pap. | 12.3/11.3 x 28 | 9.5/10 x 24 | iv | 1 | 37 |

| | | | | | | | | |
|---|---|---|---|---|---|---|---|---|
| ***M3** | Magic | *PGM* II xiii – P. Lugd. Bat. 'W' Leemans I 395 | pap. | 15/16 x 26.5/27 | ? | iv | 1 | 33, 34, 36, 47 |
| ***M4** | | P. Lugd. Bat. 'X' Leemans I 397 | pap. | 17 x 30 | | iv | 1 | 28, 41, 44 |
| ***M5** | | O. Lagercrantz, *Papyrus graecus holmiensis* (Uppsala, 1913). (P. Holm) | pap. | 16.5 x 29/30 | | iv | 1 | 41–48 |
| **Misc. 1** | Tax register | P. Lond. iv 1419 | pap. | 26 x 33.8 | | viii (after A.D. 716) | 1 | 24–26 long lines |
| ***Misc. 2** | Land-tax register | Forsch. & Fortschritte xxxv, 23 ff. | pap. | 11 x 21.5 | | vii | 1 | 17–18 |
| **Misc. 3** | Georgian Psalter | M. Sinai MS[125] | pap. | | | | | |
| ***Misc. 4** | Greek Mani Codex | P. Coln. inv. 4780[126] | parch. | 3.5 x 4.5 | 2.5 x 3.5 | iv or iv/v | 1 | 22–25 |
| **†*NT Apocrypha 1** | Gospel of Thomas | Logia Jesu 1897 = P. Oxy. i 1 | pap. | ? | ? | ii/iii | 1 | (21+) |
| **NT Apocrypha 1A** | *Roll* (Gospel of Thomas) | Logia Jesu P. Oxy. iv 654 | pap. | | | | | |

[121]Tjäder assesses size as [15 x 25].
[122]*Aegyptus* 30, 3.
[123]H. I. Bell, T. C. Skeat, *Fragments of an Unknown Gospel*, no. 4.
[124]C. Schmidt, *N. T. Studien G. Heinrici* 66.
[125]A. S. 'Atiyah, *A History of Eastern Christianity* (1968), p. xi.
[126]*ZPE* v (1970), Heft 2, pp. 97–216.

| 1 | 2 | 3 | 4 | 5 | 6 | 7 | 8 | 9 |
|---|---|---|---|---|---|---|---|---|
| †***NT Apocrypha 2** | Wisdom of Jesus | P. Oxy. viii 1081 | pap. | ? | 9/9.5 x [ ] | iv | 1 | (26+) |
| ***NT Apocrypha 3** | Gospel | P. Oxy. v 840 | parch. | 7.4 x 8.8 | 5.5 x 5.5 | iv | 1 | 22/23 |
| †***NT Apocrypha 4** | Gospel | P. Oxy. x 1224 | pap. | ? | ? | iv | 1 or 2? | ? |
| †***NT Apocrypha 5** | Gospel of Mary | P. Ryl. iii 463 | pap. | ? | 7.5 x [ ] | iii | 1 | (16+) |
| †***NT Apocrypha 6** | Abgar *Not* a codex, single sheet | P. Colt 7 | pap. | 29.9 x 30.5 | | vi/vii | | |
| †***NT Apocrypha 7** | Gospel? | BM Egerton pap. 2[127] | pap. | ? | ? | ii | 1 | (21+) |
| †***NT Apocrypha 8** | Acts of John | P. Oxy. vi 850 | pap. | ? | ? | iv | 1 | (19+) |
| ***NT Apocrypha 9** | Acta Pauli | G. Wahl, W. Schubart, C. Schmidt, *Praxeis Paulou*[128] | pap. | 20 x 26 | 17 x 22 | iii/iv | 1 | 33–40 |
| † **NT Apocrypha 10** | Acta Pauli | P. Mich. inv. 3788[129] | pap. | ? | ? | iii/iv | 1 | (13+) |
| †***NT Apocrypha 11** | Acta Pauli | *HTR* xxxi (1938): 73 | pap. | ? | ? | iv (E. G. T.; iii ed.) | 1 | (35+) |
| ***NT Apocrypha 12** | Acts of Paul and Thecla | P. Ant. i 13 | parch. | 7.2 x [9] | 4 x 5 | iv | 1 | 11 |
| ***NT Apocrypha 13** | Acts of Peter | P. Oxy. vi 849 | parch. | 9 x 9.8 | 6 x 7.3 | iii (iv ed.) | 1 | 14 |
| ***NT Apocrypha 14** | Protevangelium of Mary, Letter of Corinthians to | P. Bodmer. See Table 12 | | | | | | |

| | | | | | | | | |
|---|---|---|---|---|---|---|---|---|
| | Paul, + 11th Ode of Solomon (composite codex) | | | | | | | |
| † **NT Apocrypha 15** | Ezekiel Apocryphon | P. Mich. inv. 5553 + P. Ch. B. 185[130] | pap. | - | - | iv | - | - |
| ***NT Apocrypha 16** | vi Ezra | P. Oxy. vii 1010 | parch. | 5.6 x 8.4 | 3.0 x 5.5 | iv | 1 | 12 |
| ***NT Apocrypha 17** | Protevangelium | P. Grenfell i 8 | parch. | 6.5 x 9.6 | ? | v or vi | 1 | 14 or 15 |

*New Testament Papyri*

P + fig. = No. in Gregory-Von Dobschutz-Aland list; *no* P no. means not yet in that list.

| | | | | | | | | |
|---|---|---|---|---|---|---|---|---|
| ***P 1** | Matt. i 1- | P. Oxy. i 2 | pap. | 12 x [24.7] | ? | iii | 1 | 33 |
| † **P 2** | John xii 12-15 | *Studi religiosi* vi (1906): 129 | pap. | ? | ? | vi | | |
| † **P 3** | Luke vii, x (kephalaia) | *Wiener Studien* (1882), 198; (1963), 163 | pap. | ? | ? | vi/vii? | 1 | (25+) |
| ***P 4** | Luke v-vi | *MIFAO* ix, 2; *Rev. biblique* xlvii (1938): 1 | pap. | 13.5 x 17 | 10 x 13.3 | iii or iii/iv | 2 | 35 |
| ***P 5** | John i, xvi, xx | P. Oxy. 208 + 1781 | pap. | [12.5 x 25] | ? | iii | 1 | 27 |
| † **P 6** | John x, xi (Greek, Achmimic) | | pap. | | | iv-vii? | | |
| † **P 7** | Luke iv 1 - (quotation) | K. Aland, *N. T. Studies* iii (1957):262 | pap. | ? | ? | v | | |

[127]H. I. Bell, T. C. Skeat, *Fragments of An Unknown Gospel,* 1f.
[128]**OT 171** is part of same Ms.
[129]*HTR* xxxvi, 165; *JTS* xlvii, 196.
[130]C. Bonner, *Studies & Documents* XII.

| 1 | 2 | 3 | 4 | 5 | 6 | 7 | 8 | 9 |
|---|---|---|---|---|---|---|---|---|
| † **P 8** | Acts iv 31-v 2 vi, 1- | | pap. | | | iv | | |
| †***P 9** | 1 John iv 11- | P. Oxy. iii 402 | pap. | ? | [9 x 9]? | iv/v (E. G. T.) | 1 | 15 |
| **P 10** | Rom. i 1-7 *Not* a codex | P. Oxy. ii 209 | | | | | | |
| † **P 11, P 14** | 1 Cor. i- | K. Aland, *N. T. Studies* iii (1957): 268; K. Treu, *Forsch. und Fortschritte* xxxi (1957): 185 | pap. | | | v or vii? | | |
| **P 12** | Heb. i 1 *Not* a codex | P. Amh. i 3 b | pap. | ? | ? | iii | | |
| **P 13** | Heb. ii, x, xiii *Roll* | P. Oxy. iv 657 etc. | pap. | — | — | iii/iv (E. G. T.) | | |
| † **P 14** | 1 Cor. i 25– | | pap. | | | v? | | |
| ***P 15** | 1 Cor. vii 18– | P. Oxy. vii 1008 | pap. | [18] x 26.5 | [14] x 21 | iv (E. G. T.) | 1 | 37, 38 |
| **P 16** | Phil. iii, iv. Same codex as **P 15** | P. Oxy. vii 1009 | | | | | | |
| † **P 17** | Heb. ix 12– | P. Oxy. viii 1078 | pap. | ? | [ x 17.5] | iv | 1 | 15? |
| **P 18** | Rev. i *Roll* | P. Oxy. viii 1079 | | | | | | |
| ***P 19** | Matt. x 32–xi | P. Oxy. ix 1170 | pap. | [16] x 23 | [13] x 19 | iv/v (E. G. T.) | 1 | 22/23 |
| †***P 20** | James ii 19– | P. Oxy. ix 1171 | pap. | [ x 16] | [ x 13] | iii | 1 | 26 |
| †***P 21** | Matt. xii 24– | P. Oxy. x 1227 | pap. | ? | ? | iv/v | 1? | (11+) |
| **P 22** | John xv, xvi *Roll* | P. Oxy. x 1228 | | | | | | |
| †***P 23** | James i 10– | P. Oxy. x 1229 | pap. | 11.2 x [ ] | ? | iii or iv | 1 | (28)? |
| † **P 24** | Rev. v 5– | P. Oxy. x 1230 | pap. | ? | ? | iv | 1 | (8+) |
| † **P 25** | Matt. xviii, xix | | pap. | | | iv (Metzger) v-vi (Hedley) | | |

| | | | | | | | | |
|---|---|---|---|---|---|---|---|---|
| †***P 26** | Rom. i 1– | P. Oxy. xi 1354 | pap. | ?[131] | ? | vi or vii | 1 | 23 |
| †***P 27** | Rom. viii, ix | P. Oxy. xi 1355 | pap. | ? | [10 x 24]? | iii | 1 | 41? |
| ***P 28** | John vi 8– | P. Oxy. xiii 1596 | pap. | [12/13 x 20.5] | [10 x 17] | iii (iv Grenfell & Hunt) | 1 | 26 |
| †***P 29** | Acts xxvi 7– | P. Oxy. xiii 1597 | pap. | ? | ? | iii/iv | 1 | (6+) |
| †***P 30** | 1 & 2 Thess. | P. Oxy. xiii 1598 | pap. | ? | ? | iii/iv | 1 | 33 |
| **P 31** | Rom. xii 3 *Not* a codex | P. Ryl. I 4 | | | | | | |
| ***P 32** | Titus i, ii | P. Ryl. i 5 | pap. | [15 x 20] | [12 x 15] | iii[132] | 1 | 26 |
| † **P 33 + P 58** | Acts xv–, Acts vii | *SPP* xii no. 190; ***MPER*** iv 41 | pap. | ?[133] | ? | vi | 1 | ? |
| † **P 34** | 1 Cor. xvi–, 2 Cor. v, x Lectionary | *SPP* xii no. 191 | pap. | ? | ? | vii | 2 | (20+) |
| †***P 35** | Matt. xxv 12– | *PSI* i 1 | pap. | [ x 25] | [10.7 x 19] | iii/iv | 1 | (31) |
| †***P 36** | John iii 14– | *PSI* i 3 | pap. | ?[134] | ? | vi | 1? | (10+) |
| ***P 37** | Matt. xxvi 19– | P. Mich. iii 137 | pap. | [12+ x 25] | ? | iv (iii ed.) | 1 | 33 |
| ***P 38** | Acts xviii 26– | P. Mich. iii 138 | pap. | ? | ? | iii/iv (iii ed.) | 1 | 37 |
| ***P 39** | John viii 14– | P. Oxy. xv 1780 | pap. | [16] x 25.6 | ? | late iii | 1 | 25 |
| † **P 40** | Rom. i etc. | *VBP* iv 57 | pap. | ? | ? | v/vi ? (ed.) | 1 | (33+)? |
| † **P 41** | Acts Greek = Sahidic | Vienna K7541-8[135] | pap. | [24 x 30] (Weigandt) | ? | viii-ix | 2 | ? |
| † **P 42** | Luke i 54–, ii 29 | *Monumenta biblica et eccles.* v (1939): 112 | pap. | | | vii-viii | | |
| † **P 43** | Rev. ii 12–, xv 8– Lectionary | *Wadi Sarga*, pp. 43–5 | pap. | | | vi/vii | | |

[131] Ed.'s estimate [18 x 28].
[132] ii Bell-Skeat, *Frags. of an Unknown Gospel*, p. 6.
[133] Sanz suggests [22 x 28] for **P 58.**
[134] Ed. says 'piccolo formato c. 14(B) x 9(H)'. There is no parallel for such a format. Cf. further A. Carlini, *Archiv. Pap.* xxii (1973): 219.
[135] P. Weigandt in K. Aland, *Materialen* LIV.

| 1 | 2 | 3 | 4 | 5 | 6 | 7 | 8 | 9 |
|---|---|---|---|---|---|---|---|---|
| † **P 44** | Matt. xvii etc. Lectionary | Monastery of Epiphanius ii, 120 | pap. | | | vi-vii | | |
| ***P 45** | Gospels & Acts | P. Ch. B. I[136] | pap. | [20.4 x 25.4] | 16 x [19] | iii | 1 | 39 |
| ***P 46** | Pauline Epistles | P. Ch. B. II, P. Mich. 6238 | pap. | 13.5/15.2 x [26.5/27] | 10.3/12.6 x 17.8/20.3 | iii | 1 | 25–28, 28–31 |
| ***P 47** | Revelation | P. Ch. B. III | pap. | [14 x 24.2] | 10.2 x [19.5] | iii? | 1 | 25–30 |
| †***P 48** | Acts xxiii 11– | *PSI* x 1165 | pap. | ? | 10.5 x [ ] | iii/iv (E. G. T.) | 1 | (20+) |
| † **P 49** | Eph. iv 16– | *HTR* li (1958): 33 | pap. | ?[137] | ? | iii (ed., iii/iv ?) | 1 | [30] |
| † **P 50** | Acts viii 26– *Not* a codex | *Quantulacumque* 163 | | | | | | |
| †***P 51** | Galatians | P. Oxy. xviii 2157 | pap. | ? | [ x 21] | iv/v | 1 | 38? |
| ***P 52** | John xviii 31– | P. Ryl. iii 457 | pap. | [18 x 21.3] | [14 x 16.3] | ii | 1? | [18?] |
| †***P 53** | Matt. xxvi 29–, Acts ix 33– | *Quantulacumque* 151 | pap. | ? | 7.5/8 x [17] | iii | 1 | [25–26] |
| † **P 54** | John ii 16- iii 2– | P. Princeton ii 15 | pap. | ? | ? | v/vi | 1? | 25? |
| † **P 55** | John i 31– | *MPER* iv 35 | pap. | ? | ? | vi | 1 | (15+) |
| † **P 56** | Acts i 1– | *MPER* iv 39 | pap. | ? | ? | v/vi | 1? | 29? |
| † **P 57** | Acts iv 36– | *MPER* iv 40 | pap. | ? | ? | v | 1? | (10+) |
| **P 58** | Acts vii See **P 33** | | pap. | [22 x 28] Sanz | | | | |
| † **P 59** | John i 26– | P. Colt 3 | pap. | ?[138] | ? | vii | 1 | 7–19 |
| † **P 60** | John xvi 29– | P. Colt 4 | pap. | ? | ? | vii | 1 | (5–20+) |
| † **P 61** | Rom. xvi 23– | P. Colt 5 | pap. | ? | [14/15 x 20] | vii | 1? | (13+) |
| **P 62** | Matt. xi 25– Greek-Coptic lectionary | *Symbolae Osl.* xxiv (1945): 121 | pap. | 5.6 x 6.6 | ? | iv? | 1 | 7 |

| | | | | | | | | |
|---|---|---|---|---|---|---|---|---|
| ***P 63** | John iii 14– | *Biblica* 34 (1953): 13 | pap. | 18.5 x 30 | ? | v-vi | 1 | (13) |
| † **P64, 67** | St. Matt. iii–, xxvi– | **64** = *HTR* xlvi (1953): 233 **67** = R. Roca-Puig, *Un Papiro griego del evangelio de San Marco* (Barcelona, 1956) | pap. | [13/12 x 18/17]?? (assuming 2 columns) | [10.5/11 x 16/17] | ii | 2? | 36–39? |
| **P 65** | 1 Thess. i–, ii– | *PSI* xiv 1373 | pap. | | | iii | | |
| | See **P 49** | | | | | | | |
| ***P 66** | St. John i– | P. Bodmer ii | pap. | 14.2 x 16.2 | 11 x 11 | iii | 1 | 20 |
| † **P 67** | Matt. iii– See **P 64** | | | | | | | |
| † **P 68** | 1 Cor. iv 12– | K. Aland, *New Testament Studies* iii (1957): 266 | pap. | ? | ? | vii? | ? | ? |
| †***P 69** | Luke xxiii 41– | P. Oxy. xxiv 2383 | pap. | [13/12 x 33] | [9 x 28] | iii | 1 | [48 - 50] |
| †***P 70** | Matt. xi 26– | P. Oxy. xxiv 2384 | pap. | ? | ? | iv | ? | [28/29] |
| †***P 71** | Matt. xix 10– | P. Oxy. xxiv 2385 | pap. | ? | [ x 16/17] | iv | 1 | [31–32] |

136 + P. Vindob., *Aegyptus* (1933), 67.
137 Ed. suggest [18 x 25].
138 Ed. gives about [13 x 19.5], but 'state is bad.'

| 1 | 2 | 3 | 4 | 5 | 6 | 7 | 8 | 9 |
|---|---|---|---|---|---|---|---|---|
| ***P 72** | Jude, 1 & 2 Peter | P. Bodmer, vii, viii[139] | pap. | 14.2 x 15.5 | | iv (E. G. T.) | 1 | 16–18 |
| † **P 73** | Matt. xxv 43– | P. Bodmer ined. (P. Bodmer xvii p. 10) | pap. | ? | ? | vi? or vii | 1? | ? |
| ***P 74** | Acts, Catholic Epistles | P. Bodmer xvii | pap. | 19 x 31 | 13/14.5 x 25/26 | vi or vii | 1 | 31–35 |
| ***P 75** | Luke John | P. Bodmer xiv, xv | pap. | 13 x 26 | | iii (E. G. T.)[140] | 1 | 38–45 |
| **†*P 76** | John iv 9– | *Biblos* VIII (1959): 7. Hermeneia. | pap. | ? | ? | vi | 1 | (10+) |
| † **P 77** | Matt. xxiii 30– | P. Oxy. xxxiv 2683 | pap. | ? | [7 x 11] | ii | 1? | [22–23] |
| ***P 78** | Jude 4– | P. Oxy. xxxiv 2684 | pap. | 5.3 x 2.9 | — | iii/iv | 1 | 4 |
| **†*P 79** | Heb. x | P. Berlin 6774 = K. Treu, *Archiv* xviii, p. 37 | pap. | ? | ? | vii | [2] | [32] |
| **†*P 80** | John iii 34 + Hermeneia | Atti Milano, 225 - | pap. | ? | ? | v/vi (E. G. T.; iii/iv ed.) | 1? | (7+) |
| **†*P 81** | 1 Peter 2– | *Papyrologica Castroctaviana* II (1967) | pap. | [17 x 29]? | ? | iv (ed., v?) | 1 | (28+) |
| *No number | Matt. vi 10–12 (Amulet) | P. Ant. ii 54 | pap. | | | | | |
| † No number | Luke vii 32 | *ZPE* iii, 157 | pap. | ?[141] | ? | iv or v | | |
| ***NT Parch. 1** | Gospels | W = Washington (Freer) (032) | parch. | 13/14.5 x 20.5/21 | 9.7/9.8 x 15.7 | v | 1 | 30 |
| † **NT Parch. 2** | Diatessaron *Not* a codex, parch. roll | P. Doura 10 | parch. | | | iii | | |

| | | | | | | | | |
|---|---|---|---|---|---|---|---|---|
| † **NT Parch. 3** | Gospel Harmony | Cambridge, Codex Climaci | parch. | | | vii | | |
| †***NT Parch. 4** | Matt. i 21– | P. Oxy. iii 401 | parch. | ? | 7 x [8]? | v or vi (ed.; E. G. T., surely earlier?) | 1 | [16?] |
| † **NT Parch. 5** | Matt. ii 1– | Paris Copt. 129[19] fol. 73 etc.[142] | parch. | | | ix | | |
| † **NT Parch. 6** | Matt. iii 13– | Paris copt. 129[19] fol. 99[143] | parch. | | | ix? | | |
| ***NT Parch. 7** | Matt. iii 7– (Lectionary) | Vienna G 2324a-k | parch. | 32.5 x 40 (E. G. T.) | 21.5 x 26.5 | vi-vii (E. G. T.) | 2 | 35 |
| † **NT Parch. 8** | Matt. iii 13– | Cambr. Add. 1875[144] | parch. | | | vi | | |
| † **NT Parch. 9** | Matt. iv 2 (Lectionary?) | Crum, Catalogue BM Coptic 48 | parch. | | | vi-vii | | |
| † **NT Parch. 10** | Matt. iv 2– | Bodl. gr. liturg. c. 1[145] | parch. | | | x | | |
| †***NT Parch. 11** | Matt. iv 23– *Not* a codex (folded sheet used as amulet) | P. Oxy. viii 1077 | parch. | | | vi | | |
| ***NT Parch. 12** | Matt. vi 5– | P. Oxy. ix 1169 | parch. | [20 x 25] (ed.) | ? | v-vi | 2 | [27] |
| † **NT Parch. 13** | Matt. vii 28– (Lectionary) | Kahle, Bala'izah i 399 | parch. | | | iv | 2 | |

[139]Part of the composite Bodmer codex, see p. 79–80.
[140]See p. 95.
[141]Ed. suggests [15 x 21].
[142]Listed by Hedley.
[143]Listed by Hedley.
[144]Listed by Hedley and in Aland.
[145]Listed by Hedley.

| 1 | 2 | 3 | 4 | 5 | 6 | 7 | 8 | 9 |
|---|---|---|---|---|---|---|---|---|
| † **NT Parch. 14** | Matt. viii 25– | *Emerita* xxvii, 59 | parch. | ? | [20 x 23] (ed.) | iv | 2 | [23–25] |
| † **NT Parch. 15** | Matt. x 2– | Cambridge TS 16.93[146] | parch. | | | vi | | |
| **NT Parch. 15A** | Matt. x 17– (part of same Ms as **NT Parch. 51**) | *Archiv* xviii, p. 25 | | | | | | |
| † **NT Parch. 16** | Matt. xi 20– | P. Lit. Lond. 212 | parch. | ? | ? | vii-viii | 1 | (17+) |
| † **NT Parch. 17** | Matt. xiii 20– | Kopt. Arab. Urk. Berlin. Mus. i 5 | parch. | | | vi-vii | 2[147] | (8+) |
| † **NT Parch. 17A** | Matt. xiv 13– | Leningrad Public Library Gr. 6 III fol. 7–12[148] | parch. | ? | ? | vi | 2 | (22+) |
| † **NT Parch. 17B** | Matt. xiv 19 | Leningrad Pub. Lib. Gr. 277 + Harris, Sinai 7 | parch. | ?[149] | ? | vi | 2 | 34 |
| † **NT Parch. 18** | Matt. xv 12– | P. Rainer K. 8023 bis[150] | parch. | | | vi | 2 | 23 |
| † **NT Parch. 18A** | Matt. xv 15– | Harris, Sinai 10 + Kiev + Leningrad | parch. | ?[151] | ? | vi | 2 | (25) |
| † **NT Parch. 18B** | Matt. xvii 22 | Leningrad. Pub. Lib. Gr. 13 fol. 1–7 | parch. | ?[152] | ? | vi | 2 | 22 |
| † **NT Parch. 19** | Matt. xviii 18– | *Stud. Pal.* xii 189 | parch. | ? | ? | iv-v | 2 | [26?] |
| † **NT Parch. 19B** | Matt. xix 3– | Leningrad Pub. Lib. Gr. 12. 278 | parch. | ?[153] | ? | vi | 1 | 18 |

| | | | | | | | | |
|---|---|---|---|---|---|---|---|---|
| † **NT Parch. 20** | Matt. xx 3– | Leningrad, Coll. A. Papadopoulos Keramous[154] | parch. | | | vi-vii | | |
| † **NT Parch. 21** | Matt. xxiv 9– Gr. 2106 fol. 350 | Athens Nat. Lib. | parch. | ?[155] | ? | vi | 2 | 20 |
| † **NT Parch. 22** | Matt. xxiv 44– | BM Or. 4923(2) | parch. | | | ? | | |
| † **NT Parch. 23** | Matt. xxv 32– fol. 208 | Paris Copt. 129[10] | parch. | | | ix-x | | |
| † **NT Parch. 23A** | Matt. xxvi 2– | Leningrad, Pub. Lib. Gr. 280 + Harris, Sinai 11 | parch. | ?[156] | ? | vi | 1 | (17) |
| † **NT Parch. 24** | Matt. xxvi 25– | *ZNTW* xxvi, 99 | parch. | ? | ? | iv | 2 | [24?] |
| † **NT Parch. 25** | Matt. xxvi 42– | Paris Copt. 129[19] fol. 35–6 | parch. | | ix-x | | | |
| †***NT Parch. 26** | Matt. xxvi 75– | P. Ant. i 11 + addenda p. 107 | parch. | ? | [ x 8] | iv? (ed.; iv/v E. G. T.) | (2?) | (9+)? |
| † **NT Parch. 27** | Mark? Latin | Montfaucon, *Palaeographia gr.* 14 | parch. | | | vi-vii | | |
| ***NT Parch. 27A** | Mark iii 2– | *MPER* iv 32 | parch. | [23 x 33] (?) | ? | vi | 2 | (23)? |

146 C. Taylor, *Hebrew-Greek Cairo Genizah Palimpsests* . . . 89.
147 From Aland.
148 Listed by Aland.
149 Listed by Aland (084, 073), who gives size as 23 x 28.
150 Listed by Hedley and Aland.
151 Listed by Aland (064, 074, 090), who gives size as 21 x 28.
152 Listed by Aland (078), who gives size as 20 x 27.
153 Listed by Aland (087), who gives size as 26 x 34.
154 Listed by Hedley.
155 Listed by Aland (094), who gives size as 24 x 31.
156 Listed by Aland (089, 092a), who gives size as 28 x 36.

| 1 | 2 | 3 | 4 | 5 | 6 | 7 | 8 | 9 |
|---|---|---|---|---|---|---|---|---|
| † **NT Parch. 27B** | Mark v 26– | *Archiv* xviii, p. 28 | parch. | | | vi | 1 | (3+) |
| † **NT Parch. 27C** | Mark ii 23 | Damascus?[157] | parch. | ? | ? | vi | 2 | 22 |
| † **NT Parch. 28** | See **NT Parch. 7, 68** | | | | | | | |
| † **NT Parch. 29** | Mark vi 30– | Deissman, Heidelberger Septuaginta fragm. 3 | parch. | ? | ? | v/vi (Cavallo) | 2 | [26] |
| † **NT Parch. 30** | Mark viii 17– | Bodl. gr. bib. c5(P)[158] | parch. | | | v-vi | | |
| **NT Parch. 31** | Mark viii 33– | *MPER* iv 33 | parch. | [18/17 x 20] (ed.) | ? | v (Cavallo) | 2 | 24 |
| ***NT Parch. 31A** | Mark. ix 20– | *JTS* xxvii (1976): 34 | parch. | 22.5 x 29.5 | 17.5 x 19 | v/vi | 2 | 30 |
| † **NT Parch. 31B** | Mark ix | Leningrad Pub. Lib. Gr. 275(3) | parch.[159] | | | v | | |
| †***NT Parch. 32** | Mark x 50– | P. Oxy. i 3 | parch. | ? | ? | v-vi | 2? | (8+) |
| † **NT Parch. 33** | Mark xi 11– | *ZNTW* (1927), p. 100 | parch. | ? | ? | vii? | 2 | 21 |
| **NT Parch. 33A** | Number vacant | | | | | | | |
| † **NT Parch. 33B** | Mark xii 32– | Sinai, Harris 11[160] | parch. | | | vi | 1 | 18 |
| † **NT Parch. 33C** | Mark xiv 29– | Sinai, Harris 12 + others[161] | parch. | | | vi | 2 | 25 |
| ***NT Parch. 34** | Mark xv 20– | *MPER* iv 34 + *Stud. Pal.* xii 186 | parch. | [11 x 14/15] | ? | iv (Cavallo) | 1 | [18–19] |
| **NT Parch. 35** | number vacant | | | | | | | |

| | | | | | | | | |
|---|---|---|---|---|---|---|---|---|
| † **NT Parch. 36** | Mark xv 36– | *Stud. Pal.* xv 232 | parch. | | | vi | 2[162] | (23)[162] |
| † **NT Parch. 37** | Mark xvi 6– | Paris Copt. 129[8] fol. 162 | parch. | | | vii-viii | 2[163] | 32[163] |
| † **NT Parch. 38 = Bible 'R'** | Luke i 1– | BM Add. 17211 = Nitriensis ('R', 027) q. v. | parch. | | | v late | | |
| † **NT Parch. 39** | Luke i 39– | Paris Copt. 129[18] fol. 73 | parch. | | | xiii? | | |
| † **NT Parch. 40** | Luke i 68 etc.[164] | Rendel Harris, Bibl. frags. Mt. Sinai p. 53 | parch. | | | vii? | | |
| **NT Parch. 41** | Luke i 73– | *Stud. Pal.* xi 55 | parch. | 27.7 x 36 | ? | vi? | 2 | 36 |
| † **NT Parch. 42** | Luke ii 28– | Crum, Catalogue BM Coptic 502 | parch. | | | viii | | |
| ***NT Parch. 43** | Luke iii 19– | Paris Copt. 129[7 8 9 10] + BM + Vienna[165] | parch. | 28.8 x 34.4 | 20 x 25 | vi | 2 | c. 35 |
| ***NT Parch. 44 = Bible 'T'** | Luke vi 17– | Borghesi Copt. 109[65] + others | parch. | 20 x 24.6/25[166] | ? | vi? | 2 | 27–31 |

[157]Listed by Aland (072), who gives size as 15 x 20.
[158]Listed by Hedley and Aland (0143).
[159]Listed by Aland (080).
[160]Listed by Aland (092b).
[161]Listed by Aland (083, 0112, 0235) who gives size as 26 x 28.
[162]From Aland (0184).
[163]From Aland (099), who gives size 26 x 32.
[164]'Not N. T. MS' Hedley.
[165]Details in Aland (070, 0110, 0124, 0178, 0179, 0180, 0190, 0191, 0194, 0202). Cavallo p. 115 and Tavola p. 104.
[166]So Cavalieri-Lietzmann; W. P. Hatch 18.8/21 x 22.3/24.9.

| 1 | 2 | 3 | 4 | 5 | 6 | 7 | 8 | 9 |
|---|---|---|---|---|---|---|---|---|
| † **NT Parch. 44A** | Luke vi 23– | Previously Damascus[167] | parch. | | | vi | 2 | 24 |
| †***NT Parch. 44B** | Luke vii 12- Latin | Berlin P 6760 (*CLA* viii 1036) | parch. | ? | ? | vii | 1? | (4+) |
| † **NT Parch. 45** | Luke vii 37– | Paris copt. 129[7+1] [168] | parch. | | | xi | | |
| † **NT Parch. 45A** | Luke vii 20– | *Archiv* xviii, p. 29 | parch. | | | vi | 2 | (5+) |
| † **NT Parch. 45B** | Luke viii 25– | *Helmantica* xvi, 139 | parch. | ? | ? | vi (v ed.) | ? | (10+) |
| † **NT Parch. 45C** | Luke vii 39– | Leningrad Pub. Lib. Gr. 13 fol. 8–10[169] | parch. | | | vi | 2 | 22+ |
| **NT Parch. 46** | Luke ix 59– | *Stud. Pal.* xii 185 | parch. | 13.6 x 15.3 | [10.1 x 10.9] | iv/v | 1 | 26 |
| † **NT Parch. 47** | Luke xi 27– | Paris Copt. 129[a] fol. 96[170] | parch. | | | x | | |
| † **NT Parch. 48** | Luke xii 8– | Berlin P. 8771 + Borghesi Copt. 109[97] [171] | parch. | | | x | | |
| † **NT Parch. 49** | Luke xiv 25– | Budge, Misc. Coptic Texts, 249[172] | parch. | | | x-xii | 1 | 23 |
| † **NT Parch. 50** | Luke xix 17– | *Stud. Pal.* xii 188 | parch. | ? | ? | v-vi | 1? | [18/21?] |
| † **NT Parch. 50A** | Luke xx 19– | *Archiv* xviii, p. 30 | parch. | | | vi | 1 | [33–34] |
| ***NT Parch. 51** | Luke xxii 41– | *PSI* i 2 + ii 124[173] (+ **15a** = Mt. x 17-) | parch. | [12 x 15] | ? | iii/iv (E. G. T.) | 2 | [23/24] |
| ***NT Parch. 52** | Luke xxiii 3– Latin-Gothic | Giessen MS 651/20[174] | parch. | [ x 26/27] | [15/16 x 19/20] | v (vi. E. A. L.) | 2 | [24–25] |

| | | | | | | | | |
|---|---|---|---|---|---|---|---|---|
| † **NT Parch. 53** | John xix 13– | Paris copt. 129[19] + Borg. copt. 109[96] [175] | parch. | | | xi | | |
| †***NT Parch. 54** | John i 29– | *Stud. Pal.* xii 187 (Vienna G. 39780) | parch. | ? | ? | vii | 1 | [15] |
| † **NT Parch. 54A** | John i 30– | Berlin P. 5542[180] | parch. | | | vi | | |
| **NT Parch. 54B** | John i 30–33 | *Archiv* xxi, p. 83 | parch. | [7.5 x 10] ed. | 4.5 x 6.2 | vi/vii | 1 | 10 |
| † **NT Parch. 55** | John ii 2– | Paris copt. 129[10] fol. 207[181] | parch. | | | viii | 2 | 22 |
| ***NT Parch. 56** | John ii 11– | P. Oxy. vi 847 | parch. | 14.6 x 16.2 | 11 x 11 | iv | 1 | 19 |
| † **NT Parch. 57** | John iii 5– | Crum, Catalogue BM Coptic 504 | parch. | | | vi | | |
| † **NT Parch. 58** | John iii 23– | Paris copt. 132[2] fol. 92[182] | parch. | | | vii or ix | (2)? | |
| **NT Parch. 58A** | John v 44– Biblical oracle (Hermeneia) | *Biblica* xxxiv, 17 | parch. | 6 x 8.5 | ? | vii | 1 | 8/9 |

[167]Listed by Aland (0147), who gives size as 24 x 32.
[168]Listed by Hedley and Aland (1 961).
[169]Listed by Aland (079), who gives size as 25 x 31.
[170]Listed by Hedley and Aland (1 1741).
[171]Listed by Hedley and Aland (1 143).
[172]Listed by Hedley and Aland (1 1603).
[173]15a is dated by Treu to c. A.D. 300.
[174]*ZNTW* xi, 1; *CLA* viii 1200.
[175]Listed by Hedley.
[176–179]These notes omitted. (pub.)
[180]*Koptolog. Studien in der DDR* (1965), p. 95.
[181]Listed by Hedley and Aland (0127).
[182]Listed by Hedley and Aland (0193).

| 1 | 2 | 3 | 4 | 5 | 6 | 7 | 8 | 9 |
|---|---|---|---|---|---|---|---|---|
| † **NT Parch. 58B** | John vi 32– Biblical oracles (Hermeneia) | *Jahrb. öst. Byz. Gesellsch.* 14, 10 | parch. | | | viii | | |
| † **NT Parch. 58C** | John vii 10– | *Biblica* XX, 372[183] (Vienna K 8668) | parch. | | | viii | 1 | (10+) |
| † **NT Parch. 58D** | John vi 13– | Leningrad Pub. Lib. Gr. 279[184] | parch. | | | vi | 2 | c. 23 |
| ***NT Parch. 59** | John vii 27– Latin | P. Aberdeen 1[185] | parch. | [7.5/8 x 10] | ? | iv (E. G. T.) | 2? | [24?] |
| † **NT Parch. 59A** | John viii 19– | *Archiv* xviii, p. 33 | parch. | | | v | 1 | [17/18] |
| ***NT Parch. 60** | John viii 51– | *MPER* iv 36 | parch. | [12 x 19] | ? | v | 2 | [27] |
| † **NT Parch. 60A** | John xi 50– | Leningrad Pub. Lib. Gr. I 6 fol. 1–3[186] | parch. | | | vi | 2 | 29 |
| **NT Parch. 61** | John xi 57– | *MPER* iv 37 | parch. | [9 x 13] | ? | v | 1 | 19 |
| † **NT Parch. 62** | John xii 2– | *MPER* iv 38 | parch. | ? | ? | v | 2 | [27/28] |
| **NT Parch. 63** | vacant | | | | | | | |
| † **NT Parch. 64** | John xiii 16– | BM Add. 17136 fol. 117 126[187] | parch. | | | v | | |
| **NT Parch. 65** | John xiv 14– | *ZNTW* xxvi, 102 | parch. | [12 x 14] (Salonius) | ? | v-vi | 2? | [24] |
| ***NT Parch. 66** | John xvi 30– | *ZNTW* xxvi, 104[188] | parch. | 14.5 x 16.3 | 12 x 12 | vi/vii (E. G. T.) | 1 | 22 |
| See **NT Parch. 53** | John xix 13– | | | | | | | |
| † **NT Parch. 67** | John xx 4– | Paris copt. 129[10] fol. 198[189] | parch. | | | viii | 2 | 24 |
| **NT Parch. 68** | John xx 1– | See **NT Parch. 7** | | | | | | |
| † **NT Parch. 69** | John xx 24– | Paris copt. 129[21] fol. I, 10, 12, 13[190] | parch. | | | ix-x | | |

| | | | | | | | | |
|---|---|---|---|---|---|---|---|---|
| † | **NT Parch. 70** | John xx 26– | Paris copt. 129[10] fol. 196[191] | parch. | | | vii or viii | 2 | 32 |
| | **NT Parch. 71** | Acts ii 1- | *Stud. Pal.* xi 59c[191a] | parch. | 29.5 x 38.5 | ? | ix | 2 | 35 |
| † | **NT Parch. 72** | Acts ii 11– | P. Amh. i 8 | parch. | ?[192] | ? | v-vi | 2 | 23 |
| † | **NT Parch. 73** | Acts iii 5– | *ZNTW* xxvi, 97 | parch. | ? | ? | iv/v | 2 | [27] |
| † | **NT Parch. 74** | Acts iii 12– | Moscow Golenischev Ms Copt 55[193] | parch. | [18 x 22] (ed.) | ? | v | 2 | [26] |
| | ***NT Parch. 75** | Acts iii 24– | *ZNTW* xxvi, 110 | parch. | [14 x 19][194] | [11.5 x 14.5] | v (E. G. T.) | 2 | 32 |
| | ***NT Parch. 76** | Acts v 3– | *ZNTW* xxvi, 115 | parch. | 11.5 x 18 (ed.) | 9.5 x 15.5 | iv | 1 | 32 |
| | **NT Parch. 77** | Acts vi 7– | *PSI* ii 125 | parch. | [12 x 17] (ed.) | ? | v | 1 | [20] |
| † | **NT Parch. 77A** | Acts xi 29– | P. A. M. Khirbet Mird 8[195] | parch. | | | v | | |
| † | **NT Parch. 77B** | Acts xiii 28– | Sinai, Harris App. 5[196] | parch. | | | v | | |

183 Listed by Hedley's Addenda and Aland (0238).
184 Listed by Aland (091), who gives size as 28 x 32.
185 *CLA* ii 118; *PSI* xiii 1306.
186 Listed by Aland (065), who gives size as 19 x 29.
187 If = Aland 068 c v, 2 cols. 18ll. 24B x 26H.
188 Checked from plate in Wilcken, *Tafeln z. alteren gr. Pal.* VI.
189 Listed by Hedley and Aland (0114).
190 Listed by Hedley.
191 Listed by Hedley and Aland (0100).
191a Listed by Aland as *l*.1575. Same Ms as **N.T. Parch. 104**
192 About 18 x 18? (15 x 17 Aland).
193 P. Weigandt in K. Aland, *Materialen* 72.
194 Ed. [16.5 x 19].
195 Noted by K. Treu, *Archiv* xix, p. 184.
196 Listed by Aland (077), no further information.

| 1 | 2 | 3 | 4 | 5 | 6 | 7 | 8 | 9 |
|---|---|---|---|---|---|---|---|---|
| † **NT Parch. 78** | Acts xxiv 22– | Cambridge TS 12. 189, 208[197] | parch. | | | vi | 2 | 28 |
| †***NT Parch. 79** | Acts xxviii 30– | Deissmann, Heidelberger Septuaginta fragm. 4 | parch. | ? | ? | v | 2? | (9+) |
| † **NT Parch. 79A** | Acts xxviii 8– | Leningrad Pub. Lib. 6 II fol. 4[198] | parch. | | | vi | 2 | 25 |
| † **NT Parch. 79B** | Epistles Lectionary | Bodl. Copt. f. 5(P)[199] | parch. | | | iv | 2 | (20) |
| ***NT Parch. 80** | Rom. i 27– | *PSI* i 4 | parch. | [10.5 x 15] | [7 x 9.5] | v | 1 | 19 |
| † **NT Parch. 81** | Rom. ii 21– | *MPER* iv 42 | parch. | ? | ? | v | 2? | [25–30?] |
| **NT Parch. 82** | Rom. iv 23– | *HTR* 45, 81 | parch. | [12.7 x 15] | [8.5 x 11.7] | iii? | 1 | 24 |
| ***NT Parch. 83** | Rom. v 16– | *MPER* iv 43 | parch. | [ ] x 16 | ? | iv | 2 | 20 |
| † **NT Parch. 84** | 1 Cor. i 22– | Paris copt. 129[11 200] | parch. | | | ix-x | 2 | 35 |
| **NT Parch. 85** | 1 Corinthians ii 5 | *Stud. Pal.* xv 235 | parch. | ? | ? | iv-v | 2 | (6+) |
| †***NT Parch. 86** | 1 Cor. ix 5– | *MPER* iv 44 | parch. | ? | ? | vi (v Cavallo) | 2 | 20 |
| †***NT Parch. 87** | 1 Cor. x 29– | 'I' = Washington (Freer), Smithsonian | parch. | Damaged. Greatest dimensions [16 x 10.5] Hatch | ? | vi | | |
| † **NT Parch. 88** | 1 Cor. xi 17– | P. Lit. Lond. 215 | parch. | ? | ? | vi-vii | ? | (13+) |
| **NT Parch. 89** | 1 Cor. xii 2– | P. Lit. Lond. 216 | parch. | [14 x 14] | | v | 2 | (19) |
| † **NT Parch. 89A** | 1 Cor. xv 53– | Leningrad Pub. Lib. 6 II fol. 5–6 | parch.[201] | ? | ? | v/vi | 2 | 24 |

| | | | | | | | | |
|---|---|---|---|---|---|---|---|---|
| | **NT Parch. 90** | 2 Cor. i 17– | *MPER* iv 45 | parch. | [9.3 x 12] | [6 x 8.5] | vi | 2 | [17] |
| † | **NT Parch. 90A** | 2 Cor. i 20– | Leningrad Pub. Lib. Gr. 9 | parch.[202] | | | vi | 2 | 18 |
| | **NT Parch. 91** | 2 Cor. iv 5– | *Stud. Pal.* xv 256 + *MPER* iv 46[203] | parch. | ? | ? | v-vi | 2 | (17) |
| | **NT Parch. 92** | vacant | | | | | | | |
| * | **NT Parch. 93** | 2 Cor. v 1– | *MPER* iv 47[204] | parch. | 17.7 x [25] | ? | vi | 1 | 21–27 |
| † | **NT Parch. 93A** | Gal. i 1– | Formerly Damascus[205] | parch. | | | v/vi | 2 | 25 |
| † | **NT Parch. 93B** | Gal. i 9– | *Archiv* xviii, p. 33 | parch. | [ x 20] | [ x 15.3] | v | 2 | [25] |
| † | **NT Parch. 94** | Gal. ii 5 *Not* a codex, written only one side | *PSI* ii 118 | parch. | | | v | | |
| * | **NT Parch. 95** | Gal. iii 16– | *PSI* iii 251 | parch. | [7 x 12] (ed.) | 5.3 x [9.3] | v | 1 | [22] |
| † | **NT Parch. 96** | Gal. iv 15– | *SB Berl.* (1903), p. 825 | parch. | | | iv-v | | |
| †* | **NT Parch. 96A** | Eph. vi 11– Greek and Latin | *PSI* xiii 1306 | parch. | 13 x [ ] | ? | iv | 2 | (4+) |
| † | **NT Parch. 96B** | Col. i 29– | Munich. Bay. Staatsbibl. 29022 e | parch.[206] | | | vi | 2 | 31 |

[197]C. Taylor, *Hebrew-Greek Cairo Geniza palimpsests* . . . 93.
[198]Listed by Aland (066), who gives size as 15.5 x 20.
[199]Aland 0192 = l 1604.
[200]Listed by Hedley and Aland (0129).
[201]Listed by Aland (088).
[202]Listed by Aland (081), who gives size as 23 x 28.
[203]Identification by H. Klos, *Theol. Litztg.* LXXVIII, 469.
[204]Plate Gerstinger, *Wiener Genesis* T. VIII 39.
[205]Listed by Aland (0158), who gives size as 22 x 30.
[206]Listed by Aland (0208), who gives size as 16 x 23.

| 1 | 2 | 3 | 4 | 5 | 6 | 7 | 8 | 9 |
|---|---|---|---|---|---|---|---|---|
| † **NT Parch. 96C** | Eph. iv 2– | Moscow, Hist. Mus. V 108, S. 100[207] | parch. | | | vi | 2 | 25 |
| † **NT Parch. 96D** | Eph. iv 21– | Prev. Damascus[208] | parch. | | | vi | 2 | 25 |
| † **NT Parch. 97** | Col. iii 15– | P. Lit. Lond. 217 | parch. | ? | ? | vi | 1? | (7+) |
| † **NT Parch. 98** | 1 Thess. iii 6– | *Stud. Pal.* xii 192 | parch. | ? | 14 x [20] | vii | 1? | 28 |
| †***NT Parch. 99** | 1 Thess. iv 16– | *MPER* iv 48 | parch. | ? | ? | iv/v | 2 | [25] |
| † **NT Parch. 100** | 2 Thess. i 1– | Berlin P. 5013 | parch. | ? | ? | vii[209] | 2 | 24 |
| †***NT Parch. 100A** | 1 Tim. i 15 *Not* a codex: amulet | *Archiv* xviii, p. 36 | parch. | | | vii? | 2 | 6 |
| † **NT Parch. 100B** | 1 Tim. i 4– | *Archiv* xviii, p. 36 | parch. | 9.0 x [ ] | ? | vi/vii | 1 | (8+) |
| † **NT Parch. 101** | 1 Tim. iii 15– | Paris Louvre 7332[210] | parch. | | | v | 1 | 19 |
| † **NT Parch. 101A** | Titus ii 15 | Aspley Guise (formerly owned by H. Hyvernat)[211] | parch. | | | viii | | |
| †***NT Parch. 101B** | Heb. vi 2– | P. Barc. Inv. 6 | parch. | ? | [ x 15] | iv | 2? | [25+?] |
| ***NT Parch. 101C** | Titus i 4 | Tiflis Grus. Mus. 2123 fol. 193 198 (0240) | parch. and pap. | [22 x 26] | ? | v | 2[212] | 22 |
| † **NT Parch. 101D** | 1 Tim. iii 16– | unknown[213] | parch. | | | vi | | |
| † **NT Parch. 102** | Heb. xi 18– | *MPER* iv 49 | parch. | ? | ? | v | 2? | (5+) |
| † **NT Parch. 102A** | Heb. xii 19– | *MPER* iv 50 | parch. | | | iv | 1? | (9+) |

| | | | | | | | | |
|---|---|---|---|---|---|---|---|---|
| † | **NT Parch. 103** | 1 Pet. ii 7– | Crum, Catalogue BM Coptic 141 | parch. | | | vi | | |
| | **NT Parch. 104** | 1 Pet. ii 21– same codex | See **NT Parch. 71** | | | | | | |
| | **NT Parch. 105** | 1 Pet. v 5– | P. Oxy. xi 1353 | parch. | 10.1 x 13.5 | ? | iv | 1 | 17–18 |
| † | **NT Parch. 105A** | 2 Pet. i 5– | P. Ryl. Copt. 20[214] | parch. | | | vi | 2 | 36 |
| † | **NT Parch. 105B** | James i 12– | Cambr., Westminster Coll.[215] | parch. | | | vi | 1 | 27 |
| * | **NT Parch. 106** | James i 25 | *PSI* i 5 | parch. | 6 x 7.8 | ? | iv (E. G. T.; v ed.) | 1 | 9 |
| † | **NT Parch. 106A** | 1 John iii 23– | Birmingham, Selly Oak Coll., Ming. and Georg. 7[216] | parch. | | | vi | 1 | 23 |
| * | **NT Parch. 107** | 2 John i 1– | P. Ant. i 12 | parch. | [9 x 10] | 6.9 x [7.9] | iii (ed.; E. G. T. iv?) | 1 | [20] |
| * | **NT Parch. 108** | Apoc. iii 19– | P. Oxy. viii 1080 | parch. | 7.8 x 9.5 | 6.5 x 7.3 | iv | 1 | 14 |
| | **NT Parch. 109** | Apoc. ix 2– | *PSI* x 1166 | parch. | 15 x 19 | ? | iv | 2 | 29 |
| * | **NT Parch. 110** | Apoc. xvi 17– | P. Oxy. vi 848 | parch. | 9 x [11.5] | 6 x [8] | v | 1 | 17 |
| † | **NT Parch. 111** | Apoc. xviii 16– | *PSI* xiii 1296[217] | parch. | ? | ? | viii | 1 | (13+) |

[207] Listed by Aland (082).
[208] Listed by Aland (0159), who gives size as 17 x 24.
[209] Schubart, *Das Buch*$^2$, p. 186n. says iv, probably error.
[210] From Aland, who gives size as c. 12 x 14.
[211] Listed by Hedley and Aland (0205).
[212] K. Treu, *Die gr. HSS. des N. T. in den USSR*, 353 and others. Zereteli's restoration in a single column is wrong.
[213] Listed by Aland (0241).
[214] Listed by Aland (0247).
[215] Listed by Aland (0246), who gives size as 20 x 29.
[216] Listed by Aland (0245), who gives size as 20 x 27.
[217] From same codex as unidentified patristic work.

| 1 | 2 | 3 | 4 | 5 | 6 | 7 | 8 | 9 |
|---|---|---|---|---|---|---|---|---|
| ***OT 1** | Berlin Genesis | Rahlfs 911 | pap. | 18 x 25 (?+) | 16/18 x 22/22.5 | iv | 2, then 1 | 28–37 |
| †***OT 1A** | Genesis *Not* a codex cf. **OT 37A** | P. Fuad inv. 966 | pap. | | | i B.C. | | |
| † **OT 1B** | Gen. i 1–5 *Not* a codex | P. Amh. i 3c | pap. | | | iii/iv | | |
| †***OT 2** | Genesis | P. Oxy. vii 1007 = P. Lit. Lond. 199 | parch. | [16.2+ x ] | x [16.5] | iii | 2 | [33] |
| †***OT 3** | Genesis (vetus latina) | P. Oxy. viii 1073 = P. Lit. Lond. 200 | parch. | ? | ? | iv | 2? | 25 |
| † **OT 4** | Gen. v | *BKT* viii 1 | pap. | ? | ? | v-vi (?) (vii ed.) | 1 | [34] |
| ***OT 5** | Gen. ix 1– | P. Ch. B. IV | pap. | [18 x 28] | 13.3 x 21 | iv | 2 | 36–42 |
| † **OT 5A** | Gen. x 12 | Nachr. Akad. Gött. 1966, 6, 1 | parch. | | | ix | | |
| † **OT 6** | Gen. xiii 7 | P. Mich. iii 131 | parch. | ? | ? | iv | 1? | [22–23] |
| ***OT 6A** | Gen. xiii 3 | *BKT* viii 2 | parch. | 10.5 x [18] | 8.5 x [14] | iv-v | 1 | [22] |
| ***OT 7** | Gen. xiv | P. Yale I 1 | pap. | 14 x [20] (E. G. T.; x [23] ed.) | 13 x [17.5] | ii/iii (E. G. T.; A.D. 90 ed.) | 1 | [30] |
| **OT 8** | Gen. xiv *Not* a codex | P. Lit. Lond. 228 | | | | | | |
| ***OT 9** | Gen. xiv | P. Oxy. iv 656 | pap. | 11+ x 24.3+ | 8.5/9 x 20.3 | ii/iii (E. G. T.; iii, ed.; ii, Bell & Skeat, *Frags. Unknown Gospel*, p. 6) | 1 | 41/42 |
| **OT 10** | Gen. xvi 8 Roll | P. Oxy. ix 1166 = P. Lit. Lond. | | | | | | |

| | | | | | | | | |
|---|---|---|---|---|---|---|---|---|
| †***OT 11** | Gen. xxiv 13– | P. Ch. B. V = Rahlfs 962 | pap. | [17] (E. G. T.) x 21 | 13.3 x 15.3 | iii/iv (E. G. T.) | 1 | 17–20 |
| †***OT 11A** | Gen. xix 11– | P. Berlin 17213 (*Archiv* xx, p. 46) | pap. | ? | ?[218] | iii | 1 | [27–28] |
| † **OT 12** | Gen. xxv 19 | *Archiv* ii, p. 224 | parch. | ? | ? | v | 2 | [35?] |
| **OT 12A** | Number vacant | | | | | | | |
| †***OT 12B** | Gen. xxvi 13–etc. | P. Ryl. iii 460 + P. Oslo 11 | pap. | ?[219] | ? | v (E. G. T., H. I. B.; iv ed.) | 1 | (24+) |
| **OT 13** | Gen. xxvii 29 | *BKT* viii 3 | parch. | 3.5 x 5 | 3.5 x 5 | vi-vii | 1 | 10/11 |
| **OT 14** | Gen. xxvii 43 | *MPER* iv 1 | parch. | [13 x 16.5] | [9.3 x 10.7] | v | 2 | [23] |
| † **OT 14A** | Gen. xxxi 8 *Not* a codex | Cairo inv. 88747 | | | | | | |
| † **OT 14B** | Gen. xxix 17– Not a codex? (back unw[illegible]en) | *BKT* viii 23 | parch. | ? | ? | vi | 1 | (17+) |
| ***OT 15** | Gen. x[illegible]i 42 | P. Oxy. ix 1167 | pap. | [12.4 x 16.6] | [9.2 x 12/13] | iv | 1 | 22 |
| † **OT 15A** | Gen. xxxvi 14 | Actes X Congr. intern. pap. 209 | parch. | ? | ? | v/vi | 1 | (7+) |
| † **OT 16** | Gen. xxxvii 3 | *Rev. phil.* 28, 65; *GGN* 1911, 263 | parch. | ? | ? | v-vi | 2? | (32)? |
| † **OT 17** | Gen. xxxvii 35 | Münch. Septuaginta fragm. 103 | parch. | ? | ? | iv | 2 | (3+) |
| † **OT 18** | Gen. xxxviii 23 | *Stud. Pal.* ix 2 | parch. | ? | ? | iv-v | 2? | (10+) |
| † **OT 19** | Gen. xl 3 | Westminster Coll. Cambr. + Erzabtei Beuron[220] | parch. | | | vii-viii | | |
| **OT 19A** | Gen. xli 48 | P. Erl. 1 | pap. | 11 x 20 | ? | iv-v | 1? | 25–26 |

[218]Treu calculates $\beta$ [13 x 20].
[219][11 x 30] ed.
[220]See *Biblica* xi; xii, 367.

| 1 | 2 | 3 | 4 | 5 | 6 | 7 | 8 | 9 |
|---|---|---|---|---|---|---|---|---|
| † **OT 20** | Gen. xli 48 | P. Ibscher 5 (P. Hamb. [1954], p. 131) | parch. | ? | ? | iv | 1? | (14+) |
| † **OT 21** | Gen. xliii | *MPER* iv 2 | parch. | ? | ? | v | 1? | (9+) |
| ***OT 22** | Gen. xlvi 28 | P. Lit. Lond. 202 | pap. | [13.5/14 x 17] | ? | iii/iv | 1 | [16/17] |
| ***OT 23** | Exod. iv 4 | P. E. Kahle, Bala'izah I, p. 297 | parch. | 7 x [8.8+] | 4.5 x 8 (?) | v | 1 | 12 |
| ***OT 23A** | Exod. v 14– | *Archiv* xx, p. 47 | parch. | 7.8 x 9 | 4.8/5.2 x 6 | iv | 1 | 12 |
| †***OT 24** | Exod. viii 5 + Deuteronomy | *VBP* iv 56 | pap. | ? | [ x 16.5] | ii (ed.; late ii E. G. T.) | 2? | [35] |
| †***OT 24A** | Exod. viii 16– (vetus lat.) | *PSI* xii 1272 (*CLA* iii 294) | parch. | [ ] x 30 | [16?] x 18 | v | 2 | 25 |
| † **OT 25** | Exod. xv etc. *Not* a codex | Heidelb. Septuaginta fragm. 2 | parch. | | | | | |
| † **OT 25A** | Exod. xv 1–2 *Not* a codex | *Archiv* xx, p. 50 | pap. | | | vi/vii | 1 | 15 |
| **OT 26** | Exod. xvi 32 | *MPER* iv 3 | parch. | ? | ? | v | ? | (6+) |
| †***OT 27** | Exod. xix | P. Amh. ii 191 | pap. | ? | ? | vi (ed., v/vi Cavallo) | 1 | (7+) |
| †***OT 28** | Exod. xxiii 10 | *BKT* viii 4 | parch. | ?[221] | ? | v/vi | 1 | [18/19] |
| **OT 28A** | Exod. xxviii 4 *Roll* | *DJD* iii, p. 142 | | | | | | |
| † **OT 28B** | Exod. xxix 21– | P. Milan Vogliano i 22 | parch. | ? | ? | iv | 1? | (13+) [19?] |
| †***OT 29** | Exod. xxxi 13 | P. Oxy. viii 1074 | | ? | ? | iii (early, E. G. T.; G. H., others, ii/iii) | ? | (5+) |
| **OT 29A** | Exod. xxxiv 18– | *Archiv* xx, p. 51 | parch. | 7.4 x [7.4] | 4.5 x [5.0] | iv | 1 | [12] |

| | | | | | | | | |
|---|---|---|---|---|---|---|---|---|
| †***OT 29B** | Exod. xxxiv 35– | *Archiv* xx, p. 52 | parch. | ? | [ ] x 10.5 | iii/iv | 1 | 20 |
| **OT 30** | Exod. xl 26 *Roll* | P. Oxy. viii 1075 = P. Lit. Lond. 203 | pap. | | | | | |
| † **OT 31** | Exod. xl 5 | P. Reinach ii 59 | pap. | ? | ? | iii | 1 | [28] |
| † **OT 31A** | Lev. i 14 | Münch. Septuaginta fragm. p. 106ff. | parch. | ? | [10 x 16] (ed.) | v | 2? | ? |
| † **OT 32** | Lev. viii 14 | *MPER* iv 4 | parch. | ? | ? | vi | 2? | (13/15+) |
| **OT 33** | Lev. xvi 33 *Roll* | P. Oxy. x 1225 | pap. | | | iv | | |
| **OT 33A** | Lev. xxvi 2 *Leather roll* | Vetus Testamentum Suppl. 4, 157 | | | | | | |
| † **OT 34** | Lev. xxii 3 | Bibl. frags. from Mt. Sinai 15 | parch. | | | iv | | |
| †***OT 35** | Lev. xxvii 12 | P. Oxy. xi 1351 | parch. | ? | ? | iv | 2 | (7+) |
| ***OT 36** | Num. v 12–, Deut. i 20– | P. Ch. B. VI | pap. | [19/18 x 33] | 12.7 x 19 | ii/iii (E. G. T., A. S. Hunt; ii F. G. Kenyon, U. Wilcken) | 2 | 31–38 |
| **OT 36A** | Num. iii 30 *Leather roll* | Vetus Testamentum Suppl. iv, 155 | | | | | | |
| ***OT 37** | Deut. – Joshua | Freer = 'H' (Smithsonian, Washington) | parch. | 25/26 x 30.5 | x 20.5 | vi (v Devreesse) | 2 | 31/32 |
| †***OT 37A** | Deut. xvii *Roll*, cf. **OT 1A** | P. Fuad Inv. 266[222] | pap. | | | i B.C. | | |

[221] [9 x 12] ed.

[222] Bibliography in *Greek Manuscripts of the Ancient World*, 56.

| 1 | 2 | 3 | 4 | 5 | 6 | 7 | 8 | 9 |
|---|---|---|---|---|---|---|---|---|
| † **OT 38** | Deut. ii | P. Ryl. I 1 | pap. | ? | ? | iv | 2? | (15+) |
| ***OT 39** | Deut. xxiii 24 *Roll* | P. Ryl. iv 458 | pap. | | | ii B.C. | | |
| † **OT 40** | Deut. xxiv 15 | Giessen P. 13, 19, 22, 26[223] | parch. | [16/17 x 25] | [12.5 x 20] | v-vi | 2 | [40] |
| †***OT 41** | Deut. xxxii 3 | P. Amh. ii 192 | pap. | ? | ? | vi | 1 | (10+) |
| ***OT 42** | Josh. iv 23 | P. Oxy. ix 1168 | parch. | [9 x 13] (E. G. T.; A. S. H. 9 x 15.5) | [6 x 7.5] | iv | 1 | [19] |
| ***OT 43** | Judg. i | *PSI* ii 127 | pap. | 11.5 x 16 | 9 x 13.5 | iii early (E. G. T.; v ed.) | 1 | 19/20 |
| † **OT 44** | Judg. v 8 | Münch. Septuaginta fragm. 108 | parch. | | | vii | | |
| † **OT 45** | Judg. xvi 26 | Codex Zuqninensis rescr. | parch. | | | vi | | |
| † **OT 46** | Judg. xx 22 | *Bibl. Fragm. from Mt. Sinai,* p. 2 | parch. | | | iv | | |
| ***OT 47** | 1 Kings xviii 18 | Anz. Oest. Akad. Wiss. 1956 Nr. 15, 189 | parch. | 12.5 x 15 (?+) | 9 x 10 | iv | 2 | 25 |
| † **OT 47A** | 1 Kings xxiv 1 | *Oudtest. Stud.* xiv, 227 | parch. | | | iv-v | | |
| † **OT 48** | 2 Kings xv 35 | *Archiv* ii, p. 227 | pap. | ? | [8 x 12.5] (ed.) | iv-v | 1? | [22] |
| †***OT 49** | 1 Kingdoms (1 Sam.) xxiii 28 | *HTR* 62, 349 | pap. | ? | [ x 19] (ed.) | iv (ed.; v ? E. G. T.) | ? | ? |
| † **OT 49A** | 3 Kings xviii 26 | Nachr. Akad. Göttingen (1966), No. 6 | parch. | | | v/vi | 2 | |
| † **OT 50** | 3 Kings xxi 7 | Cambridge TS 12.184 20.50[224] | parch. | | | v-vi | | |

| | | | | | | | | |
|---|---|---|---|---|---|---|---|---|
| ***OT 51** | 2 Par. xxix 32 | P. Barc. inv. 3 | pap. | [12 x 16/17] | [8.5 x 12] | iii (E. G. T.; ii ed.) | 1 | [24] |
| **†*OT 51A** | 2 Par. xxiv 17 | Bell-Skeat, *Fragm. Unknown Gospel,* p. 52 | pap. | ? | [9 x 10.9] | iii | 1 | [25] |
| **† OT 51B** | Esther viii 10 | Nachr. Akad. Wiss. Göttingen (1966), 6, 3 | parch. | | | v-vi | | |
| **† OT 51C** | Jth. ii 19 | Nachr. Akad. Wiss Göttingen (1966), 6, 4 | parch. | | | v | | |
| **† OT 51D** | Jth. xv 1 *Ostracon* | *Rev. bibl.* liii, 534 | | | | | | |
| **† OT 52** | 2 Esd. ix 21 *Ostracon* | Mon. Epiphanius ii 119 no. 581 | | | | | | |
| ***OT 53** | Psalms | 'Λ' = Freer Psalms | parch. | [24.7 x 34.3] | ? | vi/vii (Kenyon; ed., iv/v) | 1 | 30 |
| **† OT 54** | Psalms etc. | Sinai cod. gr. 33[225] | parch. | | | viii-ix | | |
| **† OT 54A** | Psalms i 1 *Amulet, not codex* | *Annali scuola norm. sup. Pisa* xxvi, 176 | | | | | | |
| **† OT 54B** | Psalms i 1 *Amulet, not codex* | In memoriam A. Beltrami (1954), p. 227 | | | | | | |
| **† OT 55** | Psalms i 1 | BM Add. Ms 34602 fol. 10 | parch. | | | x | | |
| **OT 56** | Psalms i 1ff. | P. Rain. Führer, p. 5 | pap. | 7 x 10 | ? | v | 1 | ? |

[223] *GGN* (1911), 167.

[224] F. C. Burkit, *Fragmm. Books of Kings* . . . (1897).

[225] Benesivic, *Catalogus cod. Mss gr. qui in monasterio S. Catherinae in monte Sinai asserv.* (1911).

| 1 | 2 | 3 | 4 | 5 | 6 | 7 | 8 | 9 |
|---|---|---|---|---|---|---|---|---|
| † **OT 57** | Psalms i 3<br>Single sheet | P. Grenf. ii 112a | parch. | | | | | |
| ***OT 57A** | Psalms i 3 | *Studia Papyrologica* iv, 91 | pap. | [23 x 36.5] (ed.) | [16/17 x 24] | v/vi | 1 | 19 |
| **OT 58** | Psalms i 4 | P. Oxy. xv 1779 | pap. | 7.7 x 11.5 | ? | iv | 1 | 8/9 |
| † **OT 59** | Psalms i– | *Ztschr. ägypt. Sprache* etc. 18, 36 | parch. | | | ? | | |
| ***OT 60** | Psalms ii 3– | P. Lit. Lond. 204 | pap. | [6.3] x 7.3 | ? | iii? | 1 | 12 |
| **OT 60A** | Psalms iii 4– | P. Mich. iii 132 | parch. | 5 x 7.5? | ? | v? | 1 | 12 |
| **OT 61** | Psalms ii 7–<br>*Amulet* | *MPER* iv 23 | pap. | | | | | |
| † **OT 62** | Psalms iii– | Sahidisch-gr. Psalmen fragm., 1 | pap. | | | ? | | |
| † **OT 63** | Psalms iii 62–<br>*Amulet* | P. Ryl. iii 461 | parch. | | | | | |
| † **OT 64** | Psalms v 6– | P. Amh. i 5 | pap. | [ ] x 12.6 | ? | v or vi | 1 | 14 |
| ***OT 65** | Psalms vii– | P. Oxy. x 1226 | pap. | [15+ x 29.8] | ? | early iii (iii/iv G. H.) | 1 | [39] |
| † **OT 65A** | Psalms viii 3– | P. Mich. iii 133 | pap. | ? | ? | iii | 1 | [33–35] |
| † **OT 65B** | Psalms ix 4– | *Jahrb. öst. Byz. Gesellsch.* 14, 7 | parch. | | | vi/vii | | |
| † **OT 65C** | Psalms vii 15<br>*Roll* (on back) | *PSI* 759 | pap. | | | v | | |
| † **OT 66** | Psalms ix 22<br>*Amulet* | *MPER* iv 5 | pap. | | | | | |
| † **OT 67** | Psalms ix 6–<br>Paper! | London Or. 5465 fol. 1–19 | paper | | | xii | | |

| | | | | | | | | |
|---|---|---|---|---|---|---|---|---|
| † **OT 68** | Psalms ix 19– *Not* a codex (back blank) | *Stud. Pal.* xv 234 | pap. | | | iv | | |
| **OT 69** | Psalms ix 33– | *Stud. Pal.* ix 7 | parch. | 14 x 21.2 | 9 x 16 (E. G. T.) | vii? | 1 | 21–25 |
| †***OT 70** | Psalms x 2 | P. Lit. Lond. 206[225a] | parch. | 23.3 x [ ] | ? | vii or viii | 1 | [27] 35 |
| ***OT 71** | Psalms x 2 | 'U' = BM pap. 37 | pap. | 17.5 x 22 | ? | vii | 1 | 14–18 |
| † **OT 72** | Psalms xi 7– *Roll* | P. Lit. Lond. 207 | pap. | | | iii-iv | | |
| **OT 73** | Psalms xi 9– | *MPER* iv 6 | parch. | [12 x 13] | ? | vi | 1 | [24] |
| † **OT 73A** | Psalms xiv 1– *Not* a codex, back blank | *ZPE* i, 74 | parch. | | | v | | |
| † **OT 73B** | Psalms xv 1– | *Studia Papirologica* ix, 93 | pap. | ? | ? | v | 1 | (10+) |
| **OT 74** | Psalms xvi 15– | *MPER* iv 7 | parch. | [13 x 18/19] | ? | vii/viii | 1 | [15] |
| † **OT 75** | Psalms xvii 7– | *MPER* iv 8 | parch. | ? | ? | vi/vii | 1? | (6+) |
| ***OT 75A** | Psalms xvii 45– | P. Bodmer xxiv | pap. | 13 x 24 | 10.4/10.7 x 21/21.7 | iii/iv | 1 | 33–44 |
| † **OT 75B** | Psalms xvii 45– *Not* a codex, back blank | *BKT* viii 5 | pap. | | | iv | | |
| † **OT 76** | Psalms xviii 10– | Sahidisch gr. Psalmenfrg. 165 | parch. | | | v | | |
| **OT 77** | Psalms xviii 15– | *Stud. Pal.* ix 6 | pap. | ? | ? | iv | 1 | (11+) |
| † **OT 77A** | Psalms xx 1– *Ostracon* | *JNES* v, 181 | | | | vi/vii | | |
| † **OT 78** | Psalms xxi 15 | Cambr. TS 12. 182[226] | parch. | | | vii | | |

[225a]BM Or. 3579A(17 = **OT 84** is part of same codex.

[226]C. Taylor, *Hebrew-Gk. Genizah Palimpsests* . . ., 1.

| 1 | 2 | 3 | 4 | 5 | 6 | 7 | 8 | 9 |
|---|---|---|---|---|---|---|---|---|
| † **OT 78A** | Psalms xxi 19 *Papyrus roll* | *Jahrb. öst. Byz. Gesellsch.* 14, 9 | pap. | | | vi | | |
| †* **OT 79** | Psalms xxii 6– | Jena pap. 22[227] | parch. | ? | [20 x 23] (ed.) | v/vi (E. G. T.) | 1 | [38] |
| **OT 80** | Psalms xxv 7– | *BKT* viii 6 | parch. | [14.5] x 15.5 | ? | v? | 1 | 22 |
| † **OT 81** | Psalms xxvi *Parchment roll* | *Wien. Stud.* IV, 214 | parch. | | | vi | | |
| † **OT 82** | Psalms xxviii 6– | *BKT* viii 7 | parch. | ? | ? | iv (ed.) | 1? | [20?] |
| † **OT 82A** | Psalms xxx 3– *Ostracon* | *JNES* v, 181 | | | | vii/viii | | |
| † **OT 83** | Psalms xxx 5– *Roll* (on back) | Leipzig p. 39[228] | pap. | | | iv | | |
| **OT 84** | See **OT 70** | | | | | | | |
| **OT 85** | Psalms xxxii 9– | *MPER* iv 24 | pap. | 4.7 x 5 | | iv-v | 1 | 5–6 |
| † **OT 86** | Psalms xxxii 10– | Cairo 44800, 44802, 44804, 44810[229] | parch. | | | ? | | |
| † **OT 87** | Psalm xxxiii 2– *Ostracon* | *Mon. Epiphanius* no. 579 | | | | vi-vii | | |
| **OT 87A** | Psalms xxxiii, xxxiv | P. Bodmer ix (part of Bodmer composite codex) | pap. | 14.2 x 15.5 | | iv? | 1 | 14–17 |
| **OT 88** | Psalm xxxiii 5– | *Stud. Pal.* ix 8 | pap. | [17/18 x 23] | ? | vi-vii | 1 | [26?] |
| † **OT 89** | Psalms xxxiv 1–5 *Not* a codex, back blank | *MPER* iv p. 24 | pap. | | | iv | | |
| † **OT 89A** | Psalm xxxix 3– *Not* a codex | *Archiv* xx p. 53 | pap. | | | Byz. | 1 | 11 |
| † **OT 90** | Psalms xxxv 12– | *BKT* viii 8 | pap. | ?[230] | ? | iv | 1 | [33/34?] |
| ***OT 91** | Psalm xxxvi 5– | *PSI* xiv 1371 | pap. | 18.7 x 28 | 8.7 x 18.5 | iv | 1 | 26 |

| | | | | | | | | |
|---|---|---|---|---|---|---|---|---|
| † **OT 92** | Psalms xxxviii 8– | Sahidisch.-gr. Fragm. p. 168 | parch. | | | v | | |
| † **OT 93** | Psalms xxxix 16– | P. Bouriant 2 | pap. | ? | ?[14.5 x 21] | iv | 1 | 27 |
| † **OT 94** | Psalms xxxix 16– | *BKT* viii 9 | pap. | ?[231] | ? | vii | 1 | (24+) |
| † **OT 95** | Psalm xlii 3 *Ostracon* | O. Bodl. 2912 | | | | vii | | |
| † **OT 95A** | Psalm xliii 20– *Not* a codex, back blank | P. Harris 31 + *JTS* l, 176 | | | | iv | | |
| † **OT 96** | Psalm xlv 11–12 *Ostracon* | *Mon. Epiphanius* no. 580 | | | | vi-vii? | | |
| † **OT 97** | Psalm xlvi 1–6 | Cairo 44801 (Hedley p. 21) | parch. | | | ? | | |
| †***OT 97A** | Psalms xlviii 20– | Proc. B. A. 43, 229 | pap. | ? | ? | ii/iii (E. G. T.; ii ed.) | 1 | (10+) |
| † **OT 98** | Psalm xlix 1–7 *Not* a codex (single sheet) | P. Ross. Georg. i 1 | pap. | | | | | |
| † **OT 99** | Psalm xlix 4– | *Stud. Pal.* xv 257 | parch. | ? | ? | v-vi | 1 | (19+) |
| † **OT 100** | Psalms l 9– | *Revue de l'orient chrétien* xviii, 87 | parch. | | | ? | | |
| † **OT 101** | Psalm l 12 *Limestone* | Crum, Coptic Ostraca 512 | | | | | | |
| † **OT 102** | Psalm l 14–20 *Wooden tablet* | *BKT* viii 10 | | | | vi | | |

[227] H. Lietzmann, *Studi Heinrici,* 60.
[228] G. Heinrici, *Die Leipz. Papyrusfragm. d. Psalmen.*
[229] Listed by Hedley, p. 19.
[230] Ed. says 22 x 24, which is unparalleled.
[231] Ed. [19 x 29].

| 1 | 2 | 3 | 4 | 5 | 6 | 7 | 8 | 9 |
|---|---|---|---|---|---|---|---|---|
| † **OT 102A** | Psalms li 4– | Berlin P. 16703 = *Archiv* xx, p. 55 | parch. | ? | ? | vi/vii | 1 | (10+) [32?] |
| † **OT 103** | Psalm liv 2– *Not* a codex. Single sheet. | *MPER* iv 10 | parch. | | | vii | | |
| † **OT 104** | Psalms lviii 7– | P. Amh. i 7 | parch. | ? | ? | v | 1 | (16+) |
| † **OT 105** | Psalms lxi 8– *Not* a codex? | Berlin P. 11763[232] | parch. | | | viii | | |
| † **OT 106** | Psalms lxii 2 *Amulet* | *MPER* iv 11 | pap. | | | v-vi | | |
| † **OT 107** | Psalms lxiv 7– | BM Add. 34602 fol. 1, 2, 9 + Bodl. + Paris[233] | parch. | | | vii-viii | | |
| † **OT 108** | Psalms lxvii 2– *Not* a codex, must be single sheet | *BKT* viii 11 | pap. | [36 x 23.5?] | ? | viii | | |
| † **OT 108A** | Psalm *(Ostracon)* lxvii 1–2 | O. Tait (Bodleian) ii 2159 | potsherd | | | vii | | |
| † **OT 109** | Psalms lxvii 2– *Limestone* | *CR* xxxvi, 138 | | | | ? | | |
| † **OT 110** | Psalms lxvii 35– | *MPER* iv 12 | pap. | ? | ? | iii | 1 | [26] |
| † **OT 111** | Psalms lxviii 3– | *MPER* iv 13 | pap. | ? | ? | vi-vii | 1? | (11+) |
| † **OT 111A** | Psalms lxvii 13– | Bodl. Ms Gr. Bibl. d. 3(P)[234] | pap. | | | viii | | |
| † **OT 111B** | Psalms lxviii 13– *Not* a codex | P. Gr. Vindob. 39777 (*Stud. Pal.* xi 114) | parch. | | | iv | | |
| † **OT 112** | Psalms lxviii 30– | P. Oxy. vi 845 | pap. | [22] x ? | 18 x ? | iv-v | 1 | (10+) |
| † **OT 113** | Psalms lxix 13– *Not* a codex, back blank | Mélanges Chatelain p. 224 | parch. | | | iii-iv | | |
| † **OT 114** | Psalm lxxi 12– | P. Ant. ii 51 | pap. | ? | ? | vi | 1? | (4+) |

| | | | | | | | | |
|---|---|---|---|---|---|---|---|---|
| † **OT 115** | Psalms lxxii 11– | *Stud. Pal.* ix 9 + 10 | parch. | ? | ? | iv-v (ed.) | 1? | (13/14+) |
| **OT 116** | Psalms lxxvi 5– | P. Lit. Lond. 208 | parch. | 11 x 13.6 | 7.5 x 9.5 | vi-vii | 1 | 19–20 |
| † **OT 116A** | Psalms lxxiii 2 *Roll* | P. Bibl. Univ. Giss. iv 34 | pap. | | | iv | | |
| † **OT 117** | Psalm lxxvii 1–18 *Not* a codex (on back of document) | *PSI* viii 921 | pap. | | | ii/iii | | |
| † **OT 118** | Psalm lxxvii 1–8 *Not* a codex, single sheet | *MPER* iv 14 | pap. | | | vii | | |
| † **OT 119** | Psalm lxxix 2–16 *(Lead Roll)* | *SB Berlin* (1898), 582 | lead | | | ? | | |
| †***OT 120** | Psalms lxxxi-ii | P. Ant. i 7 | pap. | [ x 14]? | ? | ii/iii (E. G. T.; ed., H. I. Bell ii) | 1 | [24] |
| ***OT 121** | Psalms lxxxii 6– | P. Oxy. xi 1352 | parch. | 10.5 x 13.1 | 8/8.2 x 10.5 | iii/iv (E. G. T.; ed. iv) | 1 | 21, 22 |
| †***OT 122** | Psalms lxxxiii 9– *Not* a codex (back blank) | P. Oxy. xxiv 2386 | pap. | | | iv-v | | |
| † **OT 123** | Psalms xc 17– | Cambridge TS 12.187–8[235] | parch. | | | v-vi | | |
| † **OT 124** | Psalm xc *Amulet* (written on back of doc.) | P. Oxy. xvi 1928 | pap. | | | | | |
| † **OT 125** | Psalm xc 1–7, etc. *Not* a codex, amulet | Geneva, Ms gr. 50[236] | wax tablet | | | vi | | |

[232]Listed by Hedley p. 22.
[233]Listed by Hedley, p. 22.
[234]Listed by G. Maldfeld.
[235]C. Taylor, *Hebrew-Greek Cairo Genizah Palimpsests.*
[236]J. Nicole, *Textes grecques inédits*, 43.

| 1 | 2 | 3 | 4 | 5 | 6 | 7 | 8 | 9 |
|---|---|---|---|---|---|---|---|---|
| † **OT 126** | Psalm xc 1–6 *Not* a codex — strip | Berlin P. 3601 | parch. strip | | | Byz. | | |
| † **OT 127** | Psalm xc 1 *Not* a codex, amulet | Rainer 8032, cf. *Stud. Pal.* xx | pap. | | | iv | | |
| † **OT 128** | Psalm xc 1–2 *Not* a codex, on back. Amulet. | *PSI* vii 759[237] | pap. | | | | | |
| † **OT 129** | Psalm xc 1 Amulet, *not* a codex | Berlin P. 6096; *BKT* vi p. 129 | parch. | | | ? | | |
| † **OT 130** | Psalm xc 5–16 Amulet, *not* a codex | P. Ryl. i 3 | pap. | | | v-vi | | |
| † **OT 131** | Psalm xc 5–10 Amulet, *not* a codex | P. Oxy. xvii 2065 | parch. | | | | | |
| † **OT 131A** | Psalm xc 1–13 *Amulet*? | Berlin P. 3642 + 3639[238] | parch. | | | vi/vii | | |
| † **OT 132** | Psalm xc 13–16 *Papyrus roll* | Bodleian gr. bibl. e 6 (P)[239] | pap. | | | v-vi | | |
| † **OT 133** | Psalms xci 15– | *MPER* iv 15 | parch. | ? | ? | v | 1? | (6+) |
| † **OT 134** | Psalm xcii *Not* a codex, back blank | *MPER* iv 16 | pap. | | | vii | | |
| † **OT 135** | Psalm xcii 1– | *MPER* iv 17 | pap. | ? | ? | vi | 1 | (6+) |
| † **OT 136** | Psalms xciv 6 *Not* a codex | BM Or. 5297(4)[240] | parch. | | | ? | | |
| **OT 137** | Psalms xcviii 5– | *Stud. Pal.* xi 83 | parch. | 26.5 x 32.5 | 18.5 x 2 | vi? | 2 | 29 |
| † **OT 137A** | Psalms c 1– | P. Reinach ii 60 | pap. | ?[241] | ? | viii | 1 | [25] |

| | | | | | | | | |
|---|---|---|---|---|---|---|---|---|
| † | **OT 138** | Psalms ci 3– | J. Rendel Harris, Bibl. frags. from Mt. Sinai, no. 4 | parch. | | | iv | | |
| | **OT 139** | Psalm ci 12– | *Stud. Pal.* ix 17 | parch. | 26.5 x [33] | 19 x ? | vi? | 1 | 34 |
| † | **OT 140** | Psalm ciii 1– *Ostracon* | Crum, Coptic Ostraca 513 | lime-stone | | | Byz. | | |
| † | **OT 140A** | Psalms ciii 18– | *BKT* viii 22 | parch. | ? | ? | iv/v | 1 | (6+) |
| | **OT 141** | Psalm ciii 2– | *BKT* viii 14 | parch. | 14 x [14+] | ? | v | 1 | 24 |
| † | **OT 142** | Psalm ciii 24– Paper codex | P. Ryl. Copt. 62 | paper | | | x-xi | | |
| † | **OT 143** | Psalm cv 16– Not a codex | *MPER* iv 18 | paper | | | ix | | |
| † | **OT 144** | Psalms cv 20– | *Stud. Pal.* ix 11 | parch. | ? | ? | v-vi | 1? | (10+) |
| † | **OT 145** | Psalms cv 38– | *BKT* viii 15 | parch. | ? | [13 x 14] (ed.) | v | 1 | [30] |
| † | **OT 146** | Psalms cvii 14– | P. Amh. i 6 | pap. | 25.5 x [ ] | ? | vii? | 1 | (25+) |
| † | **OT 146A** | Psalms cviii 18– | Berlin P. 16390[242] | ? | | | iv-v | | |
| † | **OT 147** | Psalm cix 1–4 *Ostracon* | Crum, Coptic Ostraca p. 95 | | | | vi? | | |
| † | **OT 148** | Psalm cxiv 5– *Not* a codex, other writing on back | *Serta Eusebiana* (1958), 117 | pap. | | | v? | | |
| † | **OT 149** | Psalm cxvii 18– *Ostracon* | *Aegyptus* 15, 415 | lime-stone | | | iv | | |
| | **OT 150** | Psalms cxvii 27– *Ostracon* | Crum, Coptic Ostraca p. 81 | | | | Byz. | | |

[237] Cf. *JEA* xiii, 92; *ZAW lxxvi*, 224.
[238] Listed by G. Maldfeld.
[239] Listed by Hedley, p. 26.
[240] Listed by Hedley, p. 26.
[241] Ed. estimates [ x 23].
[242] Listed by G. Maldfeld. [Delete. Doublet of **OT 140A**].

| 1 | 2 | 3 | 4 | 5 | 6 | 7 | 8 | 9 |
|---|---|---|---|---|---|---|---|---|
| † **OT 151** | Psalms cxvii 27– | Leipzig pap. 170[243] | pap. | | | iii (ii C. H. R.) | | |
| † **OT 152** | Psalms cxviii etc. Amulet, *not* a codex | *MPER* iv 19 | parch. | | | vi | | |
| † **OT 153** | Psalms cxviii 132– | *Proc. Soc. Bibl. Arch.* 26, 217 | parch. | | | vii-viii | | |
| † **OT 154** | Psalm cxviii 155– Amulet, *not* a codex | *MPER* iv 20 | parch. | | | v/vi | | |
| **OT 154A** | *Amulet* (incl. Psalm cxxxii 1) | P. Lit. Lond. 239 | parch. | 4.5 x 6.8 | ? | vi or vii | 1 | c. 10 |
| † **OT 155** | Psalm cxxxv 10– | *MPER* iv 21 | pap. | ? | ? | vi/vii | 1? | (7+) |
| ***OT 156** | Psalms cxxxv 13– | Codex Climaci[244] rescr. fol. 26, 27 | parch. | 18.5 x [28] | 11.3 x [ ] | vii? | 2 and 1 | [28] |
| † **OT 157** | Psalms cxxxviii 17– | *MPER* iv 22 | parch. | ?[245] | ? | vi/vii | 1 | [25] |
| † **OT 158** | Psalm cxl 1– Amulet, *not* a codex | P. Reinach ii 61 | pap. | | | vii | | |
| † **OT 159** | Psalms cxli 2– *Not* a codex, single sheet | *PSI* xiv 1372 | pap. | | | vii | | |
| † **OT 160** | Psalms cxli 7– | Leningrad cod. gr. 4[246] | parch. | | | iv/v | | |
| † **OT 161** | Psalms cxliii 1– | Cambridge TS 16.320[247] | parch. | | | vi | | |
| † **OT 161A** | Psalms cxliii 7– | Nachr. Akad. Wiss. Göttingen 1966, 6, 5 | parch. | | | ix/x | | |

| | | | | | | | | |
|---|---|---|---|---|---|---|---|---|
| † **OT 162** | Psalms cxliii 14– | *PSI* viii 980 | pap. | ? | [10/11 x 21] | iii/iv Hedley (iii ed.) | 1 | 36–37 |
| † **OT 163** | Psalms cxlviii– *Not* a codex, single sheet | P. Ryl. iii 462 | parch. | | | vi-vii | | |
| † **OT 163A** | Psalms, various | Berlin P. 11763[248] | ? | | | vii/viii | | |
| † **OT 164** | Prov. ii 9– | P. Ant. i 9 | pap. | ?[249] | ? | iii? | 1 | [40?] |
| ***OT 165** | Prov. etc. | P. Ant. i 8 + iii 210 | pap. | [12 x 17] | ? | iii | 1 | [30] |
| † **OT 165A** | Prov. iv 26– | Nachr. Gött. Akad. Wiss. 1966, 6, 6 | parch. | | | v | | |
| † **OT 166** | Prov. vii 3– *Not* a codex | P. Mich. iii 134 | wax tablet | | | iv-vi | | |
| † **OT 167** | Prov. x 18– | P. Amh. ii 193 | parch. | ? | ? | vi | 1 | (18+) |
| †***OT 167A** | Prov. xxiii 26– | *BKT* viii 26 = *Archiv* xx, p. 57 | parch. | 10.7 x [ ] | ? | v/vi | 1 | (4+) |
| † **OT 168** | Prov. xxvi 11– | *MPER* iv 25 | parch. | ? | ? | v | 1? | (7+) |
| † **OT 169** | Prov. xxvii 10– | *MPER* iv 26 | parch. | ?[250] | ? | v | 1 | [20+?] |
| † **OT 170** | Prov. xxx 32– | *MPER* iv 27 | parch. | ? | ? | v (Cavallo) | 1 | [18–20?] |
| † **OT 170A** | Prov. xxxi 2 – etc. *Not* a codex, single sheet | *PSI* xiii 1297 | parch. | | | vi-vii | | |

[243] G. Heinrici, *Die Leipziger Fragmente d. Psalmen*, coll. 35 ff.
[244] Ed. A. S. Lewis, 1909; cf. *JTS* viii, 1.
[245] [13 x 15] ed.
[246] Tischendorf, Mon. Sacra ined. ii 319.
[247] *JTS* iv, 215.
[248] Listed by G. Maldfeld.
[249] Ed. [18 x 35].
[250] [13 x 18] ed.

| 1 | 2 | 3 | 4 | 5 | 6 | 7 | 8 | 9 |
|---|---|---|---|---|---|---|---|---|
| † **OT 171** | Cant., Eccl. | C. Schmidt, W. Schubart, Acta Pauli[251] | | | | | | |
| †***OT 172** | Eccles. vi 3– | P. Mich. iii 135 + P. Med. 13 (*Aegyptus* [1952], 215) | pap. | ? | ? | iii/iv (E. G. T.; iii ed.) | 1 | (9+) |
| † **OT 173** | Eccles. vi 6– | P. Oxy. xvii 2066 | pap. | ? | ? | v-vi | 1 | (13+) |
| † **OT 174** | Cant. i 6–9 | P. Grenf. i 7 | pap. | ? | ? | vii? | 1? | (4+) |
| † **OT 174A** | Cant. ii 1– | Nachr. Akad. Wiss. Göttingen 1966, 6, 7 | parch. | | | iv-v | | |
| †***OT 175** | Cant. v 12– Same codex as 503 | P. Lond. Lit. 209 | pap. | 13.1 x 19.5 | 10.5 x 15 | iv | 1 | 24, 25 |
| ***OT 175A** | Cant. v 13– | *Archiv* xx, p. 57 | parch. | [7.5 x 10] | [5.5] x 8.4 | iv | 1 | 17/18 |
| † **OT 176** | Job i 15– | P. Ryl. i 24 + P. Amh. i 4 + P. Lit. Lond. 210 | pap. | ?[252] | ? | vi or vii | 1 | (20–23) |
| †***OT 177** | Job i 19– | *PSI* 1163 | pap. | ? | ? | iv (or iii/iv? E. G. T.) | 1 | (16+) |
| † **OT 178** | Job vii 8– | P. Ryl. Copt. 3 | parch. | | | ? | | |
| † **OT 178A** | Job xxxiii 23– *Not* a codex | *BKT* viii 17 | pap. | [24 x 7] | ? | iii | 1 | (9+) |
| † **OT 179** | Wisd. i 1– | *Stud. Pal.* ix 4 | pap. | | | iv-v | 1? | (9+) |
| † **OT 179A** | Wisd. x 19– | Nachr. Akad. Wiss. Göttingen (1966), 6, 8 | parch.[253] | | | v/vi | | |
| ***OT 180** | Sirach i 1– | P. Oxy. xiii 1595 | pap. | [14] x 18 | 11.5 x 15 | vi | 1 | 16 |

| | | | | | | | | |
|---|---|---|---|---|---|---|---|---|
| † **OT 180A** | Sirach xxix 15– | *Annali Scuola norm. sup. Pisa* xxvi, 178 | pap. | | | iii/iv | | |
| ***OT 181** | Sirach xxxvi 28– | P. Ch. B. XI | pap. | 17.8 x 26.7 | 14.5 x 21.3 | iv | 1 | 35 |
| ***OT 182** | Sirach xlii 17– | *MPER* iv 28 | pap. | ? | ? | v | 1 | (8+) |
| †***OT 183** | Esther, Daniel, Ezekiel, etc. | P. Ch. B. IX + X[254] | pap. | 12.8 x 34.4 | 8.4/9 x 29.3/30 | iii (E. G. T.; Wilcken, Galiano ii) | 1 | 40–57 |
| †***OT 184** | Esther iv 1 (in Latin) | P. Ant. i 14[255] | parch. | 15.5 x [ ] | 10/10.5 x [ ] | v | 1 | [16+] |
| †***OT 185** | Tob. ii 2– | P. Oxy. viii 1076 | parch. | ?[256] | ? | vi | 2 | [10 or 11?] |
| ***OT 186** | Tob. xii 14– | P. Oxy. xiii 1594 | parch. | [8.5 x 8.5][257] | 6.7 x [5.0] | iii | 1 | [11] |
| ***OT 187** | Minor prophets | 'W' = Washington (Freer) Ms V | pap. | 14 x [32] (E. G. T.) | 10 x 26.3 | iv (E. G. T.)[258] | 1 | 46–49 |
| †***OT 188** | Hosea *Not* a codex (on back of land register) | *JEA* xi, 241 | pap. | | | iii | | |
| **OT 189** | Amos ii 6– | P. Oxy. vi 846 | pap. | [15.5 x 26.5] (ed.) | ? | vi | 1 | [22] |

251 Same codex as Acta Pauli (**NT Apocr. 9**).
252 Ryl. fr. 3 is 10.2 x 17.2 (uncertain whether any margin).
253 Palimpsest, Aristotle written *above* it.
254 + P. Princeton Scheide + Pap. Kol. 967 + P. Matr. bibl. 1.
255 Cf. *Prolegomena* ii (1952): 3; *La nouvelle Clio,* 398; *CLA* supp. 1706.
256 Calculation from photo gives [13.9 x 13]; but the parch. is badly warped.
257 Or [8 x 8].
258 See p. 59.

| 1 | 2 | 3 | 4 | 5 | 6 | 7 | 8 | 9 |
|---|---|---|---|---|---|---|---|---|
| † **OT 189A** | Jonah i– *Not* a codex: parchment roll | Vetus Testamentum suppl. x, 170 | parch. | | | i | | |
| ***OT 190** | Jonah i 11– | *PSI* x 1164 + *HTR* xxxviii, 195 | parch. | 5.5 x 6 | 4.5/4.8 x 4 | iv/v?[259] | 1 | 10 |
| ***OT 191** | Zach. iv 6– | Septuaginta Pap. aus d. Heidelb Papyrussamml. 1 | pap. | 17.5 x [30] (E. G. T.) | | vi-vii | 1 | 28(?+) |
| ***OT 192** | Zach. xii 10 | P. Grenf. i 6 | parch. | 6.3 x 8 | 3.5 x 5.2 | iv/v (E. G. T.) | 1 | 12 |
| † **OT 193** | Isa. i 18– | P. Ant. ii 52 | pap. | ? | ? | vi/vii | 1 | [21, 24] |
| † **OT 194** | Isa. vi 3 Doubtful whether codex | Patrolog. Orient. xviii 3, p. 437 | pap. | | | iv-vi | | |
| †***OT 194A** | Isa. vi 10 (quoted) | P. Oxy. iii 406 | pap. | ? | ? | iii (ed.; iii/iv ? E. G. T.) | 1 | (12+) |
| ***OT 195** | Isa. viii 18– | P. Ch. B. VII + P. Merton i 2 + *PSI* xii 1273 | pap. | 15.3 x [26] | 12.7 x 19 | iii | 1 | 25–26 |
| †***OT 196** | Isa. xxi | P. Ryl. iii 459 | parch. | [ ] x 22.7 | [ ] x 16 | v to vi | 1 | 26 |
| † **OT 196A** | Isa. xxv 4–5 | *BKT* viii 19 | parch. | ?[260] | ? | vii | 1 | [15] |
| † **OT 197** | Isa. xxxvi 16– | *BKT* viii 20[261] | pap. | ? | ? | iv | 1 | (16+) |
| † **OT 198** | Isa. xxxviii 3– | *Stud. Pal.* ix 1 | pap. | ? | ? | iii | 1 | (9+) |
| †***OT 198A** | Isa. xlviii 6– *Roll* | *Annali sc. norm. sup. Pisa* (1972), 489 | pap. | | | iii/iv | | |
| **OT 199** | Isa. xlii 3– | P. Oslo ii 11 | pap. | ? | ? | iv | 1 | (9, 10+) |
| † **OT 200** | Isa. xlix 16– Roll? Or last page of codex? | *BKT* viii 21 | pap. | ? | ? | iii-iv | 1 | (10+) |

| | | | | | | | | | |
|---|---|---|---|---|---|---|---|---|---|
| † **OT 201** | Isa. lviii 11– | P. Amh. ii 191[262] | pap. | | | vi | 1 | | (11, 8+) |
| †***OT 201A** | Jer. ii 2– | *Archiv* xx, p. 60 | pap. | ? | [?9/10 x 27] | iii | 1 | | [37?] |
| ***OT 202** | Jer. iv 30– | P. Ch. B. VIII | pap. | [15.2 x 30.5] | [11.5 x 25.5] | iv (E. G. T.; ii or ii/iii Kenyon) | 1 | | [48] |
| † **OT 203** | Jer. xii 9 | *Stud. Pal.* ix 5 | parch. | ? | ? | v | 2 | | (13+) |
| **OT 204** | Jer. xiii 16– | *MPER* iv 29 | parch. | [17 x 21] | ? | vi | 2 | | (23, 22) |
| †***OT 204A** | Jer. xvii 26– | *Recherches de Pap.* i 113 | pap. | [17/18 x ?] | ? | iv | 1 | | [27–36?] |
| †***OT 204** | Jer. xviii 15– | *Aegyptus* 45, 70 | pap. | x [25] | x [16.5] | iv | 1 | | (25)? |
| † **OT 204C** | Jer. xxv 10– | Nachr. Akad. Wiss. Göttingen (1966), 6, 9 | parch. | | | vi | | | |
| † **OT 205** | Jer. xxviii–xxxii | P. Ant. ii 53 | pap. | ? | ? | vi/vii | | ? | (8+) |
| † **OT 205A** | Ep. of Jeremiah *Not* a codex — papyrus roll | *DJD* iii, p. 143 | pap. | | | c. 100 B.C. | | | |
| † **OT 206** | Ezek. i 9– | Vat. Syr. 162 + BM Add. 14665[264] | parch. | | | vii-viii | | | |
| †***OT 207** | Ezek. v 12– | P. Grenf. i 5 | pap. | [15?] x ? | 11 x ? | iii/iv | 1 | | (15+)? |
| ***OT 207A** | Ezek. xi 25, Daniel, Susanna, Bel, Esther | P. Ch. B. IX + X[263] | pap. | 12.8 x 34.4 | 8.4/9 x 29.3/30 | iii E. G. T. (Wilcken ii) | 1 | | 49–57 |
| †***OT 208** | Ezek. xxxiii | P. Ant. i 10 + *Emerita* 39, 51 | parch. | ? | [10 x 13] (ed.) | iv | | ? | (24)? |
| † **OT 209** | Ezek. xxxvi 20– | Rome Vat. Syr. 162 rescr. Syr.[264a] | parch. | | | vi | | | |

[259]Cavallo p. 83 'not earlier than vi.'
[260]Ed. suggests [9 x 12].
[261]Listed by Hedley as ii-iii.
[262]Identified by A. Deissmann.
[263]+ Princeton + Kol. 967 + Madrid. Same Ms as **OT 183.**
[264]E. Tisserant, *Codex Zuqninensis* (1911).
[264a]E. Tisserant, *Codex Zuqninensis* (1911).

| 1 | 2 | 3 | 4 | 5 | 6 | 7 | 8 | 9 |
|---|---|---|---|---|---|---|---|---|
| † **OT 210** | Dan. i 17–<br>*Not* a codex, back blank | P. Lit. Lond. 211 | parch. | | | iv | | (8) |
| † **OT 211** | Dan. iii 23–<br>*Not* a codex (different hand and text on back) | *MPER* iv 30 | pap. | | | v | | |
| † **OT 211A** | Dan. iii 62–<br>*Not* a codex | *MPER* iv 31 | pap. | ? | ? | vii | 1 | (6+) |
| † **OT 212** | Dan. vi 20<br>*Not* a codex; homily? Different text on back | Bodl. gr. bib. c. 2(P) | pap. | | | vi-vii | 1 | (5+) |
| ***OT 213** | Bel 20– | Bodl. gr. bib. d. 2 (P) | parch. | [ ] x 12.6 | [ ] x 8.8 | iv-v | 1 | 18/19 |
| † **OT 214** | Oden | Rainer K8706[265] | | | | vi | | |
| † **OT 215** | Oden i 1–<br>*Not* a codex—back blank | *Stud. Pal.* ix 3 | pap. | | | vi | | |
| † **OT 216** | Oden iva 9<br>*Not* a codex—Arabic on back. Amulet | P. Mich. iii 136 | pap. | | | vii-viii | | |
| **OT 217** | Daniel iii 62–66<br>*Not* a codex | *MPER* iv 31 | pap. | | | vii | | |
| † **OT 218** | Oden x<br>*Not* a codex | *Mon. Epiphanius ii, p. 299* | pap. | | | vi-vii | | |
| † **OT 219** | Oden x<br>*Not* a codex: Arabic legal doc. on back | *Bessarione* VI (1899): 514 | pap. | | | viii-ix | | |

| | | | | | | | | |
|---|---|---|---|---|---|---|---|---|
| † **OT 220** | Oden x *Ostracon* | *Mon. Epiphanius* ii, p. 119 | | | | vi-vii | | |
| ***OT 221** | Enoch i 1– | *MIFAO* ix, 1 (1893) | parch. | 12 x 15 | 9/10.5 x 10.2/13.5 | vi[266] (E. G. T.) | 1 | 19 |
| ***OT 222** | Enoch xcvii– | P. Ch. B XII + P. Mich.[267] | pap. | 14 x [27] | 11 x 23 | iv | 1 | 41–46 |
| ***OT 223** | 'Ascension of Isaiah' | P. Amh. i 1 | pap. | 13.2 x 23 | 8.5 x 17.5 | v | 1 | 26–32 |

[265] Listed by Hedley, p. 38.
[266] Hedley viii-ix. Is it not earlier?
[267] Campbell Bonner, *The Last Chapters of Enoch in Greek*. Same Ms as Melito = **543.**

# Technical Index